Putting Transfer of Development Rights to Work in California

Rick Pruetz

Solano Press Books
Point Arena, California

Putting Transfer of Development Rights to Work in California

November 1993

Solano Press Books
Post Office Box 773
Point Arena, California 95468
Phone (707) 884-4508/Fax (707) 884-4109

Book and cover design by Canterbury Press, Berkeley, California
Index by Paul Kish, Mendocino, California
Cover photograph by Rick Pruetz
Text photographs by Rick Pruetz, except where noted
Printed by Braun-Brumfield, Inc., Ann Arbor, Michigan

ISBN 0-923956-29-8

Trees are one of nature's renewable resources.
To preserve this invaluable resource for future
generations, Solano Press Books makes annual
contributions to the *American Forests Global
Releaf Program. American Forests* is the nation's
oldest non-profit citizens' conservation organization.

✪ Printed on partially recycled paper

NOTICE
Before you rely on the information in this book,
be sure you have the latest edition and are aware
that some changes in statutes, guidelines or case
law may have gone into effect since the date
of publication. The book, moreover, provides
general information about the law. Readers
should consult their own attorneys before
relying on the representations found herein.

Preface

Transfer of development rights allows communities to achieve numerous land use goals—including the preservation of natural areas, hillsides, historic landmarks, and agricultural land—at little or no expense. Using TDR, development rights which are not used at a sending site can be transferred to a receiving site where additional development is consistent with community objectives.

Communities benefit from TDR because important resources can be preserved at little or no cost. Likewise, landowners and developers can profit even though some of the transferred property remains undeveloped. For difficult land use problems, since both public and private sectors benefit, TDR has often been described as a "win-win" solution.

Besides familiarizing planners, elected officials, landowners, and other citizens with the technique, the purpose of this book is to encourage the use of TDR in California.

Although traditionally thought of only as a technique for planners, TDR can be of value to anyone interested in creating a better community within the reality of shrinking budgets—city managers; utility, public works, and other elected and appointed officials; park directors; finance and budget managers; attorneys; property owners and developers; environmentalists; historic preservationists; and others.

The book is designed to accommodate readers with varying levels of interest or familiarity. The chapters proceed from general information to case studies and, finally, to specific recommendations for preparing a TDR program. Readers who already know about existing programs may want to proceed directly to the California survey results in Chapter IV. Others who have a general knowledge of TDR may prefer to see how various communities have put TDR to work in California (see Chapter III). The general content of each chapter is described below. In addition, a glossary of terms and an index follow the appendices at the end of the text.

*　*　*

Chapter I summarizes the main points of the book while familiarizing the reader with various aspects of transferable development rights—the concept, components, and advantages, along with the many reasons for using TDR, legal issues involved, and associated economic considerations.

Chapter II begins with a brief history of TDR programs in other states and then provides case studies from three programs which have been in existence since at least the 1970s—New York City; Collier County, Florida; and the New Jersey Pinelands program which has already preserved more than 5,800 acres of ecologically significant land.

In Chapter III, "The California Experience," case studies of 27 communities with TDR programs are described. These programs are designed to achieve various objectives ranging from the relatively unexpected goal of providing for flexibility in concentrating density to the more traditional objectives of preservating hillsides, unique habitat, agricultural land, and historic landmarks.

Chapter IV records the responses to a survey mailed by the author in early 1992 to every city and county in California. This survey revealed that many communities use TDR-like techniques in specific plans, planned developments, and subdivision ordinances which encourage clustering of development. However, many communities do not use any form of development right transfer even when they acknowledge that preservation goals cannot be met under existing codes and budget constraints.

In Chapter V, "Ingredients for a Successful TDR Program," the experiences of the 30 case studies are used to explain why some programs are successful while others are not. Key components for a successful program include: identifying the goals of a program; imposing development restrictions in sending and receiving areas which assist in meeting those goals; creating incentives such as transfer ratios, TDR banks, and exemptions from development requirements; and implementing TDR through public education, developer assistance, and program refinements.

Finally, Chapter VI predicts the increased use of TDR in California. Many communities already use preservation techniques similar to, but less comprehensive than, TDR. Moreover, the general plans of several California communities call for the adoption of TDR ordinances, and—particularly during recessionary and post–Proposition

13 periods—more and more communities are likely to turn to TDR to achieve their goals without the expense of public acquisition.

Acknowledgments

The "Legal Issues" section of Chapter I was written by Donald I. Berger. Mr. Berger is a partner in the Los Angeles office of the law firm Morrison & Foerster. He specializes in land use and real estate law and represents clients throughout California on development and land use regulation issues.

In addition to the numerous planners mentioned in the text and footnotes, I want to thank especially the following people for their valuable assistance in reviewing drafts and helping out in other ways—Jeannie Coughenour, JoAnn Davis, Madelyn Glickfeld, Greg Herrmann, Paul Krueger, Charles Loveman, Bill Lundgren, Margaret Sohagi, and Steve Somers.

And extra special thanks to Adrian, Jay, and Erica for their support and patience.

About the Author

Rick Pruetz is currently the Chief Assistant Community Development Director/City Planner for Burbank, California. Prior to joining Burbank in 1985, he was a planner with the City of Waukesha, Wisconsin where he worked in the areas of historic preservation and redevelopment as well as planning. Before that, Mr. Pruetz worked as a project planner for the Milwaukee, Wisconsin office of Camp Dresser McKee, an environmental engineering planning firm.

Mr. Pruetz received his Master of Urban Planning degree from the University of Wisconsin, Milwaukee in 1979. He is a former Vice-Director-at-Large of the Los Angeles Section of the American Planning Association.

In his position in Burbank, Mr. Pruetz is responsible for advance studies and transportation planning as well as current planning work. He was the principal author of Burbank's Media District Specific Plan. This plan uses transfer of development rights to allow concentrations of development on key sites while maintaining an overall limit on growth to ensure that it can be accommodated by transportation and public service systems.

Contents

Feature Articles

Introduction to TDR: Description, Advantages, Uses, and Issues

The technique of transferable development rights, or TDR, allows development rights which are unused on one parcel of land to be severed from that parcel and transferred to another parcel. TDR can be used to achieve numerous land use goals ranging from growth management to the preservation of open space, historic landmarks, natural areas, and agricultural land. Communities benefit from TDR because they can preserve important resources at minimal expense. Likewise, landowners and developers can benefit from TDR because they can make a profit from the transfer, even though some of the property involved remains undeveloped. The purpose of this book is to familiarize planners, elected officials, landowners, and other citizens with this technique and urge them to consider putting TDR to work in California.

TDR = Transferable Development Rights

A. What is TDR?

1. The TDR Concept

a. Development Rights and Credits. The TDR concept recognizes that parcels of land can be assigned a "right to develop" a certain amount of development. This "development right" is typically established by a community's general plan and zoning code. These development rights can be expressed in familiar terms such as dwelling units or square feet of commercial floor area.

Some communities use the term "development credits" (TDC) instead of "development rights." Since, for all practical purposes TDC is the same as TDR, this book uses the terms "development rights" and

TDC = Transferable Development Credits

"TDR" when referring to the transfer concept and process. However, this book uses the term "TDC" whenever a community uses that term for its own program.

b. Transferring Development Rights. Under TDR, a community can treat development rights as a commodity which can be transferred from one site to be used on another site. Because of this transfer, the community prevents development on a site it wants to preserve and gains development on a site which the community has determined is appropriate for that development. Likewise, the landowners and developers involved in the transaction are able to use their development rights even though in the process some land has been preserved for nonuse. Since both the public and the private sector benefit from these transfers, TDR has often been described as a "win-win" solution for difficult land use problems.

For example, if a community wants to preserve an undeveloped hillside, it can create a program in which the hillside to be preserved is designated as a TDR "sending area." The development rights from the sending area can be transferred to a designated "receiving area" and used to increase the density of that receiving area beyond the level otherwise allowed. After the transfer of development rights, parcels in the sending area are protected from development by conservation easements, development agreements, or conveyance of ownership of the property to a public agency. Alternatively, the sending areas may be protected by land use regulations which are in effect prior to the transfer. As a result, the owners of the sending parcel are able to gain economic compensation, even though their property remains undeveloped because the development right or credit has a value that can be "traded" or sold. Likewise, the community benefits from the protection of valuable assets without spending public funds.

2. TDR Components

This section provides a summary of the important components of a TDR program. These issues are explored in greater detail in Chapter V.

a. Sending Sites. The parcel of land from which the development rights are transferred is called the "sending site." The sending site typically contains a resource that the community wants to save such as an important natural habitat, a scenic area, hillsides, historic landmarks, open space, or agricultural land. Many successful TDR programs strongly encourage transfers by making development difficult or impossible on sending sites, while recognizing that depriving the sending owner of all development opportunities could be found to be a "taking."

b. Receiving Sites. The parcel of land which receives the transferred development is known as the "receiving site." In adopting a TDR program, a community designates as receiving sites areas of land where the increase in density resulting from the transfer would be beneficial and acceptable to the community. Successful programs often provide a strong incentive to transfer development rights by making it difficult or impossible to achieve additional density on receiving sites without using the TDR method.

c. Implementation Tools. Some TDR programs offer additional incentives for property owners to transfer development rights. These include—

> Transfer ratios which multiply development rights if they are transferred to the receiving site rather than being used at the sending site

> Exemptions from fees or other requirements for developments which use TDR

> TDR banks which buy development rights from sending sites and hold them until a developer purchases them in order to build on a receiving site; the bank facilitates transfers by eliminating the need for TDR buyers and sellers to find each other and engage in case-by-case negotiations

In general, the most successful TDR programs also involve substantial public education, an investment of staff time to assist developers in using TDR, plus a willingness to monitor the program and make whatever adjustments are needed.

3. Advantages of TDR

a. Community Benefits. The land use goals for a community often include the preservation of natural areas, open space, scenic views, hillsides, historic landmarks, and agricultural land, but usually these goals are not completely reached. Often, communities are reluctant to restrict development on the sending sites without providing some kind of compensation to the property owner, and usually there is little or no public funding to provide this compensation.

TDR solves this problem by providing transfer of development rights as compensation. The community saves the sending site with little or no public expenditure. (This is particularly important in an era in which public funding for land acquisition is likely to remain scarce.) In addition, if the general plan and TDR program have been well-coordinated, the community also receives the added bonus of concentrating development in receiving areas that can benefit from the increased density.

b. Benefits to Property Owners and Developers

1) Benefits to Owners of Sending Sites. The owners of sending sites typically have difficulty making maximum economic use of

their properties. Usually development is restricted or even prohibited by open space, agricultural or landmark designations, or some other form of zoning requirement. In some cases, the land use restrictions are less of a hindrance to development than physical constraints such as slope instability or lack of infrastructure. TDR allows these property owners to achieve some or all of the economic return which would have occurred from the development of the sending site by allowing the development rights to be transferred to an appropriate receiver site.

Above

The City of Morgan Hill, 20 miles southeast of San Jose, has four distinct TDC programs each with the same objective of saving the higher elevations of the city's most prominent geographic feature, El Toro Mountain. The Morgan Hill TDC program combines various incentives with an outright prohibition of development on the top of El Toro Mountain; as a result, over 100 acres have been preserved so far.

2) Benefits to Owners of Receiving Sites. Transfers of development rights occur because the owners of receiving sites can enjoy greater economic return through additional development on these sites. If land use restrictions only allow additional development through the TDR process, these developers will buy development rights as long as the additional profit from these denser developments is greater than the cost of acquiring the additional development rights.

B. Who Should Know about TDRs?

1. Local Officials

a. Municipal Uses for TDR. TDR can be put to a wide range of uses—

► Preserving environmentally sensitive areas

► Protecting historic landmarks

► Saving open space and agricultural land

- Prohibiting development on steep slopes, flood plains, fire-prone areas, and other hazardous locations
- Allowing concentrations of density needed to achieve urban design goals while maintaining overall development at a level that can be accommodated by the public service system

b. Municipal Officials Who Should Know about TDR

1) Planners. Planners are responsible for implementing the general plan and enforcing the zoning code. These two documents establish all land use goals and regulations including the maintenance of development limits and the preservation of natural areas, historic landmarks, open space, agricultural land, and hazardous areas. Consequently, planners have the greatest range of applications for TDR.

2) City Managers/County Executives. City managers and county executives, being responsible for all municipal activities, should also be familiar with a technique which can control development at minimal public expense.

3) Public Works Directors. Public works directors could advocate the use of TDR to steer development away from areas where the cost of infrastructure maintenance and other public works activities is likely to be high.

4) Utility Managers. Electric and water utility managers could use TDR to promote compact services areas, which are more efficient to operate and which might lead to lower overall utility rates.

5) Park Directors. Park directors could use TDR as a means of acquiring expensive parkland and open space in an era when land acquisition budgets are limited at best.

6) Finance/Budget Directors. City and county finance and budget directors should be able to remind community development directors and park directors that, because of TDR, land acquisition goals do not necessarily require enormous budgets.

7) Municipal Attorneys. Municipal attorneys are responsible for advising elected officials about litigation which could result from proposed land use regulations. Consequently, they should be aware that TDR can be used to mitigate restrictive land use controls and avoid successful legal challenges.

2. Regional, State and Federal Agencies

a. Regional Planning Agencies. Regional planning agencies typically do not exert direct control over the use of land, deferring to the long-standing desire of cities and counties to regulate their own land uses. Nevertheless, regional agencies can get involved in TDR. For example, the Tahoe Regional Planning Agency (TRPA) runs one of the most successful TDR programs in California. While TRPA may be an extreme and atypical case, other regional planning agencies could adopt ambitious goals for the preservation of greenbelts, natural areas, open space, and agricultural land. Furthermore, these agencies could promote transferable development rights as a means to implement these regional goals and even facilitate their use by creating regional TDR banks which purchase rights from sending sites and sell them for use on receiving sites.

b. State Agencies. There are numerous opportunities for branches of state government to use TDR. In fact, one of the most successful TDR programs in the country—the New Jersey Pinelands Program described in Chapter II—is run by a branch of the state of New Jersey. At least three TDR programs in California—in Monterey County, in the Santa Monica Mountains, and in San Luis Obispo County—were at least assisted by state programs (see Chapter III). And, of course, tremendous opportunities exist for greater state involvement in various ways, including—

 ▶ Identifying areas in need of preservation which could benefit from the use of TDR

 ▶ Encouraging TDR to preserve natural areas, open space, agricultural land, and other resources of statewide importance

 ▶ Facilitating their use through the creation of TDR banks and other means

To increase the use of TDR at the state level, planners, program managers, finance directors, and attorneys should increase their familiarity with TDR. While these professionals could be employed by almost any branch of state government, the most likely agencies are the Department of Agriculture, the California Coastal Commission, the Department of Fish and Game, the Housing and Community Development Department, the Parks and Recreation Department, the Department of Transportation, the State Historic Preservation Office, and the Governor's Office of Planning and Research.

c. Federal Agencies. A significant portion of the land area of California is owned by the federal government and managed by federal agencies such as the U.S. Forest Service, the National Park Service, and the Bureau of Land Management. As with local and state agencies, these federal agencies have land acquisition objectives which have to be met within constrained budgets. The U.S. Forest Service, for example, looks for opportunities to acquire privately owned land within designated forest boundaries. TDR programs which combine the regulatory authority of federal agencies and local government could be used to acquire these privately owned parcels while at the same time achieving land use goals for receiving sites.

3. Elected and Appointed Officials

This book is intended not only to advise governmental agencies about how to create and manage a TDR program, but also to encourage governments to consider using transferable development rights or to consider improving their existing TDR programs.

Too often, land use plans and open space elements are not implemented because of various inaccurate assumptions. One assumption is that public funds will be needed to preserve natural areas, open space, and other important assets. Another is that restrictive land use controls would require public funds to compensate the owners of the restricted properties or that, at the very least, such increases in land use restrictions would be too unpopular politically to adopt. This book urges that these assumptions be challenged. The "win-win" quality of TDR reduces the potential liabilities inherent in attempting to use limited public funds to purchase property or trying to severely restrict development without compensation.

4. Property Owners/Developers

This book allows property owners and developers to learn about TDR, its various uses, where it has been successful, and the ingredients needed for an effective program. Once familiar with the concept, property owners and developers can suggest the preparation of a program to a city or county government and even offer to participate in its development.

a. Owners/Developers of Sending Sites. In many cases, property owners and developers benefit most from TDR. The owners of a sending site, for example, may actually be receptive to an alternative to developing that site. They often realize that the development approval process will require time (in some cases several years) and money (for out-of-pocket expenses for environmental studies and technical reports), yet may not ultimately result in an approval.

b. Owners/Developers of Receiving Sites. The benefits of TDR are equally great for owners and developers interested in increasing density on a receiving site. As with the owner of the sending site, without a TDR program this developer faces delays, expenses, and uncertainty.

5. Environmental Organizations, Historic Preservation Societies, and Other Preservation Groups

Individuals and organizations routinely call on governments to save natural areas, preserve historic landmarks, protect open space, and accomplish a wealth of other land use goals. A common government response is that money isn't budgeted for land acquisition and that implementation of land use goals will have to be delayed until funding is available. Individuals and groups who are fully aware of TDR could urge these governments to adopt programs which use this technique.

C. Why Use TDR?

Many communities admit that they do not expect to achieve all their land use goals given the limitations of their current zoning and their inability to preserve land through public acquisition (see Chapter IV). TDR can address these problems because compensation is provided at little or no public expense. This compensation factor allows communities to adopt more effective zoning requirements to help communities meet numerous land use goals from growth management to the preservation of open space, historic landmarks, natural areas, and agricultural land. In addition, active TDR programs promote appropriate development on receiver sites and consequently implement several land use goals at the same time.

Right
Monterey County adopted a TDC program in conjunction with the viewshed protection provisions of the Big Sur Land Use Plan. The Plan prohibits new development which would be visible from Highway 1, providing a strong incentive for property owners to use TDC. The program also features a revolving fund for the purchase and sale of TDCs. The creation of this TDC program helped affected property owners as well as the general public understand the need to preserve the unique character of Big Sur.

I. Current Zoning Restrictions Will Not Achieve All Land Use Goals

Less than 20 percent of the communities responding to a statewide survey believed that their community's land use goals would be completely achieved given current regulatory authority and funding levels (see Chapter IV). Addressing regulations first, it is apparent that zoning restrictions are not strong enough in most communities to completely implement the community's general plan. The inadequate zoning restrictions could result from a lack of real commitment to the community goals and/or a reluctance to impose zoning restrictions which might reduce, or be seen to reduce, property values.

a. TDR Can Help a Community Commit to Its Goals.
It is relatively easy to insert lofty goals in a general plan without implementing them. However, some communities find that the process of preparing and adopting a TDR program helps to focus public attention on important community resources and strengthen the community's resolve to achieve its land use goals. For example, the process of preparing and adopting a TDR ordinance in Monterey County helped the citizens and elected officials to reach a consensus on the need to preserve the Big Sur area (see Chapter III).

b. Compensation Can Help a Community Adopt Effective Zoning Regulations.
Land use restrictions can cause economic impacts. For example, the owner of hillside property could experience a reduction in the value of that property if the property is "downzoned," or rezoned so that less development is allowed. In some cases, the zoning could be so restrictive that a court might conclude that a regulatory taking had occurred.[1] Regardless of legal responsibilities, many elected officials, and many communities in general, simply have difficulty in imposing an economic loss on a property owner without providing some kind of compensation.

When considering how to compensate owners for reduced property values, many communities primarily think of acquisition with the use of public funds. And since public funding for land acquisition is scarce, these communities often decide to retain their current, less effective zoning.

---

[1] The legal aspects of takings, compensation, and TDR are discussed at length in the "Legal Issues" section of this chapter.

2. Land Acquisition Funds Are Limited

Often compensation may be needed to adopt land use controls which actually achieve a community's goals. One method of compensation is to acquire the property using grants or other public funds. However, according to the statewide survey discussed in Chapter IV, most communities believe, partly because of current funding levels, that their land use goals will not be completely achieved. These funding levels are not expected to completely—or, in some cases, even partially—provide for the acquisition of natural areas, agricultural land, and other community assets.

In addition, there is no reason to believe that land acquisition funding levels will improve in the foreseeable future. With the lingering recession in California, limited budgets are likely to be oriented toward job-creating activities (such as infrastructure improvements) rather than property acquisition, especially property acquisition for open space purposes.

3. TDR Can Make Effective Zoning Possible

Outright land acquisition by public agencies is difficult if not impossible for most communities given rising property values and increased competition for limited land acquisition funding sources. However, TDR does not rely on public funds for compensation—the value of the transferred development rights provides the compensation. As suggested in Chapter VI, more communities will turn to TDR as the preferred—and often the only realistic—method for providing compensation for land use restrictions.

a. TDR Provides Compensation. Throughout most of this book, the term "compensation" simply means payment. In the "Legal Issues" section, the legal implications of the term compensation are fully explored because there are unresolved questions about the ability of TDR to provide "just compensation," as required by the U.S. Constitution, if a regulation is so restrictive that a "taking" has occurred. To summarize the discussion in the "Legal Issues" section, transferable development rights can be used to address the adverse effects of restrictive zoning regulations in two ways.

If a zoning regulation only partially restricts an owner's ability to use his or her property, TDR can provide some economic return which otherwise would not occur. This economic return can be considered in determining whether there has been a deprivation of all economically beneficial use of property or undue interference with the property owner's reasonable investment-backed expectation.

The second application, which is more problematic, involves the use of TDR to provide "just compensation" when a regulation is so restrictive that it constitutes a "taking." The ability of TDR to provide "just compensation" remains an open question for the courts to resolve in future decisions. The U.S. Supreme Court has so far only noted that the ability of a specific TDR ordinance to provide "just compensation" can be limited if the TDR ordinance contains too many restrictions on the transfer process such as few eligible receiver sites, complex approval procedures, and an uncertain market for development rights.

b. TDR Compensation Allows Communities to Adopt Effective Zoning Regulations. The compensation mechanism provided by TDR is beneficial to all parties involved in the transaction. Sending site owners can enjoy an economic return by transferring TDRs, even though development on the property from which the credits are transferred is severely restricted. Owners and developers in receiving areas are able to increase density on these sites and, consequently, boost economic return. And, of course, communities benefit because they are able to impose the zoning restrictions which actually achieve their land use goals while providing compensation in a way that does not require public funds for land acquisition. For these reasons, TDR has been described as a "win-win" solution to difficult land use problems.

4. TDR Helps Implement Entire Land Use Plans

Widespread recognition of the need to increase development in receiving areas is critical to the success of a TDR program (see Chapters III and IV). The preparation of a TDR program is an ideal opportunity for communities to examine their land use plans and identify areas which are appropriate for higher densities. The TDR program can then include incentives which generate transfers of development to the receiving sites. In the process, TDR is not only providing a mechanism for protecting the sending areas but is also helping to implement various aspects of the community's land use plan.

5. TDR Has Numerous Potential Uses

Seven potential uses for TDR are discussed in this section. In Chapter III, case studies from 27 California TDR programs are organized into these same seven categories so that readers can explore each of these potential uses in greater depth.

a. Preserve/Restore Natural Areas. At least six California communities have TDR programs designed primarily to preserve unique natural or scenic areas such as coastal bluffs, beaches, and stream environments. Monterey County, for example, has prohibited future development within scenic areas of Big Sur. In the Monterey County program, TDR allows the owners of these properties to transfer an unused development right plus a bonus right to an appropriate receiver site.

The Tahoe Regional Planning Agency and the City of South Lake Tahoe have two of the most successful TDR programs in the state. In these programs, the number of dwelling units are reduced in sensitive natural areas. In order to transfer rights from the program's Stream Environment Zone, the TDR program requires the elimination of all existing development. Consequently, the program has gone beyond preservation to restoration.

b. Protect Hillsides. At least eight TDR programs in California are designed to protect hillsides from inappropriate development. In many cases, these TDR programs are attempting to achieve multiple goals—

▶ Protection of the natural environment

▶ Provision of open space

▶ Preservation of scenic views

▶ Reduction of potential landslide and wildfire hazards

▶ Correction of substandard lots created by antiquated subdivisions

The Santa Monica Mountains program has accomplished more than 500 transfers in the coastal mountains west of Los Angeles, making it one of the most successful TDR programs in the nation. On a smaller scale, the City of Morgan Hill's TDR program has preserved more than 100 acres of hillside land.

c. Preserve Historic Landmarks. At least three California TDR programs are designed to preserve historic landmarks. The most successful program is in downtown San Francisco, where more than ten landmarks have been saved by transferring the unused density potential from the landmark site to allow new buildings elsewhere within downtown to exceed the density allowed by zoning.

d. Protect Agricultural Land. San Mateo County's program uses TDR to preserve land for agricultural uses. It also promotes the preservation of agriculture itself by offering bonus density credits for agricultural improvements such as water storage facilities.

e. Promote Urban Form. Many cities impose uniform density restrictions over large areas to ensure that future development will not overwhelm the transportation and public service systems. Some cities use TDR to allow concentrations of density at appropriate locations despite the overall density cap. In Burbank, for example, development

Below

Since the 1960s, the City of San Francisco has used TDR to preserve historic buildings like the designated landmark pictured below. The owners of historic properties have a strong incentive to sell or transfer TDRs since San Francisco's landmark regulations make it very difficult to demolish a historic structure. Similarly, since it is the only method available for new developments to exceed downtown San Francisco's density limits, there is a strong demand for TDC. As a result, more than ten San Francisco landmarks have been preserved using this program.

rights have been transferred allowing increased density at two important focal points without an increase in total growth capacity.

f.   Encourage Development of Housing. Many communities want to encourage housing in or near employment centers to improve their job/housing balance. The City of Irvine created a TDR program which encouraged housing in the Irvine Business Center by providing an incentive for developers to build housing and transfer unused office development rights to an appropriate receiving site.

g.   Promote Revitalization. Many cities would like to implement their land use goals by encouraging the removal of older, nonconforming structures to make way for new buildings and uses which are consistent with community plans. In many instances, this recycling process is hindered by the fact that the obsolete structures are larger than the buildings which would be allowed under current zoning restrictions. Consequently, the owners of these properties are reluctant to give up the revenues from this additional space. To deal with that problem, the City of Santa Barbara adopted a Transfer of Existing Development Rights (TEDR) program. Under this program, the difference between the development rights of the larger building and the development rights of the smaller building replacing it can be transferred to an appropriate receiving site.

TEDR = Transfer of Existing Development Rights

D. Legal Issues[2]

The use of TDR as a mechanism to control or focus development gives rise to a variety of legal issues. Some of these issues relate to the nature of the transfer itself and the relationship between owners of the sending and receiving sites. Among other legal questions which may need to be addressed in documenting a TDR transaction are the effect of taxes, and the extent to which title encumbrances on the sending site limit the transferability of TDR to the receiving site.[3]

The use of transferable development rights also presents a number of legal issues for the governmental agency which has adopted the ordinance. Although a comprehensive discussion of these legal ramifications

[2] This section was written by Donald I. Berger, a partner in the Los Angeles office of the law firm Morrison & Foerster.

[3] In *Mitsui Fudosan (U.S.A.) v. County of Los Angeles*, 219 Cal. App. 3d 525 (1990), the court held that transferable development rights constitute an interest in real property and, when transferred, properly result in the reassessment of the receiving site owner's real property taxes. The court also suggested that the transfer should result in a corresponding decrease in the real property taxes of the sending site.

is beyond the scope of this study, two frequently encountered legal issues are addressed—the relationship between the TDR ordinance and the local governmental agency's general plan, and the role TDR may play in determining whether a restrictive zoning regulation constitutes a taking of private property without just compensation.

1. Consistency with General Plan

a. Consistency of Goals. Like all zoning provisions, a TDR ordinance must be consistent with the community's general plan. In the broadest sense, TDR ordinances must promote the goals of the general plan, such as the preservation of open space and maintenance of character in single-family residential neighborhoods. More specifically, the TDR ordinance should be coordinated with the general plan to allow and encourage transfers.

b. Consistency of Density Limitations. To encourage transfers, a TDR ordinance will often allow increases in density beyond the limits allowed by the zoning in effect at the receiving site. If the density allowed by the zoning is exactly the same as the density called for in the general plan, an increase in density on the receiving site might not be consistent with the general plan unless provisions in the general plan allow for density increases as a result of TDR actions. For example, when Burbank adopted its Media District Specific Plan, a general plan amendment provided for exceptions to density limitations in order to allow for transfer of development rights. The overall development capacity of the Media District is not changed by that exception.

In some communities, the densities allowed under the zoning code are lower than the densities provided in the general plan. In these cases, general plan consistency is met as long as the general plan densities are not exceeded and as long as the transferred density promotes the overall goals of the general plan.

c. Prepare TDR Ordinances in Conjunction with General Plan Amendments. The consistency issue is more than a legal technicality. The ability to significantly increase density on a receiving site can be critical to the success of a TDR program. The TDR programs in some communities have been dormant largely because their general plans do not allow a sufficient density increase on receiving sites to motivate transfers (see Chapter III). The need to adopt TDR programs in conjunction with complementary general plan amendments is discussed in greater detail in Chapter V.

2. TDR and Regulatory Takings

a. TDR Ordinances Are Typically Adopted in Conjunction with Zoning Restrictions Derived from a Local Agency's Police Power. In many states, TDR is specifically mentioned in state law as a function of local government planning, zoning, or land use regulation.[4] California state law does not specifically authorize local agencies to adopt TDR ordinances. Consequently, those cities and counties which adopt these ordinances must rely on the argument that TDR is an extension of police powers and that local governments are thereby inherently enabled to adopt TDR ordinances under California law.[5]

For example, the TDR ordinance in the City of Oxnard states that "The authority to establish a transfer of development rights program is within the scope of the police power established in Article XI, Section 7 of the State Constitution." The City of Pacifica ordinance cites the constitution and also states that the TDR program "... is necessary to the exercise of the City's planning and zoning authority as set forth in the State Planning and Zoning Law, Title 7, Division One of the California Government Code."

By its very nature, a TDR ordinance is typically adopted in conjunction with some other zoning law which regulates the density, intensity, or use of the receiving and sending sites. It is by virtue of these restrictions on the use of private property that the incentives for transferring development rights are created.

b. In Certain Instances, Zoning Restrictions May Result in a Regulatory Taking. A governmental agency's imposition of zoning restrictions on the use of private property can result in a regulatory taking of such property. This issue has been addressed in numerous court cases and is the subject of many articles and books. While a detailed discussion of the law of regulatory takings is well beyond the purview of this book, a brief overview of certain general legal concepts is necessary to understand the role TDR may play in determining whether and when a regulatory taking has occurred.

As noted above, the local governmental agency's authority to regulate the use of private property through the adoption of zoning measures derives from a state's police power to protect the public health,

---

[4] Richard J. Roddewig and Cheryl A. Inghram, *Transferable Development Rights Programs* (Chicago, Illinois: American Planning Association, 1987).

[5] Madelyn Glickfeld, "Wipeout Mitigation: Planning Prevention," in Joseph DiMento, ed., *Wipeouts and Their Mitigation: The Changing Context for Land Use and Environmental Law* (Cambridge, Massachusetts: Lincoln Institute of Land Policy, 1990).

safety, and general welfare. However, despite its broad authority to regulate pursuant to these police powers, government action remains subject to the Fifth and Fourteenth Amendments of the United States Constitution, which preclude government from taking private property for public use without "just compensation," and from depriving individuals of their private property without "due process of law." Thus, "while property may be regulated to a certain extent, if the regulation goes too far, it would be recognized as a taking."[6]

The courts have been generally reluctant to rely upon any set formula for determining when a governmental regulation constitutes a taking, opting instead for an ad hoc, case-by-case, factual analysis. However, several recent cases do provide some guiding principles.

First, as the United States Supreme Court recently clarified in *Lucas v. South Carolina Coastal Council*, if the effect of a zoning regulation is to deny a property owner all economically beneficial use of his or her property, that regulation constitutes a taking without just compensation unless the restricted uses could have been prohibited under the state's nuisance or property law.[7] Although the courts have not clearly defined when the deprivation of all economically feasible use occurs, the Lucas opinion suggests that requiring land to be left substantially in its natural state (i.e., open space) would constitute such a deprivation.

Second, the "property interest" against which the economic impact of the regulation is to be measured may constitute something less than the property owner's entire property holding. To the extent state law has accorded legal recognition and protection to a particular interest in property (for example, an easement or air rights), a regulation which deprives the property owner of that interest may constitute a taking.[8]

6 *Pennsylvania Coal Co. v. Mahon*, 260 U.S. 393 (1922).

7 *Lucas v. South Carolina Coastal Council*, 112 S. Ct. 2886, 120 L. ed. 2d 798 (1992). The *Lucas* court went on to explain that to the extent "background principles" of nuisance and property law would otherwise have prohibited the same use of the property prohibited by the governmental regulation, such use was, in effect, *always unlawful,* and the governmental agency could properly make such prohibition explicit through the adoption of the regulation without paying just compensation to the landowner. The court noted that the inquiry as to whether state nuisance law would otherwise excuse a "total taking" would ordinarily entail an analysis of the degree of harm to public lands and resources (or adjacent private property) posed by the property owner's proposed activities, the social value of the property owner's activity, and the suitability to the locality in question, and the relative ease with which the alleged harm could be avoided through measures taken by the property owner and the governmental agency.

8 The court in *Lucas* specifically criticized the view espoused in *Penn Central Transportation Co. v. New York City* that the diminution in a particular parcel's

Finally, even in the absence of a total taking, zoning regulations may so substantially interfere with a property owner's "reasonable investment-backed expectations" that a taking of property has occurred.[9] Among other factors considered by courts in making this determination are—[10]

- The severity and extensiveness of regulations at the time the property was purchased

- The past regulatory history of the specific property

- The degree of impairment of the uses of the property

- The uses available before the enactment of the challenged regulation

- The novelty or expectedness of the governmental actions

- Whether existing uses were permitted to continue

- The ability to sell the property to others at a fair price

- The ability to obtain a reasonable return or profit on one's investment in the property

- Whether any development rights were substituted for those impaired by the zoning regulation

It is this last factor—the substitution of development rights—that sets the context for the application of TDR in the regulatory takings arena. Specifically, one must consider the extent to which underlying zoning restrictions on either the receiving or sending sites are sufficiently onerous to interfere with the property owner's reasonable investment-backed expectations. Then, to what extent does the right to enhance one's use of the property through the acquisition of TDR (in the case of the receiving site owner), or the selling of TDR as a means of compensation for the proportional loss of use of one's property (in case of the sending site owner), reduce the risk that a taking will be found? These issues are explored below.

value is to be determined in light of the total value of the property owner's interests. The comment suggests that, in certain circumstances, the court might be willing to find that the deprivation of all use of a parcel's air rights may constitute a taking which requires just compensation. *See also, Nollan v. California Coastal Commission,* 483 U.S. 825 (1987), in which the Supreme Court invalidated a permit condition which required the property owner to grant an easement as a condition to rebuilding a home. In *Nollan,* the Supreme Court found that the forced grant of an easement constituted a "permanent physical occupation" and hence was a taking "per se."

[9] *Lucas v. South Carolina Coastal Council,* 112 S. Ct. 2886, 120 L.ed. 2d 798 (1992) footnote 8.

[10] See Berger, "Happy Birthday Constitution, the Supreme Court Establishes New Ground Rules for Land Use Planning," 20 *Urban Lawyer,* (1988).

c. Penn Central and the Use of TDR as Mitigation or Compensation.

In *Penn Central Transportation Co. v. New York City*, the U.S. Supreme Court in 1978 upheld a challenge to New York City's landmark preservation law by Penn Central, the owner of the historic Grand Central Railway Terminal. Under New York's Landmarks Law, once a building was designated a "landmark," any modification to the exterior required the approval of the Landmarks Preservation Commission. Because substantial limitations on the property owners' use of their property was anticipated, the city also adopted a TDR program which allowed the property owners to transfer development rights to other parcels in the vicinity of the landmark. After it had been denied permission to construct an office building within the air space above the terminal, Penn Central sued the city on the grounds that the effect of the Landmarks Law was to take their property (the air space above the terminal), claiming that the right to transfer development density did not constitute "just compensation."

In finding that the Landmarks Law did not amount to a taking of Penn Central's property, the court held that the regulation would not interfere with Penn Central's present use of the terminal and did not unduly interfere with its air rights because its ability to use these rights was made transferable pursuant to the TDR ordinance.[11] As stated by the court—

> While these [transferable development] rights may well not have constituted "just compensation" if a "taking" had occurred, the rights nevertheless undoubtedly mitigate whatever financial burdens the law has imposed on appellants and, for that reason, are to be taken into account in considering the impact of the regulation.

The *Penn Central* decision suggests that there are two contexts in which TDR may be used to address potential impacts of restrictive zoning regulations: 1) as "mitigation" which should be considered in determining whether there has been a deprivation of all economically beneficial use of property or undue interference with the property owner's reasonable investment-backed expectation; and 2) as "just compensation" in certain circumstances where the zoning regulation is sufficiently onerous to constitute a "taking."

---

[11] The Supreme Court cited a second factor in support of its conclusion that Penn Central had not been denied the use of air rights over the terminal: that the only use which Penn Central had requested the Landmarks Commission to approve was for a 50-story office building, and that it had not sought approval for a smaller structure which, if approved, may have provided an additional return on Penn Central's investment.

The differences between the mitigation and just compensation role of a TDR program relate principally to the level of restriction imposed by the underlying zoning designation and the potential value of TDR in restoring the property owner's economic interest.

If a zoning regulation only partially restricts a property owner's right to use his or her property (for example, preserves the owner's right to maintain existing commercial uses, as in *Penn Central*), TDR may serve as a mechanism to supplement the investment return which otherwise would be realized by the property owner (by providing an additional source of income through the transfer of development rights). Depending upon whether air rights or other similar interests are considered a separate property interest, TDR may also serve as a mechanism to restore some economic value to those interests.

By contrast, if a regulation is so restrictive that a "taking" has occurred, the ability of the governmental agency to rely on a TDR program as just compensation is more problematic. The compensation due the affected property owner may not be merely an approximation of the value of property taken, but "a full and perfect equivalent."[12] Thus, the court in *Penn Central* seemed to acknowledge that limitations on the use of transferable development rights under the New York City law may have reduced their value to the landowner to the point that they could no longer serve as "just compensation." Among other factors cited which could limit the value of TDR as just compensation were the area to which the transfer is permitted, the complexity of the procedures required to obtain a transfer permit, and, more generally, the "uncertain and contingent market value" of the TDR.[13]

Above

The City of Belmont adopted a TDR ordinance to solve the problem of antiquated subdivisions on unstable slopes. In one instance, the city was able to transfer development from a landslide area and consequently preserve the sensitive hillside.

   d. Considerations in Maximizing the Benefits of TDR as a Means to Avoid Takings Claims. The *Penn Central* decision and other recent regulatory takings cases suggest that a number of factors should be weighed in determining when and how a TDR ordinance may be used to reduce the risk that a restrictive zoning designation will result in a regulatory taking claim.

---

[12] See *Monongahela Navigation Co. v. United States*, 148 U. S. 312 (1893); *United States v. Lynah*, 188 U.S. 445 (1903). *See also, Penn Central, supra*, 438 U.S. at page 150 (dissenting opinion).

[13] *See Penn Central, supra*, 438 U.S. at 151-152 (dissenting opinion).

First, the more restrictive the underlying zoning regulation on the permissible uses of the sending or receiving site, the more substantial the risk that takings issues will arise, and the more important the TDR program may be in determining the adequacy of mitigation or compensation.

Second, the adequacy of a TDR program as mitigation or compensation will depend in large part on how valuable the transferred development rights are perceived to be. Among other factors affecting the marketability, and hence the value, of TDR are the following—

- The area to which a transfer may be permitted

- The incentives provided to the receiving site owner to acquire TDR

- Whether the transfer of development rights is subject to any additional discretionary governmental action which may undermine the ability of the receiving site owner to use the TDR

- Whether the ordinance is sufficiently complex that the ability to transfer or use the TDR in any particular instance is difficult to determine

- Whether the development rights to be transferred are discounted or enhanced prior to use by the receiving site owner

- Whether a market for TDR transactions actually develops

Finally, a well-crafted TDR program may produce political and other practical benefits which reduce the risk that a takings lawsuit will be filed. To the extent a free market in TDR can be promoted through the adoption of an ordinance, sending site owners would receive meaningful compensation, thereby assuaging concerns that the zoning restrictions are too harsh; and receiving site owners would obtain the right to develop their property at a density or intensity not otherwise permitted, thereby easing the burden of having to purchase development rights. These factors and other techniques affecting the success of a TDR program are highlighted in Chapter III and discussed at greater length in Chapter V.

E. Economic Issues

1. Economics of Receiving Sites

The use of TDR increases when the demand for development rights and their price is attractive to both buyers and sellers.

a. Demand for TDR

1) Health of Local Economy. A developer must be able to profit from the additional development transferred to the receiving site (see Chapters III and V). This profit will only be generated if the developer can sell the additional units or lease the additional floor area in a reasonable period of time. Conversely, in some markets, the demand for additional development is so low that the marginal profits from developing at a higher density do not exceed the additional cost incurred in purchasing the right to develop at that density. In other words, the better the health of the local economy, the greater the demand for additional development.

2) Development Controls. If they can obtain additional density through some other means, owners of receiving sites will have little or no need to acquire development rights. As pointed out in Chapter III, many TDR programs fail because the community offers additional development to proposed projects at less expense than the cost of TDRs for various reasons. These include—

- Desirable design features
- Project amenities
- Completion of infrastructure improvements
- Consistency with the general plan

A well-designed TDR program will eliminate or minimize ways to increase densities of receiving sites without the use of TDR.

b. Price of Development Rights. Even if the demand for development rights is high, transfers may still not occur if the price is not attractive to both buyers and sellers. The price of TDRs must be low enough that the developers of receiving sites can realize equal or greater profits from a higher density development, even after incurring the added expense of buying development rights. Conversely, the price of TDRs must be high enough to induce the sending site owners to sell these rights.

2. Economics of Sending Sites

a. Ability to Develop Sending Sites. When development regulations on sending sites become increasingly restrictive, the owners of these properties have a greater incentive to transfer.

b. Ability to Find Buyers of TDRs. The sending site owners, in addition to wanting to sell their TDRs, must be able to find receiving site property owners who want to buy them. The particular characteristics of the TDR market are important to determining whether sending site owners are successful in locating interested buyers.

c. Price of Development Rights. For a supply of development rights to be created, the amount of profit which the owner of a sending property can realize from selling or transferring development rights must exceed the profit to be made by developing on the sending site. To ensure that transfers occur, TDR programs should operate in a highly active TDR market and/or provide market interventions.

3. Market Characteristics

Some characteristics of a good TDR market have already been addressed—a healthy local economy which provides a demand for additional development, motivated buyers and sellers of development rights, and attractive TDR prices. In addition, an ideal market will have enough potential buyers and sellers to ensure that optimum TDR prices will be maintained. If the number of potential receiving site owners is relatively small, there will be less competition, and the TDR price could decline to a level which is not attractive to potential sellers. Conversely, if there are relatively few owners of potential sending sites, the lack of competition may cause TDR prices to increase to a level at which these purchases are no longer profitable.

Since TDR markets are not always ideal, many communities include various market interventions in their TDR programs.

4. Market Intervention

a. Transfer Ratios. To induce both buyers and sellers to use transfer of development rights, many programs multiply the number of development rights allowed on the receiving site for each development right transferred from the sending site. Four of the programs summarized in Chapter III use these "transfer ratios." Oxnard, for example, recognized that the value of being able to build one beachfront home on a sending site is much higher than the value of being able to build one apartment unit at an inland receiving site. Using appraisals to estimate these relative values, Oxnard set the transfer ratio at 6:1, or six units at a receiving site for every development right transferred from a beachfront sending site.

Transfer ratios should be designed so that developers of receiving parcels make at least as much profit by developing sites at the higher densities allowed through TDR. Because several factors must be taken into consideration, this calculation can be more difficult than it might at first appear.

1) Construction Costs at Higher Densities. Construction costs at the densities being considered for receiving sites should be evaluated by a contractor or developer. In some instances, construction costs per square foot of building area can decrease because a greater amount of building area can share common structural features. But other factors may increase the construction costs per square foot—such as the need to meet more expensive building code requirements, the expense of providing multiple levels of parking, or the requirement for additional building features such as elevators.

2) Market Demand for Higher Density Development. On the revenue side, each community should consider the marketability of the type of development which would result from the proposed transfer ratio. In some communities, the post-transfer density would still be well within the range of development densities with a proven record of success. In communities where the proposed density of development is an untested commodity, some additional analysis of demand would be needed to determine whether projects at the proposed densities could be readily sold at a profit.

3) Adding TDR Costs to Other Receiving Site Costs. After estimating the relative costs and revenues of developing at higher receiving site densities, the community can determine the additional cost a developer would be willing to pay for the development rights needed to allow additional development.

4) Costs of Developing Sending Sites. The cost-revenue analysis of the sending sites can be as complicated as those needed for the receiving sites. In many cases, the sending sites are natural areas or hillsides, and the transfer-ratio analysis must address numerous development cost questions—

> ▶ What are the costs of geotechnical, environmental, engineering, and other studies which the community will require prior to approving development?

> ▶ What are the holding costs associated with loan and tax payments while the studies noted above are performed, sometimes over the course of several years?

> ▶ What are likely costs of development given the possible need to pay for extensive grading and installation of streets, sewers, utilities, and other infrastructure?

Below

In the 1970s and early 1980s, lawsuits with claims for more than $40 million were filed against the City of Oxnard by organizations both in favor of and opposed to further development of a beachfront area known as Oxnard Shores, shown below. In response, Oxnard adopted a TDR ordinance designed to encourage property owners to forego beachfront development and transfer the development rights to inland receiver sites. The Oxnard ordinance had an impressive array of incentives including a six-to-one transfer ratio and exemptions from various development fees. However, after a few transfers occurred in the mid-1980s, a settlement agreement resolved the lawsuits and minimized the need for the TDR program.

5) Sales Price of Development on Sending Sites. In some communities, the likely sales price of development at the sending site is well-established, while in others, the issue may not be so clear. If the estimated sales prices are significantly higher than the average selling prices for the community, appraisers may question the high expectations of sending-site property owners. And lenders may be concerned about the length of time needed for environmental studies, permit approvals, site preparation, and installation of infrastructure.

6) Selling Price of Sending-Site TDRs. By projecting a sensible sales price for development at a sending site and deducting all the development costs mentioned above, a reasonable profit can be estimated. Theoretically, the owner of a sending site will be willing to sell development rights for that amount or more.

For the purpose of a simple demonstration, assume that a community's typical sending site TDR value is $50,000. If $10,000 is the amount a typical receiving-site developer would be willing to pay for a TDR, the break-even ratio would be five to one.

7) Setting the Transfer Ratio. In order to stimulate transfer activity, communities should set the actual transfer ratio higher than the break-even point. The bonus amount added to the transfer ratio will depend on several factors which are specific to the community.

For example, a high transfer ratio may be warranted if numerous owners of smaller properties in the sending area purchased their properties in anticipation of building personal residences. Another consideration is how well the TDR program as a whole is designed. Less reliance needs to be placed on a high transfer ratio if other components of the TDR program are in place, including—

- The need to use TDR in order to achieve desired densities on both sending and receiving sites

- The market demand for more development on receiving sites

- The existence of other incentives such as fee waivers

Finally, how badly does the community want transfers to occur? If the TDR program was merely developed to comply with a general plan policy, a community may not mind if relatively few transfers occur. But if it resulted from strong community commitment, the TDR program should be monitored. If the level of transfer activity is weak, the community can explore various ways to make the program more effective, including use of the transfer ratio.

b. Time Is Money. Holding costs—such as loan and tax payments—can be a significant factor in the economics of development.

Consequently, the owners and developers of both sending and receiving sites will be apprehensive of any TDR program which may add time delays to the approval process. This apprehension will grow to aversion if the process is discretionary, meaning that elected or appointed officials have the authority to deny a proposed TDR transaction for any number of reasons.

1) Administrative Approval Eliminates Uncertainty. Whenever possible, TDR programs should be ministerial with the rules spelled out so clearly that developers know that transfers will be approved if all the steps are followed. A completely ministerial program would be one which involves no discretionary judgment.

The South Lake Tahoe TDR program approaches this goal. South Lake Tahoe's ordinance lists the requirements needed for the granting of a TDR permit, and the city offers guidelines to assist developers in understanding the approval process. The South Lake Tahoe TDR permits are issued by city staff. The staff may impose conditions, but the decision is final unless appealed to the City Council. Because a staff decision can be appealed, the South Lake Tahoe program should be considered administrative and not completely ministerial.

Most California TDR programs require discretionary approval (see Chapter III). In these programs, the communities are unable or unwilling to address the potential impacts of the transfer program as a whole, and these programs retain the right to examine the effects of each transfer on a case-by-case basis.

2) Certainty of Approval Time Benefits Developers. In addition to certainty of approval, developers benefit from knowing how long the approval of a TDR permit will take. This time period can then be built into the financial analysis of a project. For example, the City of South Lake Tahoe promises a response to a TDR permit request within two weeks.

c. Incentives. Many communities also adjust the demand for TDRs by offering incentives (see Chapters III and V). These incentives have the effect of increasing the value of transferred rights and consequently increasing supply and demand.

1) Exemption from Dedication Requirements. To make the use of TDR more economically attractive, some communities, such as Pacifica, exempt projects involving transfers from dedication requirements.

2) Waiver of Fees. Many communities charge new development fees to pay for necessary street improvements and the expansion of infrastructure and public service systems. In some communities, these development fees can be substantial. As an incentive to use transferable development rights, some communities, including Pacifica and Oxnard, exempt TDR-related projects from these fees.

3) Relaxation of Development Standards. As a financial inducement to use transferable development rights, some communities, such as Pacifica and Irvine, specifically allow TDR-related projects to deviate from code requirements such as open space, parking, and setback standards.

4) Exemption from Building Quotas. Some communities limit the number of homes that can be built each year. Exempting TDR-related projects from these quotas creates a significant financial incentive. In the Tahoe Regional Planning Agency and South Lake Tahoe TDR programs, for example, transfers of existing development rights are not subject to the permit quota system. In Morgan Hill, receiving site developers who purchase transferable development credits can be exempted from the city's development control system. In a similar program, developers who purchase TDCs can be given high scores in Morgan Hill's Residential Development Control System, thereby moving their projects toward the top of the list of projects to be permitted.

5) Ability to Bypass Infrastructure Allocation Systems. In some cities, developers must receive an allocation for water, sewer, or some other public service system before being allowed to build. Since these allocations can sometimes take years to obtain through normal channels, the ability to bypass these allocation systems offers a significant economic incentive to use TDR. In Morgan Hill, one TDR program provides sewer allocations to the purchaser of TDCs.

d. TDR Banks. A TDR bank, which buys development rights from the owners of sending parcels and sells them to the developers of receiving parcels, can be an important economic component of a TDR program both as an incentive to transfer development rights and as a mechanism to influence prices. TDR banks are discussed in greater detail in Chapter V.

1) TDR Banks Are an Incentive to Transfer. In communities where potential sending and receiving sites are in numerous small ownerships, any individual property owner or developer could be overwhelmed by the prospect of finding a potential TDR seller and trying to negotiate a fair price. A TDR bank actively promotes the sale of development rights whenever a sending site owner wishes to sell. Moreover, the bank has TDRs available to sell to potential receiving site developers whenever those developers choose to buy them. In effect, these banks not only alleviate the need for buyers and sellers to find one another but also allow greater flexibility in the timing of TDR sales.

This service is more than mere convenience. With a TDR bank, the developers of receiving sites are assured that development rights will be available when needed, thereby reducing the economic concerns of uncertainty and delay. TDR banks can also greatly reduce transaction costs, because they can assist with legal and real estate procedures such as the placement of covenants or easements on the sending site or the actual transfer of ownership of that site.

2) TDR Banks Can Influence TDR Prices. As mentioned above, if the price of TDRs is either too high or too low, transfer activity can be greatly reduced. Some programs use TDR banks or similar devices to influence and stabilize prices.

As discussed in Chapter III, the Mountains Restoration Trust has been instrumental in influencing the value of TDCs in the Santa Monica Mountains program. In the early 1980s, the price of TDCs in the program was so high that the Trust held an auction of TDCs under its control to increase the supply and reduce prices. However, by the mid-1980s prices had dropped so low that sending site owners were not interested in selling TDCs. To increase the supply, the Trust increased the price of TDCs, and the supply is now adequate to handle the demand.

3) TDR Banks May Not Be Appropriate for Every Community. Because they do not want to compete with the owners of sending sites, some communities, like San Francisco, have chosen not to establish a TDR bank. However, the San Francisco program is still a success because the developers of office towers in downtown San Francisco are capable of finding TDR sellers without the assistance of a bank (see Chapter III).

4) TDR Banks Can Coexist with Private Transactions. The New Jersey Pinelands Development Credit Bank is credited with greatly increasing transfer activity in the Pinelands (see Chapter III). However, the program still encourages private transactions of PDCs (Pinelands Development Credits) and assists private transactions by maintaining lists of potential buyers and sellers.

PDC = Pinelands Development Credit

F. Alternative Means of Transferring Development Rights

Most of the case studies presented in Chapter III describe TDR programs which were created by city ordinances. Transfer of development rights can also be accomplished in at least two other ways—through specific plans and development agreements.

1. Specific Plans

Under California state law, a community can adopt a specific plan which implements the general plan for all or any part of the community. The specific plan must include a program of implementation measures needed, including regulations, programs, public works projects, and financing mechanisms. Consequently, a specific plan by itself can clarify open space protection, historic preservation, and other land use goals and also impose the regulations and programs needed to implement those goals, including TDR.

Specific plans typically focus on a limited portion of the city and directly address the important issues of that area. Consequently, a specific plan is more likely to produce a better understanding of the objectives of the TDR program, the identity of the sending and receiving sites, and the nature of the process itself.

2. Development Agreements

Transfers of development rights can be accomplished on a case-by-case basis using techniques which allow flexibility in creating land use regulations for individual sites. Using techniques referred to as planned developments or planned unit developments, a developer can propose a project on one site which requires one or more exceptions from the zoning code. In return for being granted these exceptions, the developer can offer to preserve an important community asset on another site such as a sensitive natural area or an historic landmark. If it ultimately decides that the proposal promotes the goals of the general plan, the community may approve the proposal.

Although the process may differ from community to community, the plans approved for the receiving site can be memorialized through a "development agreement" between the property owner and the city. The development agreement typically spells out the way the sending site will be preserved from future development. California land use statutes define and prescribe the contents of development agreements.

Below

In the 1970s the City of Claremont adopted a TDC program to preserve its undeveloped hillsides, shown below. Although no transfers have occurred to date, the owners of this hillside land should eventually be motivated to use the program since Claremont's general plan does not allow any further subdivision of undeveloped hillside land. As an alternate method, the city is also marketing an approved specific plan which achieves the same objectives of clustering development in an accessible location while preserving hundreds of acres of higher-elevation hillside land as open space.

▌▌ TDR Programs in Other States

The first section of this chapter discusses the historical foundations and development of transferable development rights. Readers familiar with the TDR concept may wish to proceed directly to the other sections which deal specifically with three TDR programs from other parts of the country.

A. History of Transferable Development Rights

1. Government Actions Affect Property Owners

Throughout time, government actions have benefited some property owners and harmed others. When a government rezones a parcel of land for higher density development, the owners of that land benefit from higher land values. Conversely, when a property is rezoned for lower density, the owner typically suffers a loss in land value.

2. Forerunners of Transferable Development Rights

England's 1947 Town and Country Planning Act allows governments to charge developers for the increase in land value created by permission to develop. Although the United States has no comparable legislation, precedents for TDR can be found in our urban renewal and redevelopment laws which allow a government to recapture the increased value of land caused, at least in part, by development regulations and approvals.[1]

---

1 Madelyn Glickfeld, "Sale of Development Permission: Zoning on the Auction Block," in Donald Hagman and Dean Misczynski, eds., *Windfalls for Wipeouts* (Chicago, Illinois: American Society of Planning Officials, 1978).

In the 1960s and 1970s, various communities considered selling the permission to develop since this permission benefits the property owner. Experts had also identified at least three land use practices which used the same principles as transfer of development rights: the transfer of air rights, the sale of water rights, and specific regulations on oil and gas production.

3. Windfalls and Wipeouts

In 1978, a classic land use book, *Windfalls for Wipeouts*, coined the term "windfalls" to describe the increase in property value enjoyed by landowners when their properties benefit from a governmental action such as a rezoning allowing additional development.

Conversely, the term "wipeouts" was used to describe the loss in property values which results from governmental action, such as a rezoning which reduces or prohibits development on a parcel of land. The book developed and analyzed several techniques for capturing increases in land value created by government action, or windfalls, and using that recaptured value to compensate landowners who suffer damages, or wipeouts, caused by harsh land use regulations. Among those techniques was transferable development rights. The TDR concept was identified as a broader, multiple-owner application of commonplace techniques, such as cluster subdivisions and planned unit developments which also transfer density, but within a land parcel under one ownership. And the TDR process was summarized as follows:

> A planning authority which uses TDR establishes conservation zones and transfer zones. Development is not allowed in conservation zones, and the development potential of the parcels is severed. Transfer zones are the receiving areas for the development potential — thus, transferable density. These transfer zones are areas suitable for more intense development based on planning theory, available public facilities and utilities, and overall compatibility with both the built and natural environment. There is an allowed maximum density in transfer areas, but that density may be exceeded by the purchase of development rights from conservation zone landowners. This transference allows the marketplace to compensate the owner of land where development is restricted by allowing him to sell that density to transfer zone landowners.[2]

---

[2] Frank Schnidman, "Transferable Development Rights (TDR)," in Donald Hagman and Dean Miscznski, eds., *Windfalls for Wipeouts* (Chicago, Illinois: American Society of Planning Officials, 1978).

The book suggested a variety of uses (as a method for preserving historic landmarks or for protecting open space and agricultural land and as an alternative to traditional zoning) and examined existing TDR programs in each of these three categories—[3]

- ► Historic Preservation—New York City
- ► Open Space/Agricultural Land Protection—Collier County, Florida
- ► Alternative to Zoning—New Jersey Pinelands

Each of these three TDR programs is described and examined in the following sections.

B. Examples of TDR Programs in Other States

This section provides an update on the three TDR programs discussed in *Windfalls for Wipeouts*: New York City; Collier County, Florida; and the New Jersey Pinelands.

1. New York City

a. Purpose. The New York City TDR ordinance is designed to preserve historic landmarks.

b. Background. The history of TDR in New York City began in 1961 when the city allowed transfers of density between adjacent properties under the same ownership in order to compensate for the economic impact of designations under the Landmarks Preservation Law.

In 1969, the city denied a request to build a 59-story tower on top of the Grand Central Terminal, a designated historic landmark. The law suit resulting from this denial was eventually heard by the U.S. Supreme Court, which affirmed that the city did not have to allow for maximum economic return on the property and that the development rights above the terminal could be transferred to other sites, thereby mitigating the economic impact of the historic preservation restrictions.[4]

Below

One objective of the Oakland TDR ordinance is the preservation of summer homes built at the turn of the century in the Adams Point neighborhood. However, since the existing zoning allows high density development on potential receiving sites, there is little incentive to transfer even more density from historic properties. The program is also partly hindered because sending and receiving sites must abut one another, similar to the restrictions found in the New York City program.

---

[3] Ibid.

[4] Ibid.

c. **Procedural Features.** At first the city only allowed transfers through a technique called "zoning lot mergers." In a zoning lot merger, a zoning lot is essentially one city block. Adjacent parcels within the block can be given single-lot status so that unused development rights on one parcel can be used on the adjacent parcel. But, in 1968, New York expanded to a TDR program which permitted transfers to properties which are either adjacent or across a street or intersection. And in 1969, the ordinance was changed again to allow transfers to properties which are even farther away, as long as all the intervening properties are under common ownership.

The New York City program ensures not only that the landmark will be protected through preservation/conservation easements, but also that the price paid to the landmark owner is sufficient to maintain the landmark.

The receiving site is limited to 20 percent more density after transfer than the density which would be permitted under the zone designation. The transfer is at a 1:1 ratio. While the zoning lot merger is an administrative procedure, a proposed TDR requires the review of the Planning Commission, which is authorized to evaluate its benefits any adverse effects it may have on the surrounding area.[5]

d. **Transfer Activity.** While zoning lot mergers and other techniques have been used extensively during the first 18 years of the program, the TDR provisions were used only a dozen times .[6] According to Khalid Afzal of the New York City Planning Department, as of 1992 a solution to the Grand Central Terminal situation had still not been found. Suitable receiver sites have not been identified adjacent to the station. Some appropriate sites six or more blocks away may be available, but the city considers a transfer over this distance to have too many complications. The city believes that the receiver site should ideally be in the same zoning district and as close as possible to the sending parcel.[7]

e. **Program Weaknesses.** The New York City TDR program has been hampered by the ability of developers to gain additional density on receiving sites through other means such as rezoning.[8]

Approval of a TDR requires a long review process which most developers try to avoid.[9] Almost 700 landmarks in New York City

[5] Roddewig and Inghram.

[6] Ibid.

[7] Phone conversation with Khalid Afzal, Department of City Planning, City of New York, January 8, 1992.

[8] Roddewig and Inghram.

[9] Ibid.

create a combined supply of TDRs estimated to be more than 20 million square feet. This huge supply tends to reduce the price of TDRs, making the owners of potential sending sites less enthusiastic about selling.[10] And the program offers few incentives—

- The transfer ratio is 1:1
- Additional density on the receiving site cannot exceed 20 percent of the density allowed by zoning
- Transfers are limited to adjacent properties, properties across streets, or properties linked to the landmark by a continuous chain of properties under common ownership

f. Program Strengths. The demand for additional development in New York City would make the TDR program extremely successful if the review process could be streamlined and if the city would minimize non-TDR methods of allowing increased density.

Sometimes alternative methods of obtaining additional density are even more time-consuming than the approval process for TDR. As explained by Khalid Afzal of the New York City Planning Department, in return for additional density, developers may consider proposing an amenity. If, for example, a developer proposes the amenity of subway access, considerable time could be used to acquire the necessary discretionary permits from the transit authority. In the end, despite the necessary approval process, the purchase of TDR from a landmark could take less time.[11]

Since the TDR program in New York City has been in existence since the 1960s, its longevity gives the program legitimacy and ensures that most developers and public officials are familiar with TDR goals and procedures.

2. Collier County, Florida

a. Purpose. The TDR program in Collier County is designed to preserve open space and ecologically sensitive areas—specifically islands, marshes, and coastal areas outside of Naples.

b. Background. In 1974, Collier County approved a revised zoning ordinance, which contained both a growth-control provision to prevent leap-frog development and a new land use designation known as Special Treatment (ST). More than 80 percent of the land area of the county was designated ST, and any development in an ST zone required a

ST = Special Treatment

[10] Ibid.
[11] Afzal.

special permit. An owner could transfer the development rights from the ST land to contiguous land which is not designated ST. The owner of the ST land could either donate the sending parcel to the county or restrict the land by covenant to be used only for open space and recreational uses.[12]

c. Procedural Features. The ST zone regulates but does not prohibit development. Landowners have the option of transferring development to non-ST land at a rate of 0.5 dwelling units per acre of ST land to be preserved. Additional development on the receiving site can be 10 or 20 percent higher than the density allowed by zoning, depending on the receiver site zoning. And, to allow for additional density, landscaping, parking, and open space requirements on the receiving site may be waived.[13]

d. Transfer Activity. Despite numerous program refinements, the only activity in the Collier County TDR program occurred between 1977 and 1981 when 526 development rights were transferred, preserving 325 acres of environmentally sensitive land. A single transaction of the Deltona Corporation accounted for 350 of these transferred development rights.[14]

Statistics on transfer activity do not reflect the fact that some preservation occurs within the ST zones even when no transfer activity occurs. In accordance with land use regulations, developers often protect particularly sensitive areas with on-site open space features, shifting the unused density to other locations on-site.[15]

e. Program Weaknesses. The motivation to transfer TDRs out of a special treatment zone is reduced by the ability to develop in that zone. Because developers in Collier County typically do not build to the densities allowed by the zoning code, the demand for TDRs is reduced. In addition, the owners of receiving area properties have expressed concerns about increased density in their neighborhoods due to TDR.

Another program weakness is that the staffing levels of the County Community Development Division do not allow for extensive promotion.[16, 17]

---

[12] Schnidman.

[13] Roddewig and Inghram.

[14] Ibid.

[15] Letter from Ronald F. Nino, Senior Project Planner for Collier County, December 3, 1991, confirming and augmenting information in Roddewig and Inghram.

[16] Roddewig and Inghram.

[17] Nino.

f. Program Strengths. Since the Collier County program has been in existence since 1974, its longevity has given sufficient time to property owners and developers to become familiar with TDR.

The county has shown a willingness to make changes to the program, including increasing the bonus density and reducing development potential in the ST area. By making even more significant adjustments to the land use controls in sending and receiving areas, Collier County may generate more transfers out of the ST areas.

3. New Jersey Pinelands

a. Purpose. The New Jersey Pinelands TDR program is intended to preserve significant environmental or agricultural areas within the New Jersey Pinelands, which is both a National Reserve and an International Biosphere Reserve.

b. Background. New Jersey Pinelands is a huge expanse of cedar swamps, oak forests, and stands of pine. With approximately one million acres, or almost one quarter of New Jersey's total land area, it constitutes the largest stretch of open space on the mid-Atlantic coast.

1) Protection Status. In 1978, Congress established the Pinelands National Reserve. In 1979, the State of New Jersey adopted the Pinelands Protection Act which created a Pinelands Comprehensive Management Plan encompassing all or part of 52 municipalities. And, in 1983, the United Nations designated The Pinelands as an International Biosphere Reserve.[18]

2) Pinelands Comprehensive Management Plan. The Plan establishes an inner Preservation Area and a surrounding Protection Area. In the Preservation Area, the Plan's goal is to preserve large, contiguous tracts of land either in their natural state or in agricultural and recreational uses compatible with the natural environment. In the Protection Areas, the Plan seeks to maintain the existing character of the Pinelands while accommodating necessary and orderly development. The Plan calls for public acquisition of 100,000 acres of land.[19]

c. Procedural Features

1) Pinelands Development Credit Program. The Pinelands Comprehensive Management Plan (CMP) created the Pinelands Development Credit Program, which is intended to preserve significant

---

NEW JERSEY PINELANDS

◆ *The New Jersey Pinelands, with one million acres of forests and cedar swamps, is both a National Reserve and an International Biosphere Reserve*

◆ *A comprehensive management plan for the entire Pinelands area established preservation areas and protection areas and called for acquisition of 100,000 acres of land*

◆ *Incentives include a transfer ratio which allows four dwelling units to be built on a receiving site for each unit transferred from a sending site*

◆ *A Development Credit Bank stabilizes prices and assists TDR transactions*

◆ *The Pinelands Commission prevents local governments from using non-TDC methods to increase density on receiving sites*

◆ *More than 5,800 acres of land have been preserved so far*

CMP = Comprehensive Management Plan

---

[18] "The Pinelands of New Jersey," brochure with no author credit (New Lisbon, N.J., The Pinelands Commission, 1985).

[19] Ibid.

environmental or agricultural areas by allowing landowners to transfer development rights from the preservation areas to Regional Growth Areas. The number of Pinelands Development Credits (PDCs) allocated to each sending parcel varies according to the nature of the property. For example, uplands in the Preservation Area District have one credit for each 39 acres, while all uplands and active agricultural areas in the Agricultural Production and Special Agricultural Production Areas are allocated two credits per 39 acres. Each credit represents a "right" to build four residential units. Consequently, the 5,625 PDCs available in the preservation areas could be used to construct 22,500 homes in the Regional Growth Areas.[20]

2) Development Credit Bank. To determine the exact number of PDCs available on a property, the owner must receive a Letter of Interpretation from the Pinelands Commission. These PDCs are formally severed when a property owner records a conservation or agricultural easement on the property. As of June 30, 1991, 3,203 rights (or 800.75 PDCs) had been formally allocated while 659 rights (or 164.25 PDCs) had been severed.[21]

Severed PDCs may be sold to a private developer or to the New Jersey Pinelands Development Credit Bank (NJPDCB), which occasionally auctions its credits to private developers. As of June 30, 1991, the NJPDCB owned 227 rights (or 56.75 PDCs) while 323 rights (or 80.75 PDCs) had been sold to private developers.[22]

3) Public Outreach. An extensive public outreach program is an integral part of the Pinelands Development Credit Program. Not only has the Pinelands Commission prepared a color brochure explaining the Comprehensive Management Plan, but also the Pinelands Development Credit Bank has disseminated an instructional guide, "Selling and Buying Pinelands Development Credits," explaining all the procedures and forms needed to make use of the system (*See* Appendix B).

In addition, the Bank has prepared a handbook entitled, "Benefits of the Pinelands Development Credit Program," explaining why landowners and developers should use the program, and sends letters to hundreds of landowners advising them of program benefits.

4) Program Evaluation and Adjustments. In 1986 and 1987, the Pinelands Commission hired a real estate consultant to interview landowners, developers, and public officials about the Pinelands

---

[20] "Pinelands Development Credit Program," report from The Pinelands Development Credit Bank, 1991.

[21] Ibid.

[22] Ibid.

Development Credit Program. The consultant found that few of those interviewed were familiar with either the details or even the purpose of the program and recommended that the commission should place more emphasis on public information.[23]

In 1988, the commission completed a study which outlined thirty four potential changes to the Pinelands Development Credit Program. Although the commission decided that it was too early to make major program changes, some minor improvements were implemented. These included reexamination of municipal zoning when rezonings are proposed to ensure that opportunities for transfers remain in existence, improved marketing and public education, and simplification of program requirements.[24]

In 1990, the commission adopted comprehensive amendments which refined the calculation procedure, clarified requirements, and adjusted maximum densities in specified areas to take special circumstances into consideration.[25]

Above
The San Mateo County TDC program is designed to promote agriculture as well as preserve coastal agricultural land such as the farm pictured above. Under this program, bonus density credits can be acquired for consolidating land parcels and for building agricultural water storage facilities.

d. Transfer Activity

1) Early Activity. Although the Pinelands Development Credit Program was established in 1981, in its first two years there was relatively little activity due to various factors. These include the fact that property owners were unfamiliar with the program, municipalities were still adjusting their land use requirements to accept transfers, and the credit "bank" had not yet been established.[26]

2) Activity since 1983. After 1983, transfer activity increased dramatically, because the program became widely known, and

23 Ibid.

24 Ibid.

25 Ibid.

26 Ibid.

municipalities adopted commission-approved zoning ordinances. In addition, in 1988, the Pinelands Development Credit Bank began operations.[27]

The marketing efforts of the Credit Bank may be the primary reason for the dramatic rise in allocations since 1988. In the two-and-a-half year period between January 1, 1989 and June 30, 1991, 240 allocations occurred—or more than 60 percent of all the allocations which transpired in the ten-and-a-half year history of the program.

In 1989 and 1990 alone, more than 1,200 rights were allocated and 261 rights were actually severed from the land. The 3,203 rights severed since the program began represents the permanent protection of 5,876 acres of land. In the receiving areas, as of June 30, 1991, 132 development projects using 1,897 transferred rights had been approved.[28]

e. Program Weaknesses. According to John T. Ross, Acting Executive Director of the Pinelands Development Credit Bank, the program could be even more successful with certain modifications.

Additional staff could be used to work individually with developers, particularly smaller developers, to convince them that the benefits of the program are worth the extra paperwork. Increased promotional efforts would also increase the transfer activity, and public funding of infrastructure in conjunction with transfers could offer a further incentive.[29]

f. Program Strengths

1) Comprehensive Framework. The program was carefully and comprehensively crafted from the start. Instead of grafting a development credit system onto an existing set of land use plans and controls, the Pinelands Comprehensive Management Plan began with clear goals for the entire region and objectives for each of the subareas within that region. The density of development credits allowed in the preservation areas was low enough so that a bonus ratio could be established which allows four dwelling units to be built in growth areas for each development credit transferred from a preservation area. This created an incentive to transfer which is missing from many TDR programs.

2) Evaluation and Improvements. The program was not just established and then set adrift. Instead, the program was periodically

---

27 Ibid.

28 Ibid.

29 Telephone conversation with John T. Ross, Acting Executive Director, Pinelands Development Credit Bank, January 1992.

analyzed and improvements, such as the creation of the Development Credit Bank, were implemented.

3) Development Credit Bank. The Development Credit Bank helped to stabilize the price of PDCs, consequently reducing some of the uncertainty about the program. Moreover, the Bank seeks out potential buyers and sellers through promotional campaigns and individual contacts. Even though it has the authority to buy and sell TDCs, the bank encourages private sector transactions and maintains a list of potential TDC buyers and sellers.

4) Stability. The stability of the program has resulted in increased transfer activity. At first, some municipalities resisted the idea of using only transferable development credits to increase density. Prior to the TDC program, these communities used the PUD process, granting density bonuses to achieve various planning objectives. But the Pinelands Commission has been steadfast in preventing local governments from using non-PDC density bonuses since the ability to achieve a higher density without PDCs would effectively eliminate the incentive for developers to buy them.

PUD = Planned Unit Development

e. Longevity. Over time, municipalities have come to appreciate the need to maintain demand for PDCs in order to make the program work. And, because more property owners and developers have become familiar with the program, they feel more comfortable using it.[30, 31, 32, 33]

[30] Ibid.

[31] "Pinelands Development Credit Program," report from The Pinelands Development Credit Bank, 1991.

[32] Telephone conversation with Rich Osborn, Program Consultant, New Jersey Pinelands Development Credit Bank, April 8, 1993.

[33] Roddewig and Inghram.

III The California Experience

In the 1990 Edition of *The California Planners Book of Lists*, the California Governor's Office of Planning Research (OPR) listed 25 cities and 10 counties in California as having transferable development rights programs. When each of these communities was contacted, it turned out that some had never adopted TDR programs or had adopted programs with techniques similar to TDR, such as clustering of development on parcels of land under the same ownership. On the other hand, some communities not on the OPR list actually have TDR programs.

OPR = California Governor's Office of Planning and Research

This chapter examines 27 TDR programs in California which have been grouped into seven categories—Preserve/Restore Natural Areas, Protect Hillsides, Preserve Historic Landmarks, Protect Agricultural Land, Promote Urban Form, Encourage Development of Housing, and Promote Revitalization. While this categorization is intended to help those who are interested in a particular type of TDR program, some of these programs do not entirely fit their categories, while others are actually designed to meet multiple objectives.

Within each category, the individual TDR programs are presented in the approximate order of the transfer activity which has occurred. While transfer activity is not the only measure of success, programs which have generated a higher number of transfers will tend to be of greater use to those who want to learn about various TDR techniques.

A. Preserve/Restore Natural Areas

I. Tahoe Regional Planning Agency[1]

a. **Purpose.** The Tahoe Regional Planning Agency (TRPA) TDR program is designed to protect and restore sensitive natural areas.

TRPA = Tahoe Regional Planning Agency

[1] Jim Allison, Associate Planner, Tahoe Regional Planning Agency; and an eight-page handout on TRPA's TDR program without date, author, or title.

- *The Tahoe Regional
  Planning Agency
  (TRPA) is responsible
  for protecting and
  restoring natural areas
  in the Lake Tahoe
  Basin which covers
  207,000 acres of land
  in six jurisdictions and
  two states*

- *One TRPA program
  allows for the transfer
  of the right to cover
  land with impermeable
  surfaces*

- *Another program
  allows transfers of
  the right to build
  new dwelling units*

- *Annual building quotas
  create a demand for
  transferred develop-
  ment rights*

- *The TRPA program
  processes from 25 to 35
  transfers per year*

b. Background. The Tahoe Regional Planning Agency imposes environmental regulations on 207,000 acres of land in the Lake Tahoe basin, which includes one incorporated city and portions of five counties in California and Nevada. Although the transferable development rights provisions date back to 1980, TRPA seldom used TDR in the early 1980s because of ongoing litigation from both environmentalists and property owners.

In 1986, a new regional plan was adopted and, in 1987, implementing zoning ordinances were enacted which largely resolved the legal disputes. The TRPA has an agreement with the City of South Lake Tahoe allowing that city to administer most of the TDR processing in the city. TRPA administers the TDR program for other jurisdictions in the planning agency's boundaries, but some consideration has been given to having these counties shoulder some additional administrative duties.

c. Procedural Features. To minimize runoff which could result in the degradation of the lake's water quality, the TRPA strictly controls the coverage of land in the Lake Tahoe basin by structures and other impermeable surfaces. Because runoff from certain types of land are more likely to cause water quality degradation, these areas have even greater coverage controls.

The transfer program allows development to be transferred from more sensitive lands to less sensitive lands. Under the program, if they acquire coverage rights from a sending parcel, owners of receiving sites are allowed to build more land coverage than the normal maximum. There are different transfer requirements depending on the land uses involved. This program is discussed in detail in Appendix C.

In another variation, TRPA allows transfers of "allocations," which are essentially rights to build. An allocation plus a development right gives an owner the ingredients needed to construct a new building. To ensure that development remains within the capacity of the public service systems, TRPA limits the number of allocations issued in any given year.

Two kinds of transfers are involved in this variation of TDR. When an existing unit is used as the transfer, the unit must be demolished, and the sending site must be restored to its original natural state. In the other type of transfer, the sending site must be an undeveloped parcel that is ineligible for development due to environmental sensitivity. Following the transfer, the sending parcel is precluded from development through a deed restriction or by title transfer to a public agency such as the U.S. Forest Service or a nonprofit organization such as the California Tahoe Conservancy.

Due to strict limits on development in the Lake Tahoe basin, an owner may have to wait for years to receive a building allocation.

Moreover, because of environmental safeguards, a given site may only be allowed a relatively small house or building. Faced with this situation, an owner has a significant incentive to forego development altogether on a sending site and transfer the unused development rights to a receiving site.

In some situations, an owner might choose to obtain enough land to build a bigger house by acquiring an adjacent lot. When the two lots are consolidated, the unused development rights from one lot can be used immediately on a receiving site, or they can be banked. The rights are banked when TRPA verifies that they are available for transfer. This verification process should not be mistaken for a traditional TDR bank. TRPA does not buy or sell any development rights; all sales of TDRs are private transactions.

Above
The Tahoe Regional Planning Agency (TRPA) is responsible for protecting the unique environment of Lake Tahoe and the surrounding 207,000-acre basin shown above. To protect the high water quality of the Lake, TRPA imposes strict limits on land coverage. Under one of TRPA's TDR programs, site owners may acquire additional land coverage rights from a sending parcel. Under another program, the right to build a new development can be acquired by removing existing dwelling units from sensitive natural areas. The TRPA program is one of the most active programs in the state, with from 25 to 35 transfers per year. Photo courtesy of Bob and Margo Burdette.

Because the incentive to acquire TDRs is very strong both on sending and receiving sites, the demand for property in Lake Tahoe is extremely high. Although at least some modest development is allowed on every lot, in order to build more than a minimal amount, an owner will typically have to acquire TDRs. For example, TDR will usually be required for any multi-family residential proposal.

d. Transfer Activity. This is one of the most active TDR programs in the state, with an estimated 25 to 35 transfers per year.

e. Program Weaknesses. The level of transfer activity is a good indication that the program is successful and well-designed. If additional preservation/restoration of sensitive natural areas is needed, the program could be examined for possible refinements.

f. Program Strengths. Development restrictions create substantial motivation to use the TDR program because the goal of protecting sensitive natural areas is well understood in the Lake Tahoe basin. Developers could wait for years to receive from TRPA an allocation and development right to build on a site, but through TDR to a receiving site development rights can be used immediately.

In most instances, TDR is needed in order to build anything more than a minimal amount on a receiving site, and TDR is typically required for all multi-family residential proposals.

a. Purpose. The South Lake Tahoe TDR program is designed to remove existing dwelling units in environmentally sensitive areas.

b. Background. The City of South Lake Tahoe is within the jurisdiction of the Tahoe Regional Planning Agency.

Of the five counties and one city included in the TRPA boundaries, only the City of South Lake Tahoe has entered into a memorandum of understanding with TRPA to locally implement the regional agency's TDR program. And, in 1989, the City of South Lake Tahoe adopted a policy statement for Transfer of Existing Development Rights.

c. Procedural Features. The process is administrative. In fact, the city promises a response within two weeks, and a staff decision can be appealed to the City Council.

Because a development right transferred as a result of the elimination of an existing dwelling is not considered a new dwelling, this right can be used for constructing a new dwelling without having to be part of the very restrictive system of permit quotas. The ability to escape the quota system is critical to the success of the South Lake Tahoe program, since the demand for additional units is intense and the quota system tightly controls the number of new units. For example, in 1991 only 30 permits for new residential construction were granted.

Since numerous cabins and duplexes were constructed prior to the incorporation of the city, the supply of potential sending properties is relatively large. Many of these older duplexes and cabins are located in Stream Environment zones and are prime candidates for the TDR process.

Under the current program, owners of property in a Stream Environment Zone who want to transfer development rights must first remove all development from the sending property. In fact, some of the 60 transfers which have occurred to date involve the elimination of all existing development on Stream Environment sending parcels. As with transfers throughout the TRPA region, the South Lake Tahoe program consequently goes beyond preserving undeveloped land and actually creates undeveloped land from land which had previously been developed.

d. Transfer Activity. Approximately 60 transfers have occurred under this program. Typically, the owner of an older duplex will demolish one unit or permanently convert the duplex into a single-family residence. The development right created by the reduction of a dwelling

---

2 Pamela Atwood, Associate Planner, City of South Lake Tahoe, Tahoe Regional Planning Agency regulations; and City of South Lake Tahoe's "Transfer of Existing Development Rights Information" handout.

can be used to permit the construction of another dwelling without the need to wait for a permit through the allocation process.

e. Program Weaknesses. The requirement to remove all development from a Stream Environment Zone sending site in order to be eligible to transfer development may discourage some transfer activity. According to Pamela Atwood, Associate Planner for the City of South Lake Tahoe, in some instances it may be preferable to allow some development to remain in a Stream Environment Zone if this results in the elimination of other development. Providing flexibility within the Stream Environment Zone may be one of the changes considered by the city when it reviews its TDR program.

f. Program Strengths. The permit allocation system creates a strong motivation to transfer rights. Unlike most other communities, the incentive of this TDR program is not so much the ability to increase density on the receiving site, but the ability to build at all.

Given the concerns about development's potential impact on the Lake Tahoe ecosystem, the environmental protection goals of this program are well understood. In addition, the program is user-friendly, requiring only administrative approval within a two-week approval period.

3. Monterey County[3]

a. Purpose. The Monterey County TDC program is designed to preserve the unique environment of Big Sur.

b. Background. A TDC ordinance.was adopted by the county to protect Big Sur from inappropriate development

Sending parcels are lots determined by the Planning Commission to be buildable except for development prohibitions related to viewshed protection. The viewshed protection provisions of the Big Sur Land Use Plan are very strong: no new development can occur which would be visible from state Highway 1.

Following the establishment of the TDC program, California's Proposition 70 was approved, with $25 million specifically earmarked for purchase of private property subject to the Big Sur viewshed restrictions.

c. Procedural Features. Upon designation as a donor site and the dedication of an irrevocable scenic easement, the property owner of a donor site is granted two transferable development credits, while receiving sites are not allowed to be developed to a density of more than one unit per acre.

A revolving fund has been established for the purchase of TDCs. And, due to the development prohibition created by the viewshed restrictions, owners of undeveloped property along Highway 1 must turn to TDC in order to enjoy some kind of economic return from their land or else sell their land to a public or quasi-public agency.

The California Coastal Conservancy, a non-regulatory state agency designed to assist in the implementation of local coastal programs, is proceeding with a simple TDC transaction to test the effectiveness of the program. To date, the Conservancy has purchased a viewshed sending property which is capable of being approved for two dwellings. The Conservancy has also acquired a non-viewshed receiver site and is in the process of getting approval for a subdivision tract map with an additional density of four units.

---

[3] Dale Ellis, Zoning Administrator, Monterey County; portions of Monterey County's zoning code; and a telephone conversation on April 4, 1993 with Prentiss Williams, Project Analyst, California Coastal Conservancy.

d. Transfer Activity. Only a handful of requests for donor site designations have been received, representing less than 20 acres.

e. Program Weaknesses. Aside from the California Coastal Conservancy activity, no requests have been made to designate receiver sites, indicating a current low demand for transferable development credits. However, regardless of demand, Monterey County is achieving its goal of protecting Big Sur.

The availability of $25 million in property acquisition funds through the approval of Proposition 70 has made it difficult to test the effectiveness of the TDC program. The Monterey County program requires property owners to prove that sending sites are buildable, a requirement which can take considerable time and money. These owners are less likely to go through this process if they believe that Prop. 70 money can simply be used to buy their property.

f. Program Strengths. The development prohibition within the viewshed not only independently achieves the goal of protecting Big Sur, but also creates a significant incentive for the owners of restricted lots to sell or transfer TDCs.

Monterey County Zoning Administrator Dale Ellis believes the TDC program is a success for several other reasons. It has furthered an appreciation for the unique qualities of Big Sur and allowed decision makers to prohibit development in viewsheds knowing that property owners have an alternative. Property owners have accepted the loss of their development rights in return for other benefits, including TDC. Moreover, the TDC program includes an extensive public education program and an open public process which was instrumental in creating the consensus needed to gain acceptance for the viewshed protection goals.

4. Oxnard[4]

a. Purpose. The Oxnard TDR program was designed to control beachfront development.

b. Background. The Oxnard Transferable Development Rights Program was a response to a specific problem. The Oxnard Shores area of Oxnard contained 127 beachfront lots. During the 1960s, 97 of these lots were vacant and 30 were developed with residential dwellings.

In the 1970s and early 1980s, ten lawsuits were filed related to Oxnard Shores, including claims against the City of Oxnard for more

---

[4] Deanna Walsh, Coastal Planner, City of Oxnard; and portions of Oxnard municipal code.

than $40 million. These lawsuits were filed by organizations both in favor of and opposed to beachfront development.

In 1983, the "Oxnard Shores Restoration Program Project Feasibility Report" determined that a transfer of development rights system could be a feasible means of resolving the problem. And, in 1984, the city adopted an ordinance establishing a TDR program.

After the ordinance was adopted, property owners at Oxnard Shores continued to look for solutions which would allow them to build at the beach rather than be compensated for not building. According to Deanna Walsh, Coastal Planner for the City of Oxnard, because many Oxnard Shores owners had purchased their lots with the intention of building beachfront homes, they weren't interested in compensation.

The ten lawsuits pending over the inability to build at Oxnard Shores eventually resulted in a settlement agreement. The agreement restructured the area from 97 to 73 lots. As long as all requirements are met, development approval on the 73 lots is assured in accordance with the development agreement. Since the settlement agreement was concluded in 1988, 35 of the 73 lots have received approval for development.

With permission to develop almost assured, property owners would only be inclined to take advantage of the TDR program if they had no personal desire to live at Oxnard Shores and if the ability to build six additional dwellings elsewhere was more profitable than one beach house.

c. Procedural Features. Under the Oxnard TDR ordinance, seven zones are designated as receiving areas, and sites within these zones must further meet eligibility criteria. The ordinance specifies the application submittal requirements and the process of approval, which provides for an interim as well as a final determination of the development rights of the sending parcel.

Prior to final approval, the Oxnard ordinance requires that a Deed of Transferable Development Rights and an Open Space or Conservation Easement be recorded on the sending parcel. To encourage transfers, the ordinance exempts transfer units from Oxnard's Quimby Fee, Growth Development Fee, Park Tax, and plan check fee.

The Oxnard ordinance further encourages transfers by offering a 6:1 transfer ratio. For every dwelling unit which can be built on a donor parcel at the shores, a developer can build six dwelling units on a suitable receiver site. This 6:1 incentive ratio was selected based on appraisals which indicated that it would take six additional dwellings at a non-beach location to make it economically feasible for a property owner or developer to relinquish the right to build one beachfront home.

d. Transfer Activity. A handful of transfers occurred between the time the TDR ordinance was enacted in 1984 and the settlement agreement in 1988. However, the incentive package has not been sufficient to entice property owners into transfers, and no transfers have occurred.

e. Program Weaknesses. The Oxnard program was adopted after several lawsuits were filed. Under those circumstances, it was difficult for a TDR program to satisfy the numerous parties involved.

f. Program Strengths. Even though it was overshadowed by the settlement agreement for Oxnard Shores, the Oxnard TDR program has several significant features. These include a 6:1 transfer ratio and exemption from various development fees provide incentives to transfer, and a detailed ordinance specifying the application requirements and approval process.

5. Pacifica[5]

a. Purpose. The Pacifica TDR ordinance is designed to preserve open space and land subject to landslides, floods, and other potential hazards.

b. Background. In 1988, the Pacifica Open Space Task Force Report recommended a TDR program for Pacifica, a seaside community south of San Francisco. A TDR ordinance was adopted in 1989.

When the ordinance was drafted, the city had in mind a specific 20-acre coastal blufftop which was zoned for low-density residential development. Using the TDR process, the owner of this parcel could dedicate the blufftop as open space and transfer the unused development rights to gain 20 additional units of density on an inland receiving site.

c. Procedural Highlights. The Pacifica TDR ordinance designates land in the city's open space inventory and land identified as having landslide, flood, or other potential hazards as potential sending sites. These sites were zoned to permit low-density residential development.

Potential receiving sites include land within the city's residential zones, and property owners who wish to transfer rights must receive a discretionary TDR Permit from the Planning Commission. To encourage TDR, the Pacifica ordinance allows TDR-related projects to be exempt from various requirements. These include parkland dedication, capital improvement fees, and specified development standards such as open space, parking, and setbacks.

PACIFICA

♦ *Pacifica adopted a TDR ordinance in 1989 to preserve open space and land subject to landslides and other hazards*

♦ *The ordinance features numerous incentives including exemptions from parkland dedication, capital improvements fees, and development requirements*

♦ *The demand for TDR is low because site constraints make it difficult to achieve the densities allowed by zoning on vacant receiving sites*

♦ *To date, one transfer has been approved which would save a 20-acre coastal blufftop*

---

[5] Wendy Cosin, Planning and Building Director, City of Pacifica; and portions of Pacifica municipal code.

Above

Pacifica, a seaside community south of San Francisco, created a TDR ordinance to preserve open space and land subject to landslides, floods, and other hazards. To encourage transfers, Pacifica allows TDR-related projects to be exempt from numerous requirements including parkland dedication, capital improvement fees, and specified development standards such as open space, parking, and setbacks. Using the TDR program, the 20-acre coastal blufftop pictured above was preserved.

d. Transfer Activity. Only the one development project discussed above has been approved.

e. Program Weaknesses. According to Wendy Cosin, Pacifica's Planning and Building Director, the demand for TDR at potential receiving sites is low due to the fact that the remaining undeveloped sites in Pacifica are the hardest to develop and site constraints make it difficult to achieve even the density allowed by current zoning. This could change over time as land values increase to the point at which even difficult parcels can be developed at and beyond existing zoning density limits.

However, even though, from an economic standpoint, it may become feasible to develop at higher densities, there will still be physical and political restraints to higher intensity of use on these sensitive lands.

f. Program Strengths. The city is aware of the benefits of providing incentives to encourage transfers. This awareness is evident from the fact that the ordinance allows TDR-related projects to be exempt from various fees and development standards. For example, the 20-acre coastal blufftop which served as the prototype for the city's TDR ordinance could be developed as low-density residential under existing zoning. The city wanted to preserve this land as open space, but preferred to use TDR rather than simply rezoning the site to prohibit development.

Even though the program is relatively new, a major project using TDR has been approved. A successful project can counteract the tendency of some developers to avoid being the first to try a new program.

6. Pismo Beach[6]

a. Purpose. The Pismo Beach TDR program is designed to protect scenic resources, preserve open space, reduce hazard potential, and provide public access.

b. Background. The City of Pismo Beach stretches along seven miles of the Pacific coast just south of San Luis Obispo. In 1983, the city adopted a Transfer Density Overlay Zone ordinance, which identifies four undeveloped parts of the city as the Transfer Density Overlay Zone.

[6] Carolyn Johnson, City Planner, City of Pismo Beach; and portions of Pismo Beach zoning ordinance.

c. Procedural Features. Only portions of the Transfer Overlay Density Zone which are actually buildable are eligible for transfers. Unbuildable areas, such as bluff retreats and wetlands, do not qualify.

The ordinance requires a demonstration that a proposed transfer would increase preservation of scenic areas and open space. If it would result in a project which violates the density, scale, or bulk standards of the general plan/local coastal program land use plan, the transfer cannot occur.

d. Transfer Activity. A handful of transfers were approved during the first few years of the program. Only one application—for the transfer of density of a single unit—has been made in the last five years.

e. Program Weaknesses. According to City Planner Carolyn Johnson, the low transfer activity is in part due to the fact that relatively little land in the city is available to which development rights can be transferred. Conversely, many of the designated sending areas offer some of the most attractive, vacant building sites remaining in the city and, in fact, continue to be developed in an incremental fashion. In addition, because the zoning density on receiving sites matches the density of the general plan, there is little incentive, and consequently the maximum density on the receiving site, as controlled by the city's general plan, can be achieved without transfers.

f. Program Strengths. Even though only one transfer has occurred recently, the Pismo Beach program has been in existence for a decade and has an established track record. The city could build on this respectable start through a general plan amendment which increases allowable density on the most appropriate receiving sites, thereby increasing demand for TDRs.

7. Riverside[7]

a. Purpose. The TDR program in the City of Riverside was designed to acquire land for a park.

b. Background. The City of Riverside adopted a specific plan with a TDR component. The city hoped that a particular property owner would buy the development rights from a donor area to increase density within a large development proposed for the designated receiving area. The donor area was the site of a proposed regional park.

The city also studied the possibility of using TDR to facilitate the preservation of land in its 4000-acre greenbelt. The greenbelt was created by initiative in 1979 through the adoption of five-acre minimum

---

[7] Dirk A. Jenkins, Senior Planner, City of Riverside.

> **PISMO BEACH**
>
> ◆ *Pismo Beach adopted a Transfer Overlay Density Zone ordinance to reduce potential hazards and preserve public access, open space, and scenic resources*
>
> ◆ *The city's general plan does not allow additional density on receiving sites for transferred development rights, reducing the incentive to transfer*
>
> ◆ *Transfer activity is also constrained by a lack of suitable receiving sites*
>
> ◆ *Although a handful of transfers occurred in the first few years of the program, only one TDR application has been made in the last five years*

lots. A few years later, a study was completed to determine how TDR might help to preserve the greenbelt. However, a lawsuit challenging the validity of the five-acre minimum lot zoning created in the greenbelt by the initiative was brought against the city. Consequently, formal hearings were never held on the TDR proposal.

  c. Procedural Features. The TDR component of the specific plan hinged on a developer wanting more density on a receiver site than was allowed by zoning. In return for the increased density on the receiver site, the developer would be required to transfer development rights from a sending site, and in the process preserve land for a park.

  d. Transfer Activity. Instead of buying development rights, the property owner went forward with a lower density project which did not need any additional development rights. The city has since acquired the donor site for a park through other means, and the TDR provisions of the specific plan are consequently obsolete.

  e. Program Weaknesses. The program was based on an assumption that a developer desired a particular density of development, which proved to be incorrect.

  f. Program Strengths. Even though ultimately unused, the adopted TDR program provided an opportunity for developers, public officials, and Riverside citizens to become familiar with transferable development rights. This experience could be beneficial to the development of a TDR program in the future.

B. Protect Hillsides

1. Santa Monica Mountains[8]

a. Purpose. The Santa Monica Mountains TDC program is designed to reduce potential landslide and fire hazards, minimize impacts on public service systems, and avoid environmental degradation in the Santa Monica Mountains.

b. Background. The Santa Monica Mountains are coastal mountains which extend from near downtown Los Angeles 50 miles west into Ventura County. During the earlier part of this century, large portions of the mountains were subdivided into small lots which are now considered antiquated because they fail to meet typical modern standards for lot sizes, development on and preservation of slopes, and environmental preservation.

In the 1970s, there was concern that full development of these antiquated subdivisions would degrade the environment, overwhelm public service systems, and exacerbate fire and landslide hazards. Under the Local Coastal Planning process, density limits were reduced from previous county zoning.

In 1979, the Santa Monica Mountains Transfer of Development Credits Program was established and administered by the California Coastal Commission. Under this program, development can continue to occur on antiquated subdivisions, but the owners of these lots may also sell their development credits for use on receiving sites.

Since areas in the Santa Monica Mountains, like parts of Malibu, are extremely desirable, and since receiving areas are not allowed to achieve their planned density unless development credits in sending areas are retired on a one-to-one basis, there is a fluctuating demand for these TDCs.

c. Procedural Features. In the Santa Monica Mountains program, sending and receiving sites are not established prior to a transfer. Property owners who wish to sell TDCs can record deed restrictions on their properties, making them sending sites. Owners or developers who want to subdivide an existing lot or create a multiple-unit project must acquire these TDCs for their receiver sites.

The formula used to calculate the number of TDCs available on a potential sending site estimates the ability to actually build a

---

[8] Betty Wiechec, TDR Program Administrator, Mountains Restoration Trust; and R.A. Johnston and M.E. Madison, "Mitigating the Cumulative Impacts of Land Development on Habitats: Subdividing Permits Conditioned on Retiring Sensitive Parcels Nearby in the California Coastal Zone," unpublished paper, June 1992.

SANTA MONICA MOUNTAINS

◆ *In 1979, the California Coastal Commission established a TDC program to reduce environmental damage, safety hazards, and public service system problems in the Santa Monica Mountains*

◆ *TDC prices are high enough to encourage the owners of sending properties to sell*

◆ *Development restrictions on receiving sites create a demand for greater density which can only be met by TDC*

◆ *An in lieu fee program makes TDC transactions fast and predictable*

◆ *More than 500 transfers have occurred to date, making this program one of the most active in the nation*

The Santa Monica Mountains
TDC Program

The Santa Monica Mountains TDC program is one of the most successful in the nation. Of the more than 500 transactions which have occurred to date, the majority involve a few, small contiguous lots under one ownership.

For example, the Rand family owned several small lots surrounding the lot on which their house is located. In return for donating the placement of a scenic easement over five of these lots, the family received the tax benefits of a charitable contribution valued at more than $200,000. In addition to the tax benefits, the Rand family sold the development credit for a sixth lot and was assured scenic protection for the lots surrounding their home.

Three receiving sites purchased the Rand development credits. Miner Associates II purchased three of the six credits, making it possible to subdivide one parcel into four lots. Another builder used two credits to receive a coastal permit, and a third developer acquired the remaining credit in order to receive permission to build. These receiving sites could not have been developed without the purchase of development credits. In essence, development restrictions on receiving sites guarantee a demand for development credits and greatly contribute to the success of the Santa Monica Mountains program.

Information from "Mitigating the Cumulative Impacts of Land Development on Habitats: Subdividing Permits Conditioned on Retiring Sensitive Parcels Nearby in the California Coastal Zone," by R.A. Johnson and M.E. Madison

home on that site. Lots with steep slopes are assigned fewer TDCs. If it can accommodate one 1,500 square foot home, a lot will be assigned one TDC. Marginally buildable lots can be allocated 500 square feet of floor area each. So, three of these lots could be combined to achieve the 1,500 square feet of floor area needed for one TDC. For example, if three marginally buildable lots are prohibited from future development through deed restrictions, the resulting TDC can be used to build one dwelling on a receiving site.

Originally, sending and receiving sites had to be located within the same zone, but to balance supply and demand some transfers are now allowed between zones. To be allocated TDCs, the rules specify that sending sites must be at least marginally buildable.

Early in the Santa Monica Mountains program, a study recognized the difficulty for a receiving site owner to locate and purchase enough TDCs to proceed with a major development project. To resolve that difficulty, the Mountains Restoration Trust was established to manage an in lieu fee program. Developers of receiving sites can now pay an in lieu fee and the Trust prepares the necessary documents and transactions. As explained by Betty Wiechec, administrator of the TDC Program for the Mountains Restoration Trust, the goal is to make a TDC purchase simply a cost of doing business. This cost is predetermined, and typically a developer simply has to make only one visit to the Trust to complete the entire transaction.

While the demand for property in this coastal mountain area is constant, the demand for TDCs fluctuates with the real estate market. In addition, the supply and price of TDCs has been difficult to control. In the early 1980s, TDCs were priced at about $43,000 each. By that time, the Coastal Conservancy had purchased 185 substandard lots which is equivalent to 135 TDCs.

To curb rising prices, the Conservancy held a TDC auction in an effort to increase the supply and reduce prices. Following the auction, prices gradually declined to approximately $15,000 per TDC in the mid-1980s. However, due to escalating land values in the 1980s, the Mountains Restoration Trust couldn't influence property owners to sell at that price. Subsequently the price was increased to $35,000 per TDC, and the supply at that price appears to be ample.

According to Betty Wiechec, a typical TDC seller owns five small contiguous lots. The owner's home might occupy any two of the five lots, and the owner uses the other three lots as open space. Under the program, the landowner can sell the TDCs on the three open space lots and continue to enjoy them as open space. In turn, these three lots are permanently protected from development.

d.   Transfer Activity. The program has accomplished more than 500 transfers, making it the most active program in California and one of the most active programs in the entire United States.

e.   Program Weaknesses. Some owners and developers have recommended that the program be simplified, for example, by not requiring documentation stating that the sending site is buildable.

f.   Program Strengths. For the sending site, the price is adequate to entice the owners to sell their development credits and thereby protect fragile areas from overdevelopment. For the receiving site, those wanting to achieve planned densities have no choice other than to buy the TDCs.

In terms of public awareness and promotion, the program has been in existence long enough that most landowners and developers understand and accept it. To maintain acceptance, the in lieu fee process makes the TDC transaction as fast and easy as possible.

2. San Luis Obispo County[9]

SAN LUIS OBISPO COUNTY

◆ *The San Luis Obispo County TDC program was developed to decrease development on small steep coastal lots in the community of Cambria*

◆ *Zoning allows only small dwellings unless TDC is used*

◆ *By buying TDCs, the owners of receiving sites can increase the floor area of their homes*

◆ *A revolving fund administered by The Land Conservancy of San Luis Obispo County makes TDC transactions easy*

◆ *Due to land use controls and an efficient process, this program is one of the most active in California, with more than 200 transfers to date*

a. Purpose. The San Luis Obispo County TDC program is designed to reduce the intensity of development on substandard lots on steep, highly erodible coastal slopes. It is also intended to reduce development impacts on the Cambria Pine habitat.

b. Background. The community of Cambria in San Luis Obispo County contains thousands of very small lots. Many of these lots are on steep, highly erodible slopes. The largely undeveloped Lodge Hill subdivision, which contains the Cambria Pine habitat and some of the steepest slopes is of particular concern.

The county's general plan encourages preservation within the Lodge Hill subdivision but still allows small dwelling units on these 2,000 to 4,000 square foot lots. The San Luis Obispo County TDC program was developed as part of the county's local coastal program with assistance from the California Coastal Conservancy and the Land Conservancy of San Luis Obispo County. (*See* Appendix D – "Cambria Lodge Hill Restoration Program—Program Review and Status Report.")

The program was launched with a questionnaire to every property owner., and the results of this questionnaire helped to structure the program and identify the initial TDC buyers and sellers. A workshop was held with real estate professionals to explain how TDR transactions worked.

The California Coastal Conservancy granted $200,000 to establish a revolving fund, which purchased lots and sold them either as larger combined lots or as yard expansions for developed properties. The proceeds of these sales are being used to fund new lot purchases.

As part of the update to the North Coast Coastal Plan, the county is considering inclusion of a significant enlargement of the area subject to the same development standards and TDC options found in the Lodge Hill subdivision. Since thousands of undeveloped lots are in areas not likely to be served by the municipal water system for decades, the supply of TDCs is expected to be high.

c. Procedural Features. Property owners within two small specified sending areas who do not wish to build in the Lodge Hill subdivision may sell development credits to an approved nonprofit agency using the TDC program. At present, the Land Conservancy of San Luis Obispo County is the only nonprofit agency approved to buy and sell TDCs under this program.

[9] John C. Hofschroer, Senior Planner, San Luis Obispo County; Ray Belknap, Executive Director, Land Conservancy of San Luis Obispo County; portions of San Luis Obispo County code; and additional information from Madelyn Glickfeld; "Wipeout Mitigation: Planning Prevention," in Joseph DiMento, ed., *Wipeouts and Their Mitigation* (Cambridge, Mass.: Lincoln Institute of Land Policy, 1990), pp. 79-80.

Under the county's land use restrictions, some development can occur even on small steep lots. However, the size of the permitted dwelling might be quite small depending on the size and slope of the lot. TDCs can be used to increase the floor area of dwelling units on receiving sites above the limit which would otherwise be permitted. Typically, a TDC purchaser simply wants to increase the size of a single-family residential unit by one or two bedrooms.

The county's land use regulations make it difficult to increase the size of a house on either the sending or receiving sites without using TDCs.

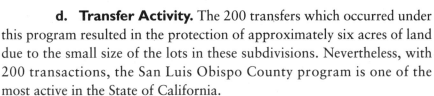

d. Transfer Activity. The 200 transfers which occurred under this program resulted in the protection of approximately six acres of land due to the small size of the lots in these subdivisions. Nevertheless, with 200 transactions, the San Luis Obispo County program is one of the most active in the State of California.

e. Program Weaknesses. John Hofschoer, Senior Planner for the San Luis Obispo County Planning Department, reports that the county's TDC effort could be improved by an expansion of the program to other parts of the county. Ray Belknap, Executive Director of the Land Conservancy of San Luis Obispo County, agrees. The Conservancy, which is running out of land to buy in the relatively small sending area, has money in its revolving fund, and needs to be allowed to purchase lots in new sending areas.

f. Program Strengths. A strong demand for transfers is created by the county's land use regulations which make it difficult to acquire additional development capacity on either sending or receiving sites without using TDCs.

The county's ordinance provided flexibility to the Conservancy to create a program that is simple and easy to use, with the Conservancy interacting with the county at only two points in the process, thereby minimizing public expense. The Conservancy is currently the only agency authorized to buy and sell TDCs under this program, which provides substantial flexibility in TDC pricing and management of the revolving fund. As a result, the revolving fund has more than doubled from the original $200,000 grant.

Above

Portions of the coastal community of Cambria in San Luis Obispo County were subdivided into very small lots, often on steep, highly-erodible slopes. To reduce development impacts, particularly to the habitat of Cambria Pines pictured above, a TDR program was established complete with a revolving fund which buys undeveloped lots and sells TDCs to property owners who want larger lots and homes. Because the land use controls make acquiring additional development capacity on either sending or receiving sites without using TDC difficult, this program is one of the most active in the state, with more than 200 transfers so far.

♦ *Morgan Hill has four TDC programs designed to preserve the top of El Toro Mountain*

♦ *In one of these programs, developers who purchase TDCs are exempt from the city's Residential Development Control System (RDCS)*

♦ *In another program, developers can achieve a higher ranking in the RDCS process by buying TDCs*

♦ *The RDCS process creates a strong demand for TDCs*

♦ *To date, 67 TDCs have been purchased, saving more than 100 acres of hillside land*

RDCS = Residential
Development Control System

3. Morgan Hill[10]

a. Purpose. The Morgan Hill TDC program is intended to preserve steeper hillside slopes, particularly the higher elevations of El Toro Mountain.

b. Background. The City of Morgan Hill, 20 miles south of San Jose, has four different TDC programs, as described below.

c. Procedural Features. One Morgan Hill TDC program is a Hillside Combining District which allows transfers of development credit from steeper parcels and promotes the preservation of open space, particularly at the top of El Toro Mountain.

Development is prohibited above the 500 foot elevation and on slopes in excess of 20 percent. To compensate for the loss of development potential, development rights can be sold or transferred at a 2:1 ratio. In order to transfer a development credit, eligible receiver sites have to be at least one acre, and the TDC cannot increase the density on the receiver site more than ten percent higher than the density allowed by the zoning code.

The second TDC program provides an incentive to transfer based on Morgan Hill's limited sewer capacity, and a building permit cannot be issued until a builder has a sewer allocation To promote hillside preservation, sewer allocations have been set aside for TDCs transferred off El Toro Mountain, and a developer may purchase a TDC as a means of receiving a sewer allocation.

In a third TDC program the city itself purchased 8.5 acres of property on El Toro. To increase their value, the city has made TDCs exempt from the city's Residential Development Control System (RDCS). Developers who purchase the city TDCs can construct a dwelling unit without having to compete in the RDCS process or wait for a sewer allocation. These development credits sell for $75,000 each, and the city can use the proceeds to purchase more property on El Toro.

In a fourth variation, development credits can be purchased by developers who have committed to the purchase of TDCs through the city's RDCS which contains a scoring category for open space. Developers trying to earn maximum points in the open space category may commit to the purchase of TDCs.

d. Transfer Activity. The level of transfer activity in the four different TDC programs varies. In the first program, as of 1990 18 TDCs had been transferred, or at least committed, to receiving sites. No one has

---

[10] Terry Linder, Associate Planner, City of Morgan Hill; Morgan Hill staff reports; letter to potential participants in Morgan Hill's TDR program; and portions of Morgan Hill's open space element and municipal code.

yet taken advantage of the second program involving the issuance of a sewer allocation in return for a TDC or the third approach which involves the sale of TDCs from property on El Toro Mountain owned by the City of Morgan Hill.

The fourth variation has seen a considerable amount of activity. So far, 49 TDCs have been purchased, representing 108.5 acres preserved from development. Of these totals, TDCs resulted in the protection of 92.5 acres on El Toro Mountain and the preservation of 16 acres of hillside land not located on El Toro.

e. Program Weaknesses. A lower price for TDCs would increase transfer activity. However, because development on the higher elevations of El Toro is prohibited, the city is meeting its hillside preservation goals regardless of the amount of transfer activity.

f. Program Strengths. The prohibition of development on the higher elevations of El Toro Mountain creates significant motivation for owners of these properties to supply TDCs for sale or transfer. The City of Morgan Hill has several ways of boosting demand. One program provides sewer allocations for TDC purchases. Another exempts developers who buy TDCs from the RDCS process, and a third offers higher scores in the RDCS process for TDC purchases. The 2:1 transfer ratio is yet another incentive to use the program.

4. Belmont[11]

a. Purpose. The City of Belmont's Hillside Residential and Open Space (HRO) zoning encourages clustering and density transfer in order to assist in reducing traffic impacts and hazards associated with steep slopes while preserving the natural terrain and visual quality of the San Juan Hills.

HRO = Hillside Residential and Open Space

b. Background. The Belmont program is designed to solve the problem of 50-year-old subdivisions approved for steep, and in some cases unstable, slopes. Development can occur on these old lots, but, if the lot is extremely steep, the floor area permitted could be as low as 1,200 square feet, or 800 square feet of living space and a 400 square foot garage. Lots with geotechnical problems, such as the potential for landslides, could be completely unbuildable without a stabilization plan approved by the Planning Commission.

c. Procedural Features. Under the Belmont program, the number of dwelling units allowed per acre decreases with the average slope of the parcel. The zoning provides maximum floor area limits for

[11] William Chopyk, Senior Planner, City of Belmont; and portions of Belmont municipal code.

BELMONT

♦ *In 1988, Belmont adopted a TDR ordinance to reduce or eliminate development in antiquated subdivisions on steep slopes*

♦ *Development is allowed on sending sites, but the size of the permitted dwelling decreases as the slope increases*

♦ *Owners of potential sending sites are encouraged to transfer by a requirement for an approved geotechnical plan for lots with possible stability problems*

♦ *Six transfers have been approved so far, including a five-lot transfer which eliminated the need to build a road through a landslide area*

dwellings and, furthermore, limits the allowable floor area according to the steepness of the lot.

By conditional use permit, the code allows the clustering of residences on smaller lots and in closer proximity than would otherwise be allowed. The zoning also allows floor area to be transferred from one lot to another on the same roadway and within the same planning sub-area. This floor area transfer is permitted upon approval of an administrative conditional use permit by the Zoning Administrator.

The application for a density transfer must include a deed restriction indicating that the sending site will be precluded from future development and remain as permanent open space.

d. Transfer Activity. Six transfers have occurred since the ordinance was adopted in March 1988. In five of the six lots involved in transfers, the road shown on the original subdivision map traversed a landslide area. Lots in the landslide area were preserved as open space by deed restrictions, and the floor area ratio was used to increase the floor area of homes built on other lots on that street.

e. Program Weaknesses. The program requires sending and receiving sites to be on the same roadway. Additional flexibility in site location might increase transfer activity. Also, the program could be improved through additional incentives such as a transfer ratio that is more generous than the current ratio of 1:1.

f. Program Strengths. The program is well-designed to encourage the owners of sending sites to sell or transfer their rights. The owners of lots with potential geotechnical problems must obtain approval of a stabilization plan from the Planning Commission. Consequently, they have a significant incentive to use TDR. Because Belmont's slope density ratios might only allow a house with 800 square feet of living area, the owners of other potential sending sites also have an incentive to transfer rather than build.

Bill Chopyk, Senior Planner for the City of Belmont, attributes the program's success to the fact that it allows owners to make some economic use of lots from antiquated subdivisions which would be very difficult or impossible to develop under modern hillside development regulations.

5. Agoura Hills[12]

a. Purpose. The Agoura Hills TDR program is designed to preserve hillsides.

b. Background. Most of the residential land in Agoura Hills was already developed, or entitled to develop by the county, when the city

[12] Michael K. Kamino, Senior Planner, City of Agoura Hills; and portions of Agoura Hills municipal code.

incorporated in 1982. A goal of the city has been to preserve as much of the remaining undeveloped hillsides as possible. The higher elevations have been zoned open space, allowing development of a residential unit only on land parcels of five or more acres. In 1987, the city adopted a transferable development credit ordinance as one method of allowing some economic return to the owners of land zoned for open space.

c. Procedural Features. Under the Agoura Hills ordinance, only parcels within the Open Space District can be donor parcels. Following a recommendation from the Planning Commission, the City Council approves the transfer via a development agreement. The receiver site can accept an additional development credit for each credit transferred from a donor parcel. However the number of units transferred may not be more than 20 percent higher than the number of units normally allowed on the receiver parcel, and the ordinance does not provide for any additional incentives to encourage transfers.

d. Transfer Activity. No transfers have occurred since the ordinance was adopted.

e. Program Weaknesses. The program limits the density increase to not more than 20 percent more than the density allowed by zoning. The city also has a Cluster Development Ordinance (CDO) which allows increases in density in return for preservation of open space as well as improvements to parks and roadways plus aesthetic enhancements which benefit the community. Furthermore, a specific plan was recently adopted for a 474 acre hillside area which will make the transferable development credit program unnecessary for that portion of the city. These programs reduce the amount of transfers which would otherwise occur.

AGOURA HILLS

♦ *In 1987, Agoura Hills adopted a TDC ordinance to preserve remaining undeveloped hillsides*

♦ *Density increases on receiving sites are limited to 20 percent of the density allowed by zoning*

♦ *As an incentive, a two-to-one transfer ratio is used*

♦ *To encourage sending site owners to sell TDCs, development restrictions in hillside areas are high and increase with the steepness of the parcel*

♦ *No transfers have occurred to date*

CDO = Cluster Development Ordinance

Left

The Agoura Hills TDR program is designed to preserve selected natural areas, such as the Palo Camado Canyon shown to the left, for open space and wildlife protection. Because it is very difficult to develop in these open space areas, the city encourages transfers by allowing two development credits at a receiving site for each credit transferred from a sending site. Despite these incentives, the program is not active, partly because there are other mechanisms which can also be used to cluster development in appropriate locations.

f. Program Strengths. The density requirements in the city's Open Space District are very restrictive, creating a motivation for owners to transfer. As an incentive, the city uses a transfer ratio of 2:1. In addition, the city's Hillside Management Ordinance allows less density on steeper slopes, which also creates an inducement to transfer.

6. Brisbane[13]

a. Purpose. The Brisbane density transfer program is intended to preserve a steep hillside area.

b. Background. The Brisbane General Plan states that density transfers should be encouraged for the steepest portion of a hillside area known as Brisbane Acres, which is designated a density of two dwelling units per acre. Due to its steepness, inaccessibility, and the limited availability of water and other public services, by modern standards many of these unrecorded lots would be considered unbuildable.

c. Procedural Features. The Land Use and Open Space elements of the City of Brisbane establish a density transfer program which allows an owner/developer to be granted additional density on a buildable site if another unbuildable site is voluntarily dedicated as open space.

The general plan encourages higher density development in those portions of the Brisbane Acres which are less steep and more accessible to roads and water. As an incentive, the general plan allows for the possibility of a bonus of greater than an "acre for acre transfer."

Brisbane's zoning code implements the general plan by allowing, for each 20,000 square feet of land dedicated as open space, one additional dwelling unit in areas with less steep slopes which are closer to roads and utilities. This transfer must be approved via the conditional use permit process.

d. Transfer Activity. In the 12 years since TDR was incorporated into the general plan, no application has been made for a transfer.

e. Program Weaknesses. The increased development potential allowed on the receiving site by the Brisbane TDR program may not be substantial enough to generate a high demand for transfers. The incentive to transfer could be increased by raising the density allowed through TDR. Brisbane Senior Planner Tim Tune also believes that the program could be improved by providing the funding and expertise needed to organize the 60 owners of property in the subject area.

f. Program Strengths. Although off to a slow start, the program has been in place for 12 years, and the city has at least established a

---

[13] Tim Tune, Senior Planner, City of Brisbane; portions of the Brisbane municipal code; and "Brisbane General Plan Report," January 28, 1980.

long-term desire to use TDR. Similarly, property owners have had a dozen years to become familiar with the concept even though they have not used it as yet. Building on this familiarity, property owners and the city could cooperate to find the program refinements which would finally lead to its use.

7. Claremont[14]

a. Purpose. The Claremont TDC program is designed to preserve hillsides.

b. Background. In the 1970s, a transferable development credit program was adopted by the City of Claremont to preserve hillsides in their natural state.

c. Procedural Features. Within Claremont's Hillside District density transferred from designated sending areas is to be clustered in designated receiver areas, which are flatter and more appropriate for development. The Claremont General Plan does not allow development in the sending areas except for the placement of a single home on a large parcel of unsubdivided land. This essentially makes the TDC program mandatory.

City staff periodically mails notices to property owners, encouraging participation in the TDC program.

d. Transfer Activity. To date, no transfers have occurred. However, to promote hillside preservation, the city obtained an option on a 1,345 acre hillside parcel. A specific plan was prepared which would preserve most of this parcel while clustering development within a 125 acre receiver area under the guidelines of the specific plan. The city is currently seeking a buyer willing to develop the area according to the plan.

e. Program Weaknesses. A demand for TDCs in the receiving areas has not yet materialized. Sharon Wood, Claremont's Community Development Director, believes that developers would be more receptive to the city's program if at least one TDC project had been approved. At this point, the procedures have not been tested nor the value of credits established, so developers may be reluctant to become pioneers.

f. Program Strengths. The Claremont General Plan does not allow further subdivision of land in the sending areas. Sooner or later, this should motivate the owners of sending area properties to sell or transfer TDCs. The city continues to promote the program through periodic mailings. Because the TDC program has been in existence since the

---

[14] Sharon Wood, Community Development Director, City of Claremont; and portions of the City of Claremont General Plan and municipal code.

♦ *Milpitas adopted a TDC program to transfer development rights from the Western Hills to the Eastern Hills*

♦ *Transfer incentives included a transfer ratio of 2.6 to 1*

♦ *This transfer ratio did not compensate for the fact that development in the Eastern Hills was more costly*

♦ *In its ten years of existence, the program generated no transfers and was eliminated in conjunction with more restrictive density requirements for the Western Hills*

1970s, property owners, developers, and the general public have had an opportunity to become familiar with the concept. This familiarity would be beneficial if the city decided to refine its program with extra incentives or additional developer assistance.

8. Milpitas[15]

a. Purpose. The Milpitas TDC program was designed to encourage the transfer of development rights from a prominent hillside area.

b. Background. Milpitas, just north of San Jose, had a TDC program in place for roughly ten years. Its purpose was to encourage transfer of development from the more prominent Western Hills to the less noticeable Eastern Hills. Donor parcels could be in either area, but receiver parcels were limited to areas in the Eastern Hills designated as appropriate for villages in the general plan.

Three years ago, a Hillside Committee was formed to investigate possible improvements to the TDC program along with other hillside issues. After two years of deliberations and more than 40 meetings, the committee recommended increasing the transfer ratio from 2.6:1 to 6:1 in order to provide a better incentive for TDCs.

The Milpitas City Council became concerned that such greater incentives could preserve the Western Hills at the possible cost of sacrificing the Eastern Hills. Ultimately, the City Council eliminated the TDC program entirely and made development in the Western Hills more difficult by changing the density from one unit per acre to one unit per ten acres.

c. Procedural Features. The PUD process used to transfer credits allowed 2.6 credits to be transferred to the Eastern Hills for every one credit relinquished in the Western Hills. Some mechanisms other than TDCs were available to exceed the zoning densities. For example, the city could grant a density bonus of up to 15 percent for projects with desirable features such as clustered development, which reduces the visibility of hillside projects.

d. Transfer Activity. No transfer occurred during the ten years of the program's existence.

e. Program Weaknesses. Wesley D. Smith, Community Development Manager of Milpitas, speculates that the inactivity in the program is partly due to the fact that numerous property owners are involved and no large development has surfaced to encourage a coopera-

[15] Wesley D. Smith, Community Development Manager, City of Milpitas; and portions of the Milpitas municipal code.

tive TDC effort. Development is typically more costly in the Eastern Hills because of the need to extend utilities and roads. Consequently, the extra costs for smaller developments could not be compensated by the 2.6:1 transfer ratio.

     f. Program Strengths. Milpitas is clearly committed to hillside preservation, as evidenced by having a TDR program in place for ten years, a favorable transfer ratio, and the adoption of more restrictive hillside controls in conjunction with the elimination of TDR as compensation. In addition, over a two-year-period a Hillside Committee participated in more than 40 meetings to propose changes to the program. While the TDR program itself was eliminated, through the discussion it engendered, prospects for hillside preservation were improved.

9. Moraga[16]

     a. Purpose. The Moraga TDR ordinance is designed to preserve the higher elevations of Moraga's hillsides.

     b. Background. The Town of Moraga lies ten miles east of Oakland. When the city incorporated in the early 1970s, environmental protection was an important goal. The TDR ordinance was intended to protect hillsides by allowing development rights from those areas to be transferred to land at lower elevations.

     c. Procedural Features. Only open space zones and land with geotechnical problems are ineligible receiver sites. In the lower hillside areas, developers have had trouble achieving even the density permitted by right given geotechnical and other development difficulties.

     The receiving areas are basically developed. One exception is a large vacant parcel. However, this parcel is zoned for a density of six units per acre, and the city allows no more than a 30 percent increase in density via TDR.

Below
A TDR ordinance was adopted to preserve the higher elevations of hillsides in the Town of Moraga, about ten miles east of Oakland. The TDR program has been hampered by low demand for additional density, since developers often find it hard to achieve the densities allowed by zoning, given geotechnical and other development difficulties.

---

[16] Jean Safir, Senior Planner, Town of Moraga.

MORAGA

♦ *Moraga adopted a TDR program to preserve hillsides*

♦ *Demand for added density is not strong because developers find it difficult to achieve the densities allowed by zoning, given geotechnical and other concerns*

♦ *There are few potential receiving sites*

♦ *Moraga allows no more than a 30 percent increase in density due to TDR*

♦ *So far, the TDR process has been largely unused*

SAN FRANCISCO

♦ *In the 1960s, the City of San Francisco adopted a TDR ordinance to preserve historic landmarks*

♦ *The owners of historic landmarks are motivated to transfer development rights because under the city's landmarks regulations it is difficult to demolish an historic structure*

♦ *TDR is the only way to exceed San Francisco's downtown density limits, creating a demand for development rights*

♦ *Ten buildings have been approved using development rights transferred from more than 10 historic landmarks*

d. Transfer Activity. To date, the TDR ordinance has been largely unused.

e. Program Weaknesses. There is insufficient demand for additional density at potential receiver sites. The lower hillside areas have geotechnical difficulties which reduce demand for increased development, and with some exceptions, other potential receiving sites are already developed.

f. Program Strengths. The longevity of the Moraga TDR program has given property owners, developers, and public officials an opportunity to become familiar with the concept. This would be beneficial if Moraga decided to make refinements to its TDR program.

C. Preserve Historic Landmarks

1. San Francisco[17]

a. Purpose. The San Francisco TDR program is designed to preserve historic landmarks.

b. Background. The City of San Francisco has used transfer of development rights in the downtown area since the 1960s. The TDR ordinance specifies the amount of development that can be transferred as the difference between the floor area of the landmark building to be saved and the floor area that would be allowed for a new building under current zoning.

c. Procedural Features. Development rights can be transferred on a one-to-one basis. Once it has relinquished development rights, a building is classified as a significant historic building, greatly reducing its likelihood of being altered or destroyed. It is very difficult to get approval to demolish a significant historic structure in San Francisco, therefore creating a supply of development rights.

San Francisco's downtown density standard of nine-to-one cannot be circumvented by bonus density for amenities or design, making the TDR program the only way to achieve higher density. The city has not created a TDR bank primarily because it does not want to compete with the owners of landmarks who may want to sell their development rights.

d. Transfer Activity. In downtown San Francisco, at least ten buildings have been approved, and four have been built using TDRs. However, more than ten historic landmark buildings were needed to transfer TDRs to the receiver projects.

---

[17] Lawrence B. Badiner, Planner/Urban Designer, Department of City Planning, San Francisco; and portions of San Francisco's municipal code.

e. Program Weaknesses. Judging by the success of the program in the downtown area, it is surprising that San Francisco has not expanded the application of TDR to other parts of the city.

f. Program Strengths. San Francisco's historic landmark regulations make it very difficult to demolish a historic structure. Consequently, the owners of landmarks are highly motivated to sell or transfer the development rights from these buildings, thereby creating a supply of TDRs. On the receiving site, TDR is the only way to exceed the density limits in downtown San Francisco, resulting in a substantial demand for TDRs.

In addition, the longevity of San Francisco's program has assured developers that the use of TDR will not be an issue, but instead is considered a technical matter that can be relied on in the approval process.

2. Los Angeles[18]

a. Purpose. The TDR program in the City of Los Angeles is designed to preserve historic structures, promote housing, improve transportation, and provide open space.

b. Background. The City of Los Angeles adopted a transfer of development rights ordinance for its central business district with the purpose of preserving historic structures, promoting housing, improving transportation, and providing public open space. The ordinance provides for increasing commercial densities on sites which are served by public transportation, particularly near transit stations.

c. Procedural Features. The ordinance requires that a transfer plan be prepared and submitted first to the Community Redevelopment Agency (CRA). Upon approval by the CRA, the transfer plan is submitted to the City Planning Commission and then to the City Council for final approval. The decision makers are required to make eight findings, including that the transfer mitigates impacts on transportation, housing, open space, historic preservation, cultural resources, community assets, and public facilities.

The program requires a public benefit payment on transfers to fund affordable housing, open space, and public transportation. The benefit payment is currently set at $35 per square foot of floor area transferred. From the developer's point of view, the public benefit payment is part of the cost of purchasing additional development rights, making it possible for office projects to be built at substantially higher densities than would be permitted by right. For example, a ratio of 6:1 is permitted by right while up to 13:1 is permitted with a transfer.

---

[18] David Riccitiello, Project Manager, Los Angeles Community Redevelopment Agency; and portions of City of Los Angeles municipal code.

LOS ANGELES

- ◆ The City of Los Angeles adopted a TDR ordinance for its downtown to preserve historic structures, promote housing, improve transportation, and provide open space
- ◆ A controversial public benefit payment of $35 per square foot is required for all transferred floor area
- ◆ Using TDR, a project can have a floor area ratio of 13:1, more than double the 6:1 ratio allowed by zoning
- ◆ So far, the program has transferred almost one million square feet of floor area in conjunction with projects having more than 3.5 million square feet of floor area

CRA = Community Redevelopment Agency

City of Los Angeles Central Library

The Central Library of the City of Los Angeles was built in 1926, designated as an historic monument of the city in 1967, and added to the National Register of Historic Places in 1970. Looking for a way to preserve, restore, and expand the Central Library as well as other historic buildings in the downtown area, the City of Los Angeles in 1985 adopted a "Designated Building Site" ordinance.

Under this ordinance, contiguous parcels of property can be classified as a "Designated Building Site," permitting much higher density limits for the site as a whole, compared to what would have been allowed for individual parcels. In return for the preservation and restoration of historic property within the designated site, an increase in the total development capacity of non-historic parcels would be permitted.

In 1985, the Community Redevelopment Agency of the City of Los Angeles and Maguire/Thomas Partners Development, Ltd., jointly filed for "Designated Building Site" status for five parcels of land in the downtown area, including the Central Library. Without this status the development of these parcels would have been limited to a total floor area of 2.5 million square feet. However, under the new status, the development capacity of the five combined parcels increased to 13 square feet of floor area for each square foot of land (a floor area ratio of 13:1), almost doubling the development capacity of the site.

This expanded density limit allowed the development of two major office towers—the First Interstate Building, the tallest building in Los Angeles, and the Gas Company Building. In addition, the Central Library was preserved, restored, and enlarged, with the top of its new subterranean parking garage developed as a public plaza providing open space for the surrounding area. And, in the process, One Bunker Hill, another existing building, was rehabilitated.

The developers paid a total of $15 million for the library parking garage and related public amenities and, in return for the increased density, paid the city an additional $50 million. Besides allowing for the development of two major office towers, the preservation of two historic structures, and the provision of public art and open space, this transaction resulted in the City of Los Angeles receiving $65 million worth of community benefits.

The information for this case study was provided by staff members of the Community Redevelopment Agency of the City of Los Angeles.

Since it is fixed rather than being tied to rising land values, the public benefit payment provides developers with a level of certainty. Nor does it need to be made until the project is ready to begin construction.

In the case of several major transfers, the agency owned a reserve of floor area which was made available to developers at a nominal price so that developers were not faced with the uncertainties and difficulties of purchasing excess floor area on the open market. This level of certainty over project costs is critical to securing financing for major developments which may require up to five years from conception to completion.

d. Transfer Activity. Since the new TDR program was enacted, three projects have been approved with a total of almost one million square feet of transferred floor area and a total project build-out of more than 3.5 million square feet of office, hotel, and retail floor area. In addition, three more projects using TDR are currently in the pipeline. Unfortunately, however, the current surplus of empty office space in downtown Los Angeles will probably mean that the demand for additional density will remain low for years to come.

e. Program Weaknesses. Some critics argue that the public benefit payment ($35 per square foot of floor area transferred) discourages transfers by increasing the cost of TDRs and the cost of development. However others claim that this payment is a reasonable price for additional density, as evidenced by the fact that almost one million square feet of floor area has been transferred thus far.

f. Program Strengths. While the demand for additional office space in downtown Los Angeles was strong, this TDR program was very effective in achieving its goals, such as the preservation of the historic central library. The program allows density to be increased from a ratio of 6:1 to a ratio of 13:1, more than doubling the allowed density on the receiver site. This creates a strong demand for TDRs.

3. Pasadena[19]

a. Purpose. The TDR program in Pasadena is designed to encourage the preservation of historic properties and mitigate the effects of an ordinance that reduced density limits.

Above

The City of Los Angeles TDR program is designed to preserve historic structures, promote housing, and provide open space in the downtown while concentrating development near public transportation centers. When the economy is healthy, developers have a strong incentive to acquire TDRs, since projects using TDR can have more than double the density than that permitted for non-TDR projects. So far the program has facilitated the development of more than 3.5 million square feet of commercial floor area. The Los Angeles Central Library, shown above, was preserved by transferring unused development rights from the library site to new office towers surrounding the library.

19 Denver Miller, Zoning Administrator, City of Pasadena; and portions of Pasadena municipal code.

b. Background. The City of Pasadena adopted a TDR program to mitigate the 1984 adoption of new height and density limits contained in the Central District regulations and Urban Design Plan for the downtown. The code section specifically states that the purpose of the TDR component is to "allow property owners to recapture a portion of the development potential which was reduced by the adoption of this ordinance." The provisions also encourage the preservation of historic properties.

c. Procedural Features. An owner of property which had been developed to a density below the level permitted prior to the effective date of the new ordinance can apply for a transfer. Also, any property owner who does not want to develop to the level permitted by the new ordinance may apply for a transfer. The sending site may be any parcel in the Central District.

The transfer may be to receiver sites either within the same planning subdistrict or to three other subdistricts identified in the ordinance. The building envelope of the proposed project on the receiver site may not exceed the envelope limits of its planning subdistrict by more than 25 percent.

The Holly Street Grill, Pasadena

An ivy-covered, red brick mortuary, built in the 1920s, stands a block away from city hall in downtown Pasadena. Since it has the status of a "contributing structure" on the city's list of historic properties, the owner wanted to preserve the building.

Using the maximum density allowed by the zoning code, the difference in size between a new building on this site and the existing mortuary would have been an increase of 558,000 square feet of floor area. To compensate for the loss of potential revenue a larger building would have provided, the property owner sold all 558,000 square feet worth of unused development rights to the builders of the Pasadena Gateway, a high-rise office tower. The Gateway project also purchased 250,000 square feet of development rights from the Pasadena Presbyterian Church.

By using the 808,000 square feet acquired through TDR, the Pasadena Gateway project was able to exceed both the height limits and density restrictions of the zoning code. At the sending sites, the city preserved an architecturally significant church as well as the historic mortuary which is now the home of the Holly Street Grill.

Information provided by Alex Khoury, Pasadena Planning Department

d. Transfer Activity. Three projects have applied for density transfers since the program was enacted.

e. Program Weaknesses. The demand for transferred density is hampered by the fact that other methods, such as a special design density bonus CUP, can be used to increase density. A growth management initiative placed a cap on yearly development, further reducing demand for transferred density.

f. Program Strengths. The 1984 ordinance imposed density limits which give the owners of both potential sending sites and potential receiving sites an incentive to transfer TDR. In addition, the ordinance offers a wide range of potential receiving sites.

4. San Diego[20]

a. Purpose. The City of San Diego's TDR program is designed to preserve historic structures in the Golden Hill Historic District.

b. Background. The Golden Hill Historic District is close to downtown San Diego and Balboa Park. In 1981, a TDR program was adopted for the Golden Hill area of the City of San Diego. Unused density from properties in the Golden Hill Historic District can be transferred to other sites within the Golden Hill area.

c. Procedural Features. The motivation to demolish historic buildings in the Golden Hill area is reduced by the fact that current zoning restrictions would often result in a new building that was smaller than the old one. At the other end, potential receiver sites in the Golden Hill area are not always easy to find since, in many cases, the densities desired by developers can be achieved without purchasing development rights. In fact, the City Council made the policy decision to maintain density limits in the zoning code which allow development to occur without having to purchase development rights.

Acceptable receiving sites in other San Diego neighborhoods have been hard to find. Moreover, residents were opposed to accepting higher-than-planned densities in their neighborhoods in order to preserve historic structures in other neighborhoods.

d. Transfer Activity. In its first few years, the program allowed for transfers of at least two properties representing a transfer of from five to ten residential units. Since that time, there has been little interest in the program. Recently the subject of TDR has been raised again, but which neighborhoods to designate as receiving sites continues to be a concern.

[20] Michael J. Stepner, City Architect, City of San Diego; and City of San Diego staff report numbers 89-313 and 90-005.

PASADENA

♦ In 1984, Pasadena adopted a TDR program to mitigate the economic effects of new downtown height and density restrictions

♦ The program also promotes the preservation of historic properties

♦ The new density limits provide an incentive to sell and buy development rights

♦ But non-TDR methods allow density limits to be exceeded

♦ An annual growth cap has reduced demand for transferred development

♦ So far, three projects have been approved for transfers

SAN DIEGO

♦ In 1981, the City of San Diego adopted a TDR program to preserve landmarks in the Gold Hill Historic District

♦ Densities desired by developers on receiving sites can typically be met under existing zoning without the need for TDR

♦ Zoning restrictions on potential sending sites typically fail to create an incentive to transfer

♦ To date, the program has generated transfers of at least two properties

e. Program Weaknesses. Because the goals of the San Diego program are not widely accepted throughout the community, residents resist plans to transfer additional density into their neighborhoods in order to preserve landmarks in some other part of the city. Nor is the program ideally suited to zoning and pre-existing plans.

Restrictions on sending sites often fail to create excess rights to transfer, and additional density could be obtained in receiving areas without having to transfer rights from a sending site. According to Michael Stepner, San Diego City Architect, area plans should be developed with TDR in mind, and these plans should clearly state how TDR implements each plan.

f. Program Strengths. The San Diego program has been in existence since 1981. This longevity has given property owners, developers, and public officials an opportunity to become familiar with the concept. This familiarity, and the fact that at least some successful transfers have occurred, could make it easier to make needed TDR program refinements.

5. West Hollywood[21]

a. Purpose. West Hollywood uses TDR as an incentive to preserve, rehabilitate, and maintain cultural resources and as a mitigation for the Cultural Heritage Preservation Ordinance, which allows a property to be designated a cultural resource without the consent of the property owner.

b. Background/Refinements. TDR provisions were incorporated in the city's Cultural Heritage Preservation Ordinance which was adopted in 1989. A task force of the Cultural Heritage Advisory Board will be re-examining the TDR program to ensure that the incentives for the owners of sending parcels are adequate to promote transfers in the future.

c. Procedural Features. Once designated as a cultural resource, a property cannot be altered or demolished without city approval. After making various findings, the Planning Commission can approve the transfer of unusable development rights from a designated cultural resource in conjunction with granting a development permit for the receiving site. These include the finding that the transfer will not be detrimental to public health, safety, or welfare and that the use of monetary incentives had been exhausted prior to a transfer being granted.

In addition, the transfer can only occur if the sending site, or historic property, is rehabilitated to the standards of the ordinance.

---

[21] John Jacupcak, Associates Planner, City of West Hollywood; and portions of City of West Hollywood municipal code.

d. Transfer Activity. To date, no transfers have occurred. However some owners have expressed an interest in demolishing designated historic structures.

e. Program Weaknesses. Since the program is relatively new, some time will be needed to familiarize property owners, developers, and the general public with the benefits and procedures of the program.

f. Program Strengths. The TDR effort is part of a comprehensive cultural preservation program with a regular public information component and an established inventory/designation process. The Cultural Resources Preservation Ordinance requires city approval for the demolition of a designated cultural resource. This provides significant motivation for the owner of a cultural resource to sell or transfer the unusable development rights.

D. Protect Agricultural Land

▶ San Mateo County[22]

a. Purpose. The San Mateo County TDC program is designed to promote the preservation of both agricultural land and the business of agriculture itself.

b. Background. San Mateo County, which occupies the southern portion of the San Francisco peninsula, wants to keep as much of its coastal agricultural land as possible in production. The county has a Planned Agricultural District (PAD) zone which strictly limits nonagricultural uses on prime agricultural land. For example, land cannot be subdivided unless the agricultural productivity of all the resulting parcels would not be reduced in the process.

The density allowed on agricultural land ranges from one density credit per 40 acres to one density credit per 160 acres. The amount of development which can occur under a density credit depends on whether the proposed use is a single-family home, a bed and breakfast, or some other land use. When subdivisions are created, agricultural

Above
The El Mirador shown above, is a designated cultural resource of the City of West Hollywood. The West Hollywood Cultural Heritage Preservation Ordinance allows a property to be designated as a cultural resource without the consent of the property owner, and a designated landmark cannot be altered or demolished without city approval. These restrictions provide incentives for the owners of landmark buildings to transfer unused development rights to appropriate receiver sites.

PAD = Planned Agricultural District

---

22 Diane Regonini, Planner, County of San Mateo; and portions of San Mateo County zoning regulations.

SAN MATEO COUNTY

♦ *The San Mateo County TDC program is designed to preserve agricultural land and agricultural activity*

♦ *The ordinance allows bonus density credits to be created by consolidating land parcels in agricultural zones*

♦ *Density credits can also be created for building agricultural water storage facilities*

♦ *The strong agricultural zoning restrictions provide an incentive to use TDC*

♦ *Since the program started in 1988, two density credits have been transferred as a result of the construction of a water impoundment*

use is required to be protected in perpetuity through the recording of an agricultural easement.

c. Procedural Features. The PAD ordinance allows bonus density credits to be acquired for consolidating parcels and for building agricultural water storage facilities. The credits related to water storage facility development can be transferred, upon approval of the Planning Commission, to parcels in the rural Coastal Zone as long as the transfer would not convert Prime Agricultural Land or locate development within scenic corridors. Deed restrictions record the fact that the sending parcel has relinquished any bonus density credits.

In addition to bonus density credits, density credits associated with a parcel completely covered by prime agricultural land can be transferred to another parcel of land in the rural Coastal Zone in return for an easement permanently restricting the sending parcel to agricultural uses, non-agricultural uses accessory to agriculture, and farm labor housing.

d. Transfer Activity. Although the program has been in existence since 1988, thus far only two bonus density credits have been granted and transferred. This occurred when a farmer built a water impoundment and sold the resulting bonus density credits.

e. Program Weaknesses. According to Diane Regonini of the San Mateo County Planning Department, the lack of activity in the density transfer program may be explained by several factors. For example, there may not be enough parcels completely covered by prime agricultural land to stimulate the transfer of a large number of credits. In addition, the density program is dependent either upon a landowner's ability to finance the construction of agricultural water impoundments before being compensated by the sale of the bonus density credits or on the existence of large development projects which can take advantage of the lot consolidation bonus.

Moreover, both the density transfer and bonus density transfer programs may be constrained by a limited number of receiving sites that comply with the transfer criteria. And the program may also be hampered by a lack of promotion.

f. Program Strengths. The TDC program is supported by a strong agricultural zoning ordinance which demonstrates the county's commitment to agricultural preservation. The zoning code provisions offer various opportunities and incentives for landowners to supply TDCs. The demand may increase as the economy improves or could be stimulated by revising the receiving site criteria so that more sites become eligible for transfers.

E. Promote Urban Form

1. Cupertino[23]

a. Purpose. The Cupertino TDR program allows for reasonable flexibility in concentrating development while maintaining an overall growth limit which can be accommodated by the street system.

b. Background. Twenty years ago, Cupertino adopted a Traffic Intensity Performance Standard (TIPS) regulation, which limits density within its DeAnza Boulevard/Stevens Creek Boulevard commercial area to 16 one-way, peak-hour trips per gross acre in order to maintain acceptable traffic flow. To maintain development flexibility within this density limit, the property owner may retain, sell, or transfer trips to other properties in this commercial area if a development does not use the entire 16-trip-per-acre capacity.

c. Procedural Features. Transfers can only be approved by the Planning Commission or City Council through a use permit for the receiving site. The use permit cannot be approved if the transfer significantly reduces the future development options for either the sending or receiving sites.

Cupertino also imposes floor area ratio (FAR) restrictions within three commercial areas which are not subject to TIPS. As in the TIPS area, FAR transfers may occur within a defined area through a use permit approval for both the sending and receiving parcels.

Cupertino has prepared a "Development Intensity Manual" which clearly describes these density and transfer regulations and provides sample calculations.

d. Transfer Activity. Robert Cowan, Cupertino's Community Development Director, estimates that from 30 to 40 transfers have occurred under this program. In fact, almost all the trip capacity of the program has been allocated to development projects, either approved or completed. According to Cowan, only five trips are currently not assigned to a completed or approved project. Some developers acquired trip rights realizing that their value would increase over time. At one point, the value of a trip was estimated at $50,000.

e. Program Weaknesses. With only five trips currently not assigned, the 20-year-old Cupertino program has effectively accomplished the city's original goals. Thanks to the success of this program, some thought might be given to using TDR to achieve other land use objectives in Cupertino.

---

[23] Robert Cowan, Director of Community Development, City of Cupertino; and "Development Intensity Manual," City of Cupertino, May, 1990.

CUPERTINO

♦ *Twenty years ago, Cupertino adopted density limits on a commercial corridor to keep traffic within the capacity of the street system*

♦ *To maintain flexibility, property owners may sell unused development rights to other owners who wish to exceed the density limits*

♦ *The program benefits from comprehensive instructional materials and a well-informed development community*

♦ *Some developers acquired development rights early in the program, knowing their value would increase over time*

♦ *Between 30 and 40 transfers have been approved, leaving very few development rights left to be transferred*

TIPS = Traffic Intensity Performance Standard

FAR = Floor Area Ratio

Cupertino's Research and Development Campus

Sobrato Development Companies owns a total of 55 acres of land within Cupertino's De Anza Boulevard/Stevens Creek Boulevard commercial zone. A Traffic Intensity Performance Standard (TIPS) system limits development in this zone through a restriction on trips-per-acre, but, in order to provide flexibility in concentrating development, also allows property owners to transfer trips to other properties.

In addition to the office and commercial buildings already on their land, Sobrato proposed a 785,000 square foot office park adjacent to the I-280 freeway, which was eventually named the Apple Research and Development Campus.

According to the TIPS system, the Sobrato project would generate 1201.4 trips, but the formula only allowed for 884 trips. To make up the difference, Sobrato purchased an additional 322 trips from three other properties in the zone and transferred the excess 4.6 trips to yet another property.

Using the TIPS system, Cupertino was able to maintain a level of development within the corridor that could be accommodated by the transportation system and still provide the flexibility needed to allow an important, higher-density project at an appropriate site adjacent to a freeway.

Right

The Cupertino TDR program allows for flexibility in concentrating development while maintaining an overall growth limit which can be accommodated by the street system. During the 20-year life of the program, more than 30 transfers have occurred, accounting for almost all of the available development capacity. Most recently, the Apple Research and Development Campus was developed using transferred development rights.

f. Program Strengths. Because developers in the program area cannot exceed density limits without acquiring trip rights, this creates a strong demand for transfers. In turn, this strong demand increases their value, providing a significant incentive for landowners to create a supply.

The program is supported by reader-friendly instructional materials. Consequently, the majority of the property owners and developers in Cupertino understood the trip control/transfer program from the beginning. With a 20-year history, longevity itself increases confidence and encourages property owners and developers to use the program.

2. Burbank[24]

a. Purpose. The City of Burbank TDR program is designed to promote appropriate concentrations of development while maintaining overall development capacity within limits which can be accommodated by the transportation and other public service systems.

b. Background. In order to keep future growth in Burbank's Media District from adversely affecting public service systems and surrounding single-family residential neighborhoods, the Media District Specific Plan established a relatively low density limit. Recognizing that concentrations of development could benefit the city as well as property owners, the plan allows transfers of development rights between properties within the district. The overall development capacity of the District remains the same despite transfers.

c. Procedural Features. A TDR proposal requires approval through the conditional use permit process. During that process, at least one public hearing is held, and the project receives environmental review to identify any potential effects resulting from the transfer.

d. Transfer Activity. To date, two transfers have been approved. In the first transaction, approximately 400,000 square feet of floor area were transferred from the main studio lot of NBC to an adjacent office-retail complex known as NBC Plaza. This transfer allowed a floor area ratio of 4:1 on a site which the Media District Specific Plan identified as the major focal point of the district. Without this transfer, the site would only have been allowed a density of 2:1.

In October 1992, the city approved a second transfer from the Warner Brothers main studio lot to a new Warner Brothers office building across the street.

e. Program Weaknesses. The Burbank program requires the approval of the Planning Board through the CUP process. This procedural

---

BURBANK

◆ *In 1991, Burbank adopted a specific plan for its Media District which features relatively restrictive density limits*

◆ *To promote appropriate concentrations of development, the specific plan allows transfers of development rights between properties in the district*

◆ *Despite transfers, the overall development capacity of the district remains constant*

◆ *The relatively restrictive density limits create a demand for added development rights*

◆ *Only TDR and one other mechanism can be used to exceed the density limits*

◆ *In two years, two transfers have been approved, with total floor area of almost one million square feet*

---

24 Rick Pruetz, City Planner, City of Burbank, Burbank's Media District specific plan; and portions of the City of Burbank municipal code.

♦ *Oakland's TDR ordinance allows for transfers between abutting properties*

♦ *The ordinance is primarily designed to preserve historic properties*

♦ *The receiving site zoning allows very high density, reducing the incentive to transfer development rights*

♦ *The requirement that sending and receiving sites abut one another also reduces the ability to transfer*

♦ *To date, Oakland's TDR ordinance has not been used*

hurdle tends to limit interest in TDR to larger projects with longer lead times for project approval. However, in Burbank this is not considered a critical problem since the specific plan includes another mitigation mechanism for smaller projects needing to exceed the plan's density limits.

f.   Program Strengths. The Burbank Media District Specific Plan has relatively restrictive density limits which can only be exceeded by TDR and one other mechanism—the allocation of density from a reserve controlled by the city. This creates a demand for density transfers.

TDR, an integral component of the specific plan since its inception, was designed both to mitigate the relatively restrictive densities and provide a means to achieve land use goals while maintaining a consistent density limit on all property in the planning area.

3. Oakland[25]

a.   Purpose. The Oakland TDR ordinance is designed to allow transfers of density between abutting properties. One primary objective is the preservation of historic properties.

b.   Background. The City of Oakland has a code provision which, by conditional use permit, allows an increase in living units or floor area ratio upon the acquisition of development rights from abutting properties.

c.   Procedural Features. The ordinance requires a determination that the proposed reduction in units or floor area be sufficient to compensate for any effects which would result from allowing additional density on the receiving site.

d.   Transfer Activity. The TDR code section has never been used.

e.   Program Weaknesses. One drawback to the program is that the sending and receiving properties must abut one another. Willie Yee, Manager of Comprehensive Planning with the Oakland Planning Department, notes that the incentive to transfer density may be low because the density allowed by the basic zoning is relatively high, in some areas as high as a floor area ratio of 7:1.

f.   Program Strengths. The existence of a TDR program has given property owners, developers, and public officials an opportunity to become familiar with the concept. This familiarity would be beneficial if the city decides to refine its program.

---

[25] Alvin James, Planning Director; Willie Yee, Manager of Comprehensive Planning, Oakland City Planning Department; and City of Oakland municipal code.

F. New Housing and Revitalization

1. Irvine[26]

    a. Purpose. The Irvine TDR program was designed to encourage development of residential uses on sites previously approved for office buildings.

    b. Background. Prior to incorporation, the Irvine Business Complex (IBC) was zoned by the county for research and development. This zoning restricted office development to less than 50 percent of the floor area of any new project in the IBC except for corporate headquarters. When Irvine incorporated, for awhile the zoning remained unchanged. By the late 1970s, however, there was considerable pressure to build 100 percent office projects in the IBC.

    While developers were increasingly interested in 100 percent office projects, the City of Irvine was increasingly interested in attracting residential development to the IBC to improve the jobs/housing balance.

    c. Procedural Features. Irvine adopted a TDR ordinance which allowed residential units to be constructed on sending sites in the IBC and allowed office development rights to be transferred from the sending sites to receiving sites.

IBC = Irvine Business Complex

Left

Irvine created a TDR program to encourage residential development in the Irvine Business Complex. In the only transfer approved under this program, a developer built the 400-unit residential project shown to the left in return for approval to transfer office development rights to another site.

---

[26] Pam Davis, Senior Planner, City of Irvine; and portions of the City of Irvine municipal code.

- ♦ *Irvine adopted a TDR ordinance to promote residential development in the Irvine Business Complex*

- ♦ *The ordinance encouraged the construction of residential units on sending sites*

- ♦ *As an incentive, development rights for office uses could be transferred to a receiving site project composed entirely of office space*

- ♦ *The program criteria were designed to promote a specific project*

- ♦ *The program facilitated only the specific project it was designed to promote, a 400-unit residential complex*

TEDR = Transfer of Existing Development Rights

As a result of a transfer, a receiving site would be allowed to be 100 percent office, and the city would get additional housing needed in the IBC.

d. Transfer Activity. The city approved only one transfer, which allowed for construction of a 400-unit residential project on the sending site and a 100 percent office project on the receiving site. However, the office component has not yet been built. Having approved only one transfer, Irvine eventually eliminated the TDR provision from its zoning code.

e. Program Weaknesses. The criteria written into Irvine's TDR ordinance were so specific that only one sending site and one receiving site qualified for approval.

f. Program Strengths. The city has enjoyed one successful transfer using TDR. This experience may encourage the city to use TDR for other purposes in the future.

2. Santa Barbara[27]

a. Purpose. The Santa Barbara Transfer of Existing Development Rights (TEDR) program promotes revitalization by offering incentives for property owners to replace older buildings with new, smaller buildings.

b. Background. In 1989, the city of Santa Barbara projected constraints on specific resources needed to suport commercial growth, such as transportation/parking infrastructure and worker housing. In response, the city adopted a program which limits commercial development to 3 million square feet over the next 20 years.

The city also realized that areas were in need of revitalization. To promote revitalization, the city adopted a Transfer of Existing Development Rights program which encourages property owners to replace older buildings with new, smaller buildings. Under this concept, the difference between the development rights of the larger building and the development rights of the smaller building replacing it could be transferred to an appropriate receiving site.

At the start of the process, Freilich, Stone, Leitner and Carlisle, the city's legal consultant, prepared a 48-page background paper

---

[27] Danny Kato, City of Santa Barbara Community Development Department; Margaret Sohagi, Freilich, Stone, Leitner, and Carlisle, correspondence of October 19, 1992; Martin Leitner and Margaret Sohagi, "Transfer of Existing Development Rights: A Discussion of Issues and Policy Alternatives," April 18, 1991; and Martin Leitner and Margaret Sohagi, "Alternative Analysis for Proposed Transfer of Existing Development Rights Program," August 21, 1991. (The latter two citations are discussion papers prepared for the Santa Barbara City Council.)

which discussed TDR in general and analyzed numerous planning and legal issues which would be important to the program.

c. Procedural Features. The Transfer of Existing Development Rights program is voluntary, with owners of sending area property able to decide whether or not they want to voluntarily replace their existing buildings with smaller buildings. Existing development rights (EDRs) are privately bought and sold, and the city should not incur the expense of purchasing EDRs for resale.

In addition to existing square footage, floor area approved, but not yet built, is transferable, with all transferable floor area not to be considered new square footage under the city's growth cap.

The city approves the development proposed for both the sending and receiving sites in conjunction with approving the transfer itself, which ensures that land use goals are achieved at both sites. And eligible sending and receiving sites are determined on a case-by-case basis.

In addition, the ordinance states that a sending site cannot be left vacant. All development rights can be transferred from the sending site only if the sending site is used for residential development or the site is dedicated to the city for use as a park, parking lot, or other public use.

d. Transfer Activity. No transfers have yet occurred.

e. Program Weaknesses. As adopted, the city approves the development proposed for the sending and receiving sites along with the transfer itself. While this allows a case-by-case examination of whether or not land use goals will be achieved, some communities have found that such requirements reduce transfer activity because separate property owners must find one another, prepare consistent development proposals, and seek approval of those proposals concurrently.

f. Program Strengths. According to Freilich, Stone, the program should be successful because the city's growth cap creates a strong market demand. Moreover, transferred floor area would not be subject to the growth cap, creating a significant incentive to use TEDR. In addition, the program should be an incentive to develop housing on sending sites.

SANTA BARBARA

◆ *Santa Barbara wants to maintain limits on future commercial growth while promoting the recycling of areas in need of revitalization*

◆ *The city adopted a Transfer of Existing Development Rights (TEDR) program, which encourages owners to replace older buildings with new, smaller buildings and transfer the difference in floor area to receiving sites*

◆ *The transferred floor area is not considered new development and is not subject to the city's growth cap*

◆ *So far, no transfers have occurred but the program appears promising because the demand for development is high and TEDR transfers are exempt from the city's growth cap*

EDR = Existing Development Right

IV Why More California Communities Don't Use TDR—A Survey

The technique of transferable development rights has been fairly well known within the planning profession since the 1970s. Publications of the American Planning Association have described how they can assist in the preservation of open space, historic landmarks, environmentally sensitive areas, and agricultural lands without the cost of public purchase. In fact, many cities, counties, and even states have preserved substantial amounts of land at minimal cost using TDR (see Chapters II and III).

Despite this favorable record, relatively few California communities have adopted TDR programs. According to *The California Planner's 1990 Book of Lists*, a publication of the California Governor's Office of Planning and Research, an OPR survey completed in 1989 shows that only 25 out of 456 cities and 10 out of 55 counties adopted TDR programs. And some communities on OPR's list do not have TDR programs (see Chapter III).

Of the responses OPR received, only 27 communities in California have TDR programs, or five percent of all the cities and counties in the state. To determine why relatively few communities use TDR despite its apparent benefits, a statewide survey was conducted.

A. Survey Process

1. Survey Implementation

The survey was sponsored by the author. In February 1992, questionnaires were mailed to the planning directors of all 431 cities and 45 counties in California which, according to OPR's *1990 Book of Lists*, have no TDR programs. By July 1992, 177 communities, or 37 percent, had responded to the questionnaire. The results are reported in the "Findings" section below.

2. Questionnaire Contents

As shown in the Sample Questionnaire (Appendix A), the survey asked questions in three general areas: about the goals of the community, the probability of achieving those goals given current regulations and funding, and why a particular community doesn't use transferable development rights.

a. What Are the Goals of Your Community? To determine the extent to which communities considered land preservation/protection activities as community goals, respondents were asked if their goals included any of the following: acquiring parkland/open space, preserving natural areas, saving historic landmarks, saving agricultural land and/or others not defined.

b. What Percent of These Goals Will Be Reached Given Funding Levels and/or Regulatory Authority? Here respondents were asked to consider what percentage of land use goals were likely to be achieved under current budgets and present codes and other regulations. The purpose of this question was to encourage planning directors to report on the adequacy of their current tools for implementing the land use goals they identified in response to the first question.

c. Why Doesn't Your Community Use Transferable Development Rights? Here respondents were offered a list of ten potential reasons for not using TDR, ranging from "we have not given TDR much serious consideration," to "our property owners are, or may be, reluctant to agree to a process that is unknown or untested." The purpose of this question was to determine the most commonly cited reasons why communities decide not to use TDR. (For a complete list of the options, see Appendix A.)

B. Findings

Of the 476 cities and counties surveyed, 177, or thirty-seven percent, responded. The tables below summarize the results of the survey in numerical form. In some instances, the number of responses may exceed the number of communities responding, because cities and counties were free to indicate whatever number of responses was appropriate. Conversely, in some categories the total number of responses is less than the total number of respondents because some declined to respond in certain categories.

1. Land Preservation/Protection Goals

Most planning directors responded that land preservation/protection activities were goals of their communities. As shown in Table 1 below, more than 70 percent of the 177 respondents reported that their community goals included the acquisition of parkland/open space, the preservation of historic landmarks, and the preservation of natural areas. About 40 percent reported that agricultural land preservation was also a community goal. In addition, approximately 13 percent of the communities reported other goals including revitalization, industrial retention, maintenance of village character, provision of affordable housing, and ridgeline protection, as well as the preservation of endangered species, wetlands, bridletrails, flood plains, wetlands, aquifers, and baylands.

2. Achieving Land Use Goals?

Most respondents reported that, given funding levels and/or regulatory authority, they did not expect to achieve all their land use goals. Some respondents balked at attempting to speculate on the probability of attaining long-range goals. However, most respondents made an attempt at quantification. Generally, less than 20 percent believed all their community's land use goals would be completely achieved, while few respondents believed that their communities would not achieve at least some portion of their goals.

Above

San Diego's TDR program is designed to preserve historic structures in the Golden Hill Historic District, such as the Villa Montezuma pictured above. The San Diego program has been hampered by the fact that zoning densities for potential receiving sites are so high that developers have little need to transfer additional density from a sending site.

Table 1

Indicate which of the following, if any, are goals of your community.

(Please circle "yes" or "no.")

		yes	no
A	Acquire parkland/open space	138	27
B	Preserve natural areas	138	26
C	Save historic landmarks	136	22
D	Save agricultural land	73	46
E	Other _____	25	3

As shown in Table 2 on page 86, the bulk of the responses indicate that the probability of achieving land use goals ranges from 25 to 75 percent. The confidence expressed is remarkably similar from one land use category to another. In each category respondents reported that at least half of their goals would be met, with slightly more optimism in the categories of saving agricultural land and preserving natural areas.

Table 2

**Roughly what percent of these goals are likely to be achieved
given funding levels and/or regulatory authority?
(Please circle a percent estimate.)**

		0	25	50	75	100 %
A	Acquire parkland/open space					
		1	39	28	33	20
B	Preserve natural areas	0	25	50	75	100 %
		8	34	28	39	24
C	Save historic landmarks	0	25	50	75	100 %
		10	38	29	35	18
D	Save agricultural land	0	25	50	75	100 %
		7	16	10	23	12
E	Other	0	25	50	75	100 %
		0	4	3	5	8

The response totals in this table are in italics so they can be differentiated from the numbers that are part of the survey form itself. For example, the number "20" at the far right of the second row indicates that 20 respondents believe that 100 percent of their parkland/open space acquisition goals will be met given funding levels and/or regulatory authority.

3. Why Don't Communities Use TDR?

As shown in Table 3 on page 87, the questionnaire offered respondents ten possible reasons to explain why their communities do not use TDR.

a. Many Communities Don't See a Need for TDR. In every category, the most common response was that the community "relies primarily on zoning and development restrictions to achieve land use goals." The second most common response was "we have not given TDR much serious consideration." In fact, these two responses accounted for more than half the total number of responses.

b. Some Communities Think of TDR as Untested, Legally Complex, and Logistically Burdensome. A smaller number of responses indicated a reluctance to use TDR for logistical reasons. Over ten percent of the total number of responses were represented by the concern that "property owners are, or may be, reluctant to agree to a process that is unknown or untested."

Respondents also reported concerns about TDR being "legally complex and/or logistically burdensome." Over ten percent of the respondents stated that their communities "cannot agree on areas suitable to accept transferred density." In fact, in margin notes several respondents pointed out that the preservation of existing or planned densities was as important to their communities as the competing goals of preserving

Table 3

Below are several reasons why communities don't use TDR.

A   We have not given TDR much serious consideration.

B   We rely primarily on zoning and development restrictions to achieve land use goals.

C   We prefer to use outright purchase to acquire land, easements and development rights.

D   Our community considers TDR to be legally complex and/or logistically burdensome.

E   Our community cannot agree on areas suitable to accept the transferred density.

F   Our property owners want to develop the land they own; they are not interested in transferring development rights even if it would result in the same monetary return.

G   Our property owners are not convinced that they would achieve as much return on investment with TDR as they would be developing their own land.

H   Our property owners are not sure there would be much demand for transferred development rights since achieving desired density is fairly easy.

I   Our property owners are, or may be, concerned about the amount of time needed for TDR projects.

J   Our property owners are, or may be, reluctant to agree to a process that is unknown or untested.

For each category in which you indicated a goal in response to Question 1, please circle the letters of the reasons why your community has not used TDR or might be reluctant to use TDR.

A   Acquire parkland/open space

A	B	C	D	E	F	G	H	I	J
71	87	28	21	21	20	10	15	8	31

B   Preserve natural areas

A	B	C	D	E	F	G	H	I	J
63	101	22	19	17	18	13	14	11	27

C   Save historic landmarks

A	B	C	D	E	F	G	H	I	J
65	79	9	19	16	18	12	8	8	27

D   Save agricultural land

A	B	C	D	E	F	G	H	I	J
32	48	7	16	6	7	9	10	4	18

E   Other

A	B	C	D	E	F	G	H	I	J
9	18	2	4	6	3	3	0	2	5

open space, natural areas, landmarks, and agricultural land. This concern about receiving areas is supported by the fact that almost 15 percent of the respondents reported that their communities "prefer to use outright purchase to acquire land, easements, and development rights."

c.   A Few Communities Avoid TDR because of Property Owner Concerns. As shown in Table 3, other potential reasons for not using TDR were cited less frequently: "our property owners want to develop the land they own; they are not interested in transferring development rights even if it would result in the same monetary return;" "our property owners are not convinced that they would achieve as much return on investment with TDR as they would by developing their own land;" "our property owners are not sure there would be much demand for transferred development rights since achieving desired density is fairly easy;" and "our property owners are, or may be, concerned about the amount of time needed for TDR projects."

As opposed to the more commonly cited reasons, these infrequently used responses deal with only one of the players in a TDR transaction—the property owners. In addition, a community would already have to be seriously considering TDR to know whether property owners are concerned about processing times, the demand for transferable density, or the relative profitability of projects involving TDR.

d. Some Respondents Believe TDR Is Not Applicable in Fully Developed Communities. The questionnaire did not include a response option for those who do not use TDR because their communities are completely developed. However, at least 15 respondents used handwritten margin notes to report that, because they are built out, their communities see no applicability for TDR. These comments result from the fact that TDR is often associated solely with the preservation of agricultural land, open space, and sensitive natural areas. In fact, TDR is commonly used in completely developed communities.

The most typical function for TDR in a developed community is historic preservation, but TDR has also been put to more exotic uses. For example, the cities of Burbank and Cupertino have programs which allow the flexibility to concentrate development in appropriate locations without exceeding the overall capacity of the transportation network and other public service systems (see Chapter III).

e. Several Respondents Emphasized That Zoning Alone Was Sufficient. One of the response choices printed on the questionnaire was, "we rely primarily on zoning and development restrictions to achieve land use goals." Nevertheless, several respondents felt the need to reinforce their response in supplemental letters and margin notes. Some respondents merely listed the types of restrictions they had in place, such as agricultural zoning. Others explained in detail that their zoning was so restrictive that essentially no excess development opportunity was available to transfer.

This is one of the most interesting aspects of the survey. Clearly, if zoning restrictions already achieve all of a community's land use goals, there is little reason to institute a TDR program. However, as mentioned above, most communities report that they aren't achieving all their land use goals, a paradox explored in the last section of this chapter.

f. Several Communities Transfer Development Only on a Case-by-Case Basis. Some respondents reported in margin notes that, even though they don't have a formal TDR ordinance, in planned developments and individual project approvals they still use density transfers and clustering on a case-by-case basis. These case-by-case solutions are possibly most appropriate in communities involving a limited number of land parcels or where the need for transfers of development are confined to identifiable segments of the community.

g. Several Communities Intend to Use TDR. At least nine respondents, or about five percent, stated that their communities might adopt TDR programs in the future. Some mentioned that their general plans call for an exploration of TDR, and others indicated that they intend to examine TDR but, at the moment, more pressing issues are on their agenda.

C. Conclusions

1. Is a Community's Zoning Adequate?

Although the most common responses given for not using TDR was, "we rely primarily on zoning and development restrictions to achieve land use goals," margin comments suggest that existing zoning is so restrictive that there is no unused development capacity on parcels which need to be protected and, consequently, no need to transfer development capacity to some other site.

a. Most Communities Will Not Achieve All Their Land Use Goals. Several communities are undoubtedly in the enviable position of having existing zoning regulations which achieve all land use goals. However the survey found that less than 20 percent of the respondents believe that the land use goals of their communities will be completely achieved given current funding levels and regulations.

b. TDR Should Be Viewed as a Means to Make Zoning More Effective. From the survey results it is clear that many respondents have the impression that TDR is an alternative to zoning and other traditional land use controls. However, TDR should not be viewed as an alternative to traditional techniques, but rather as a means of imposing zoning and other restrictions which would actually achieve all of a community's goals.

For example, Monterey County, Morgan Hill, Claremont, and West Hollywood were able to impose prohibitions on development in sending areas by providing TDR as a means of compensation. In

Below
To preserve its undeveloped hillsides, the City of Brisbane, just south of San Francisco, adopted a TDR ordinance which allows one additional dwelling unit on receiver sites for each 20,000 square feet of hillside dedicated as open space. The incentive to transfer could be increased by raising the density allowed on the receiver site through TDR.

other words, TDR made it possible for these communities to adopt controls that actually implement land use goals. The code changes for downtown Pasadena went so far as to state that the purpose of the TDR component is to "allow property owners to recapture a portion of the development potential which was reduced by the adoption of this ordinance."

2. Communities Need More Information

The second major category of reasons for not using TDR included, "we have not given TDR much serious consideration;" "our property owners are, or may be reluctant to agree to a process that is unknown or untested;" and "our community considers TDR to be legally complex and/or logistically burdensome."

Additional information about TDR could help to overcome this reluctance. For example, as more TDR success stories are circulated to the planning community and elected officials, more communities will be inclined to give TDR "serious consideration." Case studies of TDR programs could likewise demonstrate that the technique has received considerable examination and testing. And finally, these case studies could also prove that TDR programs can be relatively simple to implement, instead of being "legally complex and/or logistically burdensome." In other words, procedural for not using TDR would decline if the details of existing TDR programs were more widely publicized.

3. Coordinating TDRs with General Plans And Zoning Codes

In the third major category, respondents stated that their communities "cannot agree on areas suitable to accept the transferred density." Some respondents added margin comments, emphasizing that in their communities the desire to maintain low densities is often as strong as the desire to achieve other goals such as the preservation of open space and agricultural land. Naturally, it doesn't make much sense to attain the goal of preserving a sending parcel through TDR if it only means that the resulting project on the receiving parcel is contrary to other important community goals. This response highlights the importance of coordinating a TDR program with the community's general plan and zoning code.

a. Communities Must Agree on Sites Where Additional Development Would Be Appropriate. In many communities, there could be a general consensus that additional development is appropriate in certain areas. In fact, in some cities, areas appropriate for additional development may not only be identified but already planned for higher density. But in other cities the task of designating appropriate receiving sites will require that the community re-evaluate its land use goals, gather citizen input, and formally amend its general plan.

b. Comprehensive Plan and Code Changes May Be Needed. Identification of receiving sites is only one step in the process of coordinating TDR with general plans and zoning codes. For TDR to work well, additional development on a receiving site should only be possible through the transfer process. As discussed in detail in Chapter V, this often requires comprehensive amendments to general plans and zoning codes to clarify that additional development on the receiving site and reduced development on the sending site are both important community goals.

V Ingredients for a Successful TDR Program

In this chapter, the information from the California TDR case studies (see Chapter III) and the California TDR Survey (see Chapter IV) is used to suggest the ingredients needed for a successful TDR program. This chapter also includes the criteria considered relevant to the success of a TDR program—goals, development restrictions on sending and receiving sites, incentives, and TDR program management.

A. What Constitutes a Successful Program?

1. The Number of Transfers Is Only One Measure of Success

In Chapter III, considerable attention was given to the number of transfers which have occurred as a result of the TDR programs discussed. Other publications on transferable development rights have also emphasized the number of transfers generated under the programs summarized in those reports.

However, the success of a TDR program should not be judged solely by the number of transfers. Even exceptional TDR programs produce few transfers if either the pace of or demand for development in the sending areas is relatively low. A TDR program should not be judged as ineffective merely because it operates in a more leisurely development environment or because it was instituted in anticipation of demand that has not yet materialized.

2. A Successful Program Is One That Meets the Goals of All Participants

TDR has been called a "win-win" solution because it allows both the public sector and the private sector to achieve their goals.

a. Achieving Community Goals. In many communities, TDR is significant because it provides the compensation which makes it possible to adopt the land use restrictions needed to preserve important community resources. The Pasadena TDR ordinance, for example, specifies that TDR is intended to mitigate the downzoning of the downtown area (see Chapter III).

The adoption of a TDR program can also focus public attention on the importance of a community resource and assist in reaching a consensus on the need to preserve that resource. In the process of adopting the Monterey County TDR program, property owners, elected officials, and the general public recognized the need to preserve the unique character of the Big Sur area.

Right

The City of Pasadena adopted a TDR program in 1984 to mitigate restrictive density and height limits imposed in its downtown. The demand for transferred density has been hampered by Pasadena's overall cap on annual development plus the ability to receive additional density through means other than TDR. Nevertheless, three projects have used the TDR program including the historic adaptive reuse project pictured to the right.

b. Achieving the Goals of Property Owners and Developers. To greatly simplify the discussion, property owners and developers succeed if the opportunity to build additional development on a receiving site yields at least as much economic return as the opportunity to develop the sending site.

Developing a TDR program which allows for a fast, predictable transfer of profit-making potential requires the application of many of the techniques discussed in this chapter, including appropriate restrictions on sending and receiving sites, incentives (such as transfer ratios, TDR banks, and fee exemptions), and careful program management.

B. Development Restrictions on Sending Sites

The development restrictions placed on the sending sites are critical to determining the degree to which the goals of a TDR program will be achieved. On the "highly restrictive" end of the spectrum, some programs prohibit or come very close to prohibiting development in sending areas. These programs are often referred to as "mandatory," because development is prohibited whether or not transfers occur. At the "unrestrictive" end of the spectrum are programs in which there are no or few additional restrictions on the sending sites. These programs are sometimes called "voluntary," because the property owner can decide whether to develop on the sending site or transfer the development rights elsewhere. In California, TDR programs are at both ends of the spectrum and at various points in between.

1. Programs with Highly Restrictive Regulations on Sending Sites

a. Likely to Achieve Preservation Goals.
Complete prohibition of development in the sending areas is typically the result of overwhelming public support for the preservation of a particular resource. The most dramatic example in California is the Monterey County viewshed restriction which essentially prohibits development in the most scenic portions of Big Sur.

However, other California TDR programs also effectively prohibit development on sending sites. In Morgan Hill, development is completely prohibited on the higher elevations of El Toro Mountain and on all parcels with slopes in excess of 20 percent. In Claremont, the general plan does not allow development in hillside sending areas except for a single unit on non-subdivided land.

The historic preservation ordinance of the City of West Hollywood prohibits the alteration or demolition of a designated landmark without city approval, and it is very difficult to get approval to demolish a significant historic structure under San Francisco's historic preservation ordinance.

b. Generate Public Support for Preservation.
The process of preparing, adopting, and implementing a TDR program in itself can serve to increase the public agreement on the need to preserve a particular resource. For example, the Monterey County Zoning Administrator noted that the county's TDR program helped to promote an appreciation for Big Sur. Furthermore, it is likely that there would be more agreement on the need to preserve natural areas, open space, landmarks, and agricultural land if the general public and elected officials realized that TDR can preserve these assets without the expense of public acquisition.

c. Greater Responsibility to Mitigate Economic Impacts Effectively.

Clearly, with highly restrictive development requirements on the sending site, the hillside, scenic view, or historic landmark has a much greater chance of being saved. The flip side is that the owners of sending sites may argue that these restrictions constitute a regulatory taking. The section entitled "Legal Issues" in Chapter I addresses the ability of TDR to provide legally required compensation for a regulatory taking. Here it is sufficient to note that, as the land use controls on a sending site become increasingly restrictive, the community should correspondingly increase the ability of its TDR program to mitigate the economic impact of those restrictions effectively.

Effective mitigation involves all the concerns and techniques discussed later in this chapter including receiving site characteristics, program design, incentives, and program management. Any or all of these techniques can be used to ensure that transfers are truly a profitable alternative to developing on the sending site and that developers can rely on these transfers. At this point, it should be noted that the "voluntary" TDR programs may have less chance of achieving the goal of preserving the sending area, but may also have less of a need to ensure that the program will generate transfers.

2. Programs with Few Restrictions on Sending Sites

a. Appropriate When Absolute Preservation Is Not a Strong Community Goal.

Some California TDR programs impose few or no additional restrictions on development in the sending areas. For example, Brisbane's hillside-preservation TDR program does not use severe density limits to encourage transfers. The zoning for the steepest portions of the Brisbane hillsides allows two dwelling units per acre. Likewise, the proposed TDR program recently adopted by Santa Barbara is entirely voluntary.

The absence of severe restrictions could indicate that complete preservation of the sending site is not a strong community goal. To create a hypothetical example, Community A may merely want to reduce hillside development rather than eliminate or even minimize it. In this example, a TDR program with few restrictions on sending sites may be entirely appropriate.

b. Leads to Greater Public Support for Preservation.

A TDR program with relatively few restrictions on sending sites may pave the way for a more restrictive program. For example, the Milpitas hillside TDR program began with a one-unit-per-acre density limit on some sending sites. No transfers occurred, and hillside development continued. After two years of deliberations on how to improve the TDR program, Milpitas City Council members realized that hillside preservation had become a more important city goal, and they rezoned the hillsides to a density limit of one unit per ten acres.

c. Less Responsibility to Mitigate Economic Impacts Effectively. If a TDR program imposes few restrictions on its sending sites, from a legal perspective the community does not have to concern itself with whether or not the program is effective in generating transfers. This occurs because the weak restrictions impose few economic impacts which need to be compensated.

Even though compensation is not required, these programs may still offer a wide array of incentives to encourage transfers. For example, the proposed Santa Barbara program offers the significant incentive of allowing transferred development rights to be excluded from the city's growth cap.

3. Programs with Moderate Restrictions on Sending Sites

While some TDR programs completely prohibit development on sending sites, and other programs impose relatively few development limitations, most programs fall somewhere between these two extremes. To make TDR work, communities rely on both development restrictions and incentives to motivate property owners.

a. Appropriate for Communities That Want to Minimize but Not Prohibit Development. In many instances, complete preservation is not necessary to achieve a community's goals. In a hillside area, the reduction of density may be adequate to address concerns about slope stability and the overburdening of streets and other infrastructure.

1) San Luis Obispo County. The county's TDC program for the environmentally sensitive Lodge Hill subdivision allows small dwelling units on small lots. The dwelling sizes allowed are so small that a demand has been created to purchase TDCs (thereby preserving some lots from development) in order to increase the size of a single-family home by one or two bedrooms. The program's regulations make it difficult to yield added development capacity on either the sending or the receiving site without using TDC. As a result, the program has generated 200 transfers.

2) Belmont. Similarly, the City of Belmont allows development in the sending area, but the dwelling size allowed could be as small as 800 square feet of living space. These restrictions motivate the owners of sending sites to transfer development opportunity to increase the floor areas of homes on receiving sites.

b. Adequate Compensation for Economic Impacts. It is possible that some communities create moderately restrictive programs, not because they are not interested in complete preservation, but because they are concerned that TDR will not work well enough to provide effective compensation needed for a more restrictive program. These communities should routinely monitor their programs and find ways to improve TDR effectiveness using the design considerations and techniques discussed below. If it is demonstrated that TDR can effectively compensate economic impacts, the community may ultimately change to a program which uses more sending-site restrictions should such changes be needed to completely reach the community's goals.

C. Receiving Site Characteristics

The properties designated by a community as appropriate to receive additional development through TDR are called receiving sites. The designation of receiving sites is critical to gaining public support for a TDR program. In many cases, the identification of receiving sites should be an integral part of a comprehensive general plan amendment. The success of the entire program hinges on the demand for additional development on the receiving sites and the ability to achieve that additional density primarily or exclusively by using TDR.

1. Receiving Sites Should Be Clearly Identified and Recognized by the Community

It is critical that communities identify and officially recognize receiving sites early in the development of a TDR program. Several California TDR programs are not currently successful because the receiving sites are not capable of generating transfers (see Chapter III). And, in response to a statewide survey, many communities reported that they have not adopted a TDR program because the "community cannot agree on areas suitable to accept the transferred density" (see Chapter IV).

a. Some TDR Programs Make No Distinction between Receiving and Sending Sites. In some programs, a TDR area is defined and transfers can occur between any lots within the boundaries of the area. In the Pasadena, Cupertino, and Burbank programs, the purpose of TDR is to provide the flexibility to concentrate development at appropriate locations while still maintaining an overall development limit which can be accommodated by the public service system. A similar goal is met by historic preservation TDR programs, like those of West Hollywood and San Francisco, where the receiver site is likely to be a property in the general vicinity of the landmark building.

Some hillside TDR programs allow development rights to be transferred between any parcels in the designated transfer area. This transfer approach is appropriate for communities that only wish to reduce rather than eliminate further hillside development. On the other hand, if they actually have the goal of minimizing further development in certain sensitive areas, the communities should identify separate, appropriate receiving areas even if that requires a comprehensive general plan amendment process as suggested below.

b. Many TDR Programs Must Identify Separate Sending and Receiving Sites. Many communities want to move future development away from sensitive areas into separate receiving areas suitable for increased density.

1) Some General Plans Reserve Areas for Future Growth. Sometimes general plans indicate areas which are suitable for additional growth before a TDR program is even contemplated. In these cases, the future growth areas can be designated as the TDR receiving areas with relatively little effort.

2) Designation May Require General Plan Amendments. When the general plan does not already identify an area suitable for future additional development capacity, a community should embark on a planning process to identify and designate such an area. It may be tempting for the communities to try to rationalize why such areas cannot be found.

Some may claim that their land use densities cannot be changed since the community is already largely developed. However, this argument ignores the potential for increasing density through infill and the recycling of older, obsolete properties.

Other communities may believe that it is politically impossible to increase the allowed density in any neighborhood because of the public's generally negative perceptions about density. Certainly, density issues are very sensitive in many communities. However, in a comprehensive planning process, the general public typically realizes the need for the community to evolve, particularly to take advantage of new opportunities, such as public transportation centers. For this reason alone, the comprehensive planning process will be time and effort well spent. Without a clearly identified and recognized receiving area, a TDR program has greatly diminished chances for succeeding.

California has examples of TDR programs which are based on comprehensive general plan amendments. To date the most ambitious project in the state is the plan adopted by the Tahoe Regional Planning Agency which placed aggressive restrictions on thousands of lots in counties in both Nevada and California.

Another large program is the mammoth New Jersey Pinelands Comprehensive Management Plan which controls land uses in 52 municipalities. The Pinelands Plan established the total development capacity of the one-million acre planning area and designated both preservation areas and growth areas as well as a transfer ratio capable of ultimately saving 100,000 acres of land (see Chapter II and Appendix B for documents pertaining to this program).

2. Receiving Sites Should Generate Transfer Activity

Two basic ingredients are needed for receiving sites to generate transfer activity: demand for additional development on receiving sites and land use controls which make that additional development possible only, or primarily, through TDR.

a. Demand for Additional Development on Receiving Sites. If the demand for additional development on a receiving site is too low, the marginal profit from developing at a higher density will not exceed the added costs incurred in purchasing the TDRs needed to build at the higher density (see Chapter I). The general health of the local economy is a very important demand factor that is difficult for the community to control. However, there are still several techniques which a community can use to increase development demand on receiving sites.

1) Target Economic Development Programs at Receiver Sites. Hopefully, receiver sites are not just areas where the community would like to see additional development, but also sites where developers would like to build more development. But, even if that isn't the case, communities can focus economic development efforts on these sites using the tools generally available to them: redevelopment programs, tax abatement, loan programs, off-site improvements, and marketing and promotion.

2) Incentives Available from TDR Programs. In addition to the general development incentives listed above, the incentives often associated with TDR programs can also serve as a stimulus to develop on receiver sites: favorable transfer ratios; waiver of fees and dedications; exemptions from development quotas; permission to deviate from open space, setback, parking, and other design standards; and exemption from requirements to obtain infrastructure allocations. These incentives are discussed in detail below.

b. Allow Additional Development Only by TDR. If the demand for additional development at receiving sites can be met in a manner that is cheaper and/or faster than transferable development rights, developers will have little motivation to purchase them. Because additional density can be obtained some other way, some California programs have yet to be successful.

Clearly, developers will not need TDR if the receiving site zoning allows a higher density than the density desired by the developers. As discussed in Chapter III, permissive receiving site zoning is a problem for the Oakland TDR program. A related problem occurs when the zoning densities cannot be exceeded because a higher density is not permitted by the general plan. The Pismo Beach TDR program suffers from this inability to exceed zoning densities.

Some cities offer density bonuses for certain desirable design features or building amenities such as plazas. Even if they are more expensive than purchasing TDRs, developers may elect to pay for these amenities because they often increase the value of their properties. As discussed in Chapter III, the Pasadena TDR program may be hampered by the ability to exceed zoning density through a special design density bonus CUP.

Conversely, the TDR programs in which TDR is the only or the primary way of exceeding zoned densities tend to be successful. These include the Tahoe Regional Planning Agency, South Lake Tahoe, Santa Monica Mountains, San Luis Obispo County, Morgan Hill, San Francisco, Burbank, and Cupertino.

D. Incentives

Restrictive land use controls on both the sending and receiving site are often essential to the effectiveness of a TDR program. However, incentives can also be instrumental in making a TDR program work. Incentives can be any techniques which encourage transfers, including transfer ratios, TDR banks, and exemptions from fees and other development requirements.

Above

The City of Pismo Beach adopted a TDR program to preserve four undeveloped portions of the city, including the coastal blufftop pictured above. Although some transfers occurred early in the program, the transfers eventually declined due to a lack of potential receiver sites and the inability to exceed zoning densities on receiver sites, even when using TDRs.

CUP = Conditional Use Permit

1. Transfer Ratios Multiply Transferred TDRs

In many TDR programs, for each development right foregone on the sending site, only one development right can be transferred to the receiving site. In these cases, the transfer ratio is 1:1. More than two-thirds of the programs discussed in this study use a straight 1:1 transfer ratio.

However, in order to further encourage transfers, some programs multiply the number of development rights allowed on the receiving site for each development right transferred from the sending site. For example, Morgan Hill allows two rights to be transferred to a receiving site for each right relinquished on the sending site, or a transfer ratio of 2:1. Other transfer ratios identified in the California case studies include: Monterey County, 2:1; Milpitas, 2.6:1; and Oxnard, 6:1. As an indication of the importance placed on transfer ratios by some cities, a special task force in Milpitas studied that city's TDR program for three-years and ultimately concluded that the program would be much more effective if the transfer ratio were increased from 2.6:1 to 6:1.

a. Purpose of Transfer Ratios. Transfer ratios should encourage the use of TDRs by ensuring that the developer of a receiving site can make at least as much profit from developing at the higher density allowed by the transfer, even after paying for the TDRs which made the higher density possible.

b. Several Economic Factors Must Be Considered When Developing a Transfer Ratio. The process of developing a transfer ratio can be very complicated because per-unit costs and revenues will often differ with the size and density of a project. Consequently, the profit projections will also change with density. In attempting to develop an appropriate transfer ratio, the following factors should be considered: construction costs at higher densities; market demand for higher density development; adding TDR costs to other receiving site costs; costs of developing sending sites; sales price of development on sending sites; and selling price of sending-site TDRs. These factors are discussed in the "Economic Issues" section of Chapter I.

c. Setting the Transfer Ratio. The formulation of a transfer ratio should be done with the assistance of local developers who can create cost-revenue analyses for prototype projects under various density and transfer ratio scenarios. Local developers are in the best position to know certain key components of the analysis process, such as the market demand for projects of varying densities. One product of the analysis will be a transfer ratio "break-even" point, or a transfer ratio which generates the same profit using transferable development rights as a developer would receive by developing the receiving site at its currently allowed density without using TDR.

Communities should set the transfer ratio higher than the break-even point to encourage developers to use TDR. The extent of the bonus added to the density ratio will depend on at least the following three factors (see Chapter I).

1) Characteristics of the Sending Site. Are the sending sites characterized by numerous, smaller parcels under separate ownership? These property owners might have a strong preference to build on their own properties. A higher transfer ratio may be needed to motivate them.

2) Effectiveness of Other Parts of the TDR Program. In general, if other parts of the TDR program are designed for maximum effectiveness, less reliance needs to be placed on the transfer ratio. In general, a high transfer ratio will be less critical to a project if the following TDR components are in place: land use restrictions which discourage development of the sending sites; a high demand for additional development opportunity on receiving sites; the ability to achieve higher density on receiving sites primarily (or only) through the TDR process; the ability of the community to approve transfers administratively and rapidly; the presence of a TDR bank to buy and sell TDRs on demand and assist with the transaction process; and the availability of various incentives, such as waivers of fees and dedications, exemptions from development requirements, quota systems, and infrastructure allocation processes.

3) Community Commitment to TDR. In general, if it is very supportive of TDR goals, the community will want a program which maximizes transfer activity. Various methods can be used to improve the effectiveness of a TDR program including sending site restrictions, receiving site techniques, TDR banks, incentives, and program management. In addition, communities may decide to improve their transfer ratios in an effort to motivate transfer activity.

2. Waivers of Development Requirements Are Popular TDR Incentives

Communities often encourage transfers by offering exemptions from certain development requirements (see Chapter I).

a. Exemption from Dedication Requirements. To make the use of TDR more economically attractive, some communities, such as Pacifica, exempt projects involving transfers from dedication requirements. These include dedications during the subdivision or development process for roads, streets, parks, etc.

b. Waiver of Fees. Many communities charge new development fees to pay for necessary street improvements and the expansion of infrastructure and public service systems. In some communities, these development fees can be substantial. As an incentive to transfer development, some communities, including Pacifica and Oxnard, exempt TDR related projects from these fees.

c. Relaxation of Development Standards. As a financial inducement to use TDR, some communities, such as Pacifica and Irvine, specifically allow TDR-related projects to deviate from code requirements such as standards for open space, parking, and setback.

d. Exemption from Building Quotas. Some communities limit the number of homes that can be built every year. Exempting TDR-related projects from these quotas creates a significant financial incentive to use TDR. For example, in the Tahoe Regional Planning Agency and South Lake Tahoe programs, transfers of existing development rights are not subject to the permit quota system. In Morgan Hill, receiving site developers who purchase transferable development credits can be exempted from the city's development control system. In a similar program, developers who purchase TDCs can be given high scores in Morgan Hill's Residential Development Control System, thereby moving their projects toward the top of the list of projects to be permitted.

e. Ability to Bypass Infrastructure Allocation Systems. In some cities, developers must receive an allocation for water, sewer, or some other public service system before being allowed to build. Since such allocations can sometimes take years to obtain through normal channels, the ability to bypass these allocation systems offers a significant economic incentive to use TDR. In Morgan Hill, one TDR program provides sewer allocations to the purchasers of TDCs.

3. TDR Banks Can Make Programs More Effective

Many communities report that a major impediment to the use of TDR is the need for the owner/developer of the receiving site to find the owner of a sending site willing to sell development rights. Furthermore, once they connect, the two parties still need to agree on the value of a development right. This task might not be easy if the TDR program is new or used infrequently and the value of development rights are therefore not firmly established. To solve that problem, some programs include a TDR revolving fund or bank. A TDR bank can make the process more effective by facilitating transfers, providing certainty and speed to developers, influencing TDR prices, and providing TDR transaction services.

a. TDR Banks Facilitate Transfers. A TDR bank is a public or quasi-public institution which buys development rights and then sells them to developers of receiving sites. When it sells them to the developers of receiving sites, the TDR bank can use the sales revenue to buy more TDRs from the owners of sending sites.

With a TDR bank, sending site owners can sell their TDRs to the bank at any time rather than waiting until those TDRs are needed for a receiving site project. At the other end of the transaction, receiving site developers can purchase them from the TDR bank rather than trying to persuade a sending site owner to sell TDRs.

b. TDR Banks Increase the Certainty and Speed of Transfers. In addition to reducing the logistical problems of connecting buyers and sellers, TDR banks assure the potential developers of receiving sites that development rights will be available when needed. This assurance provides developers with certainty about the availability of TDRs and a relatively fast acquisition process. As discussed in Chapter I, certainty and speed are important to the decisions of developers, particularly in an out of the ordinary process like TDR.

c. TDR Banks Can Influence and Stabilize Prices. If TDR prices are too high, receiving site developers will not buy them. Conversely, if TDR prices are too low, sending-site owners will have less motivation to sell their TDRs. TDR banks can influence prices by controlling their supply.

Receiving site developers want certainty of price and availability. Without relatively stable prices, developers find it difficult to calculate the cost-revenue streams of proposed projects. TDR banks can provide TDR price stability. In fact, the price stability created by the New Jersey Pinelands Development Credit Bank is largely credited for the tremendous success of that program.

d. TDR Banks Provide Transaction Services. If they aren't assured that they will be assisted in the process, individual property owners and developers may avoid TDR. TDR banks can provide that assurance by offering to assist with the necessary real estate, legal, and governmental processes. In addition, these banks serve the valuable function of educating the general public about the program and promoting the use of TDR.

e. Three California Programs Have TDR Banks. The managers of three California programs have credited TDR banks for making major contributions toward the success of their programs.

The California Coastal Conservancy provided a $200,000 grant to create a revolving fund for the San Luis Obispo County TDR program. Senior Planner John Hofschroer reports that this fund made it much easier for buyers to obtain TDCs. Similarly, a revolving fund has been created for the Monterey County program. And in Morgan Hill, the city itself purchased 8.5 acres of El Toro Mountain, the sending area, and sells the development rights to this land to those developers who want to avoid the city's building permit quota system. The sales price has been set at $75,000 per development right.

f. TDR Banks Are Not Appropriate for Every TDR Program. While many program managers are enthusiastic about TDR banks, at least one city has deliberately not created one. As explained by Planner/Urban Designer Lawrence Badiner, because it did not want to compete with the owners of historic landmarks who want to sell development rights, San Francisco chose not to create a TDR bank.

The absence of a TDR bank has not kept the San Francisco program from being successful, because the other components of the program are effective. Namely, the demand for additional density is strong in downtown San Francisco—as is the demand for TDRs—because TDR is the only way to exceed San Francisco's density limits. Owners of historic landmarks are motivated to sell TDRs because San Francisco's landmarks regulations make it very difficult to demolish an historic structure, and the longevity of the city's TDR program gives developers a certainty that the program can be relied upon.

E. Ministerial or Administrative Approval

As discussed in Chapter I, developers will be more likely to use the TDR process if they are reasonably sure that TDRs will be approved in a timely manner. Assurances of certainty and speed are difficult if the decision to grant TDRs is discretionary, meaning that an elected or appointed body may approve or deny the proposed project. Conversely, in a nondiscretionary program, city staff has the authority to approve TDRs based on requirements provided in the community's ordinance.

For the purpose of this discussion, a ministerial function is one which involves no discretionary judgment, while an administrative function is a task carried out by someone who is executing adopted policies rather than creating policy. However, an administrative decision may or may not call for discretionary judgment, as discussed below.

1. Most California TDR Programs Are Not Administrative

In an administrative or ministerial program, the community must spell out the criteria for approval and the applicable conditions for countless combinations of potential transfers. In addition, the community should analyze the potential impacts of these transfers beforehand so that the necessary mitigations are incorporated into the administrative process.

Because many communities are unable or unwilling to relinquish the ability to review each requested transfer on its individual merits, most California TDR programs are neither ministerial nor administrative.

2. Ministerial Programs Provide the Greatest Certainty

In a truly ministerial program, no discretionary judgment is involved when deciding whether or not to approve a transfer. All the criteria for approval are clearly spelled out and, if these criteria are met, the transfer is approved. A good example of a ministerial program is in the Santa Monica Mountains, where the staff of the Mountains Restoration Trust handle all the paperwork in one visit, much like a banking transaction. In fact, a major goal of the Mountains Restoration Trust is to make TDC purchases simply another cost of doing business. Not surprisingly, the Santa Monica Mountains program is one of the most active in the nation, with more than 500 transfers accomplished thus far.

3. Administrative Programs Encourage Transfers

In some programs, the initial decision of whether or not to approve a transfer is made administratively by a staff person. However, that decision can be appealed to a policy-making body such as a city council, where the final decision may or may not involve discretion. This is essentially the process used by the City of South Lake Tahoe. There city staff can approve a TDR application if it meets program guidelines. Staff members also have the authority to attach necessary conditions. Unless appealed to the City Council, staff approval is final. To further promote the certainty and speed of TDR approvals, the city guarantees a response within two weeks.

In South Lake Tahoe, the administrative process encourages transfers. Even though the staff decision can be appealed, builders and property owners know that they will receive a staff decision based on written guidelines within two weeks. Partly as a result of this relatively certain and expedited process, the South Lake Tahoe program is one of the most successful in California, with approximately 60 transfers to date.

F. Program Management

The California case studies support the general observation that successful TDR programs require a substantial commitment and ongoing support in the form of public education, assistance to the development community, and a willingness to monitor the program and make necessary adjustments. In other words, a TDR program cannot simply be created and forgotten. To succeed, the program needs an ongoing infusion of attention.

Above

In 1979, a TDC program was established by the California Coastal Commission to preserve the environment of the Santa Monica Mountains. This range of coastal mountains extends from downtown Los Angeles 50 miles west into Ventura County and contains a wide variety of ecosystems including Cold Creek pictured above. Property owners are allowed to build dwelling units in the mountains, but typically need to acquire TDCs in order to have larger homes. To facilitate transactions, the Mountains Restoration Trust established an in lieu fee program which allowed developers the convenience of acquiring development rights through a simple administrative procedure. Consequently, the Santa Monica Mountains program has accomplished over 500 transfers, making it the most active TDR program in California and one of the most active programs in the entire United States.

1. Public Involvement

Some programs arise because planners are complying with general plan policies calling for the creation of a TDR program. Given the competing demands placed on planners, it is understandable if some TDR programs are developed and adopted as efficiently as possible, sometimes without citizen advisory committees or extensive public involvement. While the need for expediency is understandable, the experience of some California TDR programs suggests that public education and involvement is critical to achieving the ultimate goal of preserving environmentally sensitive land, historic landmarks, open space, agricultural land, or whatever resource the program is designed to protect.

a. Citizen Input Can Help Develop and Promote TDR Programs. In some communities, a citizens advisory committee is instrumental in recommending the preservation of open space, agricultural land, historic landmarks, and other community resources. In many cases, the same citizens committee also recommends the use of TDR and may even participate in the development of the program.

In Pacifica, the Open Space Task Force recommended the development of a TDR program. In Milpitas, a Hillside Committee met more than 40 times over the course of a three-year period to develop recommendations for improving that city's program. In Burbank, a Media District Blue Ribbon Committee met for six years to develop recommendations for the city's Media District Specific Plan including the TDR proposal which makes it possible to have flexibility in the concentration of development while still maintaining an overall limit on growth in the area. And, in West Hollywood, the TDR program is part of the city's overall historic preservation effort. This effort is supported by the local historical society and includes an award-winning landmarks program and a newsletter designed to promote historic preservation.

Another benefit of citizen advisory committees is that, following adoption of a TDR program, these groups can promote its use and support individual TDR applications as they are presented for approval.

b. Discussion of TDR Can Help Generate Support for Preservation. Just as overall preservation programs can assist a TDR effort, the preparation, adoption, and implementation of a TDR program can assist in educating the public about the need for preservation. As discussed in Chapter III, the manager of the Monterey County TDR program believes that one of its main benefits is the fact that it focuses public attention on the unique characteristics of the Big Sur area and helps property owners and the general public realize the need to protect this resource.

2. Developer Assistance Increases Transfer Activity

For the most part, the more successful TDR programs emphasize cooperation with property owners and developers in designing the program, increasing awareness of the program, and assisting developers with the process.

a. Developers Should Be Involved in Designing Programs. When designing a TDR program, developers are an invaluable source of information. They can provide advice on which transfer ratios, fee waivers, and regulation exemptions will be successful in motivating transfers from sending sites to receiving sites. In addition to offering insight into the financial aspects of transfers, developers can also inform community officials about the need to address less obvious factors such as speed and certainty.

When the San Luis Obispo County program was being developed, a questionnaire was sent to every affected property owner. The results of that questionnaire were used to structure the county's TDR program and identify the most likely buyers and sellers. In addition, a workshop for real estate professionals was held to explain the transactions.

b. TDR Programs Should Be Promoted to Property Owners and Developers. In addition to being brought into the process of designing a TDR program, property owners and developers should be notified of the benefits once a program is adopted. Property owners and developers should also be routinely reminded to consider using TDR.

Claremont periodically mails notices to property owners to urge them to use TDR. In San Luis Obispo County, the success of the TDR program was partly credited to the promotional efforts of the San Luis Obispo County Land Conservancy. And the New Jersey Pinelands Program, which has preserved over 5,800 acres of land so far, uses an extensive public outreach program, regularly sending letters to hundreds of landowners advising them of program benefits.

c. Developer Help Can Overcome Resistance. Unless the community offers some guidance and assistance, many aspects of the TDR process could be intimidating to property owners and developers. The New Jersey Pinelands Program, for example, has an instructional booklet on how to use the TDR program (see Appendix B) and offers developer assistance through the New Jersey Pinelands Development Credit Bank. Some California programs also realize the need to assist developers.

The City of Cupertino prepared and distributed a "Development Intensity Manual" which clearly describes the density and transfer regulations, complete with sample calculations. In the Santa Monica Mountains, the program has been streamlined so that the

Mountains Restoration Trust handles most of the transactional details, with the receiving site developer only having to pay a predetermined fee. And in South Lake Tahoe, the city has established its TDR program to be handled administratively and has guaranteed a staff response within two weeks after receiving an application.

Some program directors reported that their TDR programs are successful because of sophisticated property owners and developers. However, communities can greatly influence the willingness of developers to use TDR by providing information and step-by-step instructions as well as offering to assist in the actual processing of the transfer.

3. Monitoring and Improving TDR Programs

Roughly half the communities represented in the case studies reported that they had changed, or were considering changing, their TDR program. Given the complexity, it is not surprising to find that communities are routinely reviewing and refining their programs. As discussed below, sometimes this refinement process leads to the adoption of non-TDR techniques.

a. Review May Result in Improvements and Program Expansion. It is common for communities to periodically review the success of their TDR programs and consider expansion, the inclusion of additional incentives, or even a complete overhaul of the entire program.

The City of West Hollywood began reviewing its program in 1992 to ensure that its incentive package is adequate. In San Luis Obispo County, the TDR program for the Lodge Hill area has been so successful that county officials are considering expanding the program to other areas. The program director for the City of San Diego has considered the relative lack of transfers in that program and advocates that TDR be included in a comprehensive planning program designed so that TDR can implement preservation goals.

Beginning in 1992, the City of South Lake Tahoe began re-examining its TDR program. To further encourage transfers, the city is considering relaxation of one of the requirements for a transfer from a Stream Environment Zone. And the Santa Monica Mountains program has been fine-tuned through numerous changes, including the provision for greater flexibility with guidelines for the appropriateness of proposed sending sites and where development rights could be transferred. The most dramatic change occurred when the Mountains Restoration Trust instituted the in lieu fee program and the current streamlined ministerial process.

b. Review May Result in Adoption of Non-TDR Techniques. In monitoring their TDR programs, some communities conclude that other, non-TDR techniques are needed to assist or, in some cases, replace the TDR process.

Because Claremont's program experienced no transfer activity for several years, the city has obtained an option on a tract of hillside land and adopted a specific plan which contains open space and clustered development designations. The city is currently seeking a developer to implement the plan.

Agoura Hills has also adopted a specific plan for a portion of its hillsides which eliminates the need for TDR in that area. In Oxnard, the need for TDR was largely satisfied by a court settlement for a beachfront area which restructured the lot configurations and established the right to build on these lots. And in Irvine, the TDR ordinance was designed to encourage residential development in a business district. The program regulations were specific to a particular project, and, after the transfer from that project occurred, the city eliminated the TDR provisions from its code.

When no transfers occurred under the Milpitas ordinance, a Hillside Committee was formed to consider potential improvements to the TDR program. After studying the issue for more than three years and 40 meetings, the Committee concluded that the program's transfer ratio should be increased from 2.6:1 to 6:1 in order to provide a better incentive for transfers. However, the City Council became concerned that the TDR program might work so well that the Eastern Hills would be sacrificed in the process of saving the Western Hills. Consequently, the Milpitas City Council downzoned the Western Hills to a ten-acre minimum and eliminated the TDR program entirely.

As stated throughout this study, TDR is only one potential method of preservation. A city should explore all potential options and employ the option or combination of options best suited to the community's goals and circumstances.

It is equally important not to abandon a program just because it has not generated numerous transfers. An important factor in the success of a TDR program is longevity. Older TDR programs, like San Francisco's, are often successful because property owners and developers have become familiar with them and accept TDR as a dependable

process. In other words, rather than abandon a sluggish program, a community should supplement it with other preservation initiatives and/or improve the TDR program itself using some of the techniques discussed above (see Chapter III).

4. Program Management Requires Appropriate Staffing

The level of staffing required to properly manage a TDR program will vary according to the size and nature of the program.

a. Focused Programs Require No Additional Staff. In many programs, the relatively small geographical boundaries of the sending and receiving sites may result in only a handful of transfers occurring in any year. In Burbank, for example, transfers are limited to properties within the one square mile area referred to as the Media District. In the Burbank program, TDR can only be approved through a conditional use permit granted by the City Planning Board. However, development proposals which include TDR typically require other approvals as well.

Consequently the CUP requirement will rarely result in a need for additional staff, and, in fact, no additional personnel have been added as a result of the TDR program.

CUP = Conditional Use Permit

b. Comprehensive TDR Programs Can Require a Substantial Staff Commitment. At the other extreme is the New Jersey Pinelands program with jurisdiction over approximately one million acres of land, including all or part of 52 municipalities. This program requires part-time assistance from five staff members at the Pinelands Commission on an as-needed basis to process transfer applications as they are submitted. Also, additional personnel are needed at the Pinelands Development Credit Bank. Ideally, the staffing there would consist of a director, an administrative assistant, and one person to promote the TDR concept to property owners and developers.[1] Of course, most programs would not require this level of staffing. In addition to serving a huge area, the Pinelands program is one of the most active in the nation.

[1] Osborn.

VI Putting TDR to Work in California

The preceding chapters have provided an introduction to the concept of transferable development rights, described how they have been used in several communities, explained why TDR is not used more widely, and reviewed some of the ingredients needed for a successful program. This chapter predicts the future use of TDR and offers some recommendations for putting TDR to work in California.

A. Future of TDRs in California

Increased use of TDR is inevitable in California for several reasons: techniques similar to TDR are already in place in numerous California communities; TDR is proposed in the general plans of many California communities; and TDR can preserve valuable community resources despite budget cuts.

1. Techniques Similar to TDRs

Many communities allow development to be shifted within land parcels under a single ownership through clustering ordinances, planned developments, and specific plans. In addition, many communities allow development to be transferred between parcels in different ownerships on a case-by-case basis, again using techniques such as planned developments and specific plans. It is easy to foresee that many of these communities will take the next logical step and establish TDR programs which promote and facilitate transfers for a wider range of purposes and properties.

2. TDRs Specified by General Plans

As a potential method of implementing the goals of preserving open space, landmarks, environmentally sensitive areas, and agricultural land, many communities call for the use of transferable development rights in their general plans. As noted in Chapter IV, survey respondents from at least nine communities were either considering a TDR program or actually working on one.

3. Public Acquisition Funding Not Required

TDR will increasingly be recognized as one of the few methods of achieving preservation and other goals within shrinking municipal budgets. It is not entirely accurate to say that TDR is cost-free since TDR programs require staff, resources, promotional expenses and, in some cases, seed money to start revolving funds. But generally these costs are relatively minor if compared with the expense of outright acquisition of property. As California works its way out of the current recession and its associated fiscal crisis and continues to cope with the affects of Proposition 13, it is likely that more and more communities will turn to TDR as one of the few remaining options for achieving many land use goals.

B. Recommendations

If not now, at some time in the future every community in the state will want to save environmental resources, preserve open space, agricultural lands or historic landmarks, or achieve some other land use goal with little or no funding. Hopefully, these communities will at least consider the following recommendations. Communities should: consider TDR for a wide range of uses and for all facets of a project; clearly identify the goals of TDR programs and create TDR programs with the best chance of meeting those goals; and commit the staff and resources needed to implement, monitor, and improve TDR programs

1. Wide Range of Uses for TDRs

The case studies found in Chapters II and III show that TDR can be employed for many purposes other than the traditional uses of preserving landmarks, open space, and agricultural land.

The cities of Burbank and Cupertino both adopted relatively restrictive density limits in selected areas to ensure that the transportation and other public service systems could accommodate future development. In both cities, TDR allows developers to concentrate density on certain parcels without exceeding the overall capacity of the public service systems.

San Mateo County wants to encourage the preservation of agriculture as well as agricultural land. Consequently, the county's TDR program offers bonus density credits for agricultural improvements such as water storage facilities.

The City of Irvine created a TDR program to encourage the development of housing units in an office park area. And the Tahoe Regional Planning Agency program uses TDR not just to maintain existing density but to reduce or even eliminate development on the sending sites through the granting of transferable credits when housing units are removed from sensitive environmental areas.

The City of Santa Barbara's Transfer of Existing Development Rights program provides an incentive for owners to replace larger existing buildings with smaller buildings.

As the technique becomes more widespread, communities will undoubtedly find new uses for TDR, either to solve long-standing problems or tackle new issues.

2. Consider TDRs for All Facets of a Project

While the preceding section discussed how they can be used for a wide range of land use projects, transferable development rights can also be used to assist in various ways within a single project.

a. TDR Can Help Communities Recognize Valuable Resources. In Monterey County, TDR was a useful way to focus attention on the uniqueness of Big Sur and the need to preserve this area (see Chapter III). In other words, the public presentation of a TDR ordinance or program can serve as the catalyst to build popular support for preservation. TDR can perform this function even if the proposed program is not ultimately adopted.

b. TDR Can Assist in Adopting Stronger Land Use Controls. As discussed throughout this book, TDR can be used to strengthen existing codes and preservation requirements. In the California TDR survey, the most common response, when asked why a community does not use TDR, was that the community "relies primarily on zoning and development restrictions to achieve land use goals." Yet, as discussed in Chapter IV, less than 20 percent of the responding communities believed that all their land use goals would be achieved "given funding levels and/or regulatory authority."

Most of these communities could greatly improve their chances of achieving their land use goals by proposing TDR as a compensation technique in conjunction with the adoption of more restrictive preservation regulations.

Above

The City of Santa Barbara adopted a TDR ordinance to encourage property owners to replace larger, nonconforming buildings, such as the former lemon packing plant shown above, with smaller buildings which comply with current development requirements. A promising incentive in Santa Barbara's newly-adopted TDR ordinance is the provision that transferred floor area is not subject to Santa Barbara's strict growth cap.

3. The Goals of a TDR Program

TDR programs come in all shapes and sizes. Communities should avoid the temptation to simply adopt another city's ordinance without at least ensuring that there is agreement on the community's preservation goals.

a. TDR Program Should Be Comprehensive. If a community's appreciation for its natural areas, historic landmarks, or agricultural land is high, the goals of a TDR program designed to preserve these resources may be quite ambitious, perhaps as ambitious as absolute preservation. Achieving this goal will require a TDR program that is equally ambitious.

1) General Plan Amendments Should Be Considered. If a major preservation goal is envisioned, the TDR program will probably need to be prepared in conjunction with wholesale general plan amendments which create the conditions needed to make a TDR program successful. These conditions include: restricting or prohibiting development in sending areas; ensuring demand for transferred density on the receiving site; and creating incentives to transfer development including transfer ratios, TDR banks, and exemptions from fees and other development requirements.

2) Resources Should Be Committed. Wholesale general plan and code amendments of this nature can require a significant investment of time and resources. Perhaps the most extreme example is the New Jersey Pinelands program, discussed in Chapters II and V, which involves a state Comprehensive Management Plan encompassing 52 municipalities. This Plan establishes density limits, development restrictions, and transfer ratios which provide attractive incentives for transfers. The Pinelands effort is enormous, but the effort is worthwhile since the program is achieving its goals, with more than 5,800 acres of land preserved so far.

b. Communities Should Supply the Ingredients Needed for a Successful TDR Program. A community may not want absolute preservation but, instead, less ambitious goals such as a reduction of hillside density or a decrease in the conversion of agricultural land to other uses. Even with these more modest goals, a TDR program is not likely to be completely successful unless the community creates the conditions needed for success. As discussed in Chapter V, the ingredients for a successful TDR program include—

- Community consensus on the goals of the TDR program
- Controls on sending sites which are adequate to motivate transfers

- Demand for TDR on receiving sites generated both by the desire for additional density and the ability to achieve additional density primarily (or only) through TDR

- Additional incentives such as transfer ratios, waivers of development fees and other requirements, and TDR banks

- An efficient and dependable TDR procedure

- Program management which emphasizes public input, developer assistance, TDR program promotion, periodic program monitoring, regular program improvements, and adequate staffing

4. Commitment of Staff and Resources to Implement, Monitor and Improve Programs

The success of a TDR program is not guaranteed even if a community clearly identifies its goals and changes its general plan and codes to create ideal conditions in the sending and receiving areas. Developers and property owners may initially be reluctant to use TDR programs because the process is relatively unknown. Property owners and developers may also assume that TDR is time-consuming and legally burdensome. To make TDR a success, the community must commit staff and resources to the program on an ongoing basis. An education effort is important in order to inform not just the development community but the general public about the existence and benefits of TDR. Moreover, targeted correspondence with individual developers and property owners is critical to generating transfer activity.

The TDR process itself should be easy to understand, fast, and free of surprises. Ideally, the TDR program should be administrative, with printed guidelines which state that the transfer will be granted within a specified period of time if specified criteria are met. Attention to program management is labor-intensive, but it is also the most effective way to overcome the natural tendency of developers to avoid a program that is unfamiliar.

Finally, to be effective, TDR requires a careful balance of restrictions, market demand, incentives, and promotions. Consequently, it is not surprising that communities don't get the formula exactly right the first time, or perhaps even the first few times. The important point, again, is the commitment to routinely monitor the TDR program, identify its shortcomings, and make the necessary corrections. As discussed in Chapter V, roughly half the communities represented in the California case studies have changed their TDR programs or are considering changing their programs after learning from their initial experiences.

Appendix A

Transferable Development Rights Survey

Source: Rick Pruetz.

Transferable Development Rights Survey

1. **Indicate which of the following, if any, are goals of your community. (Please circle "yes" or "no".)**

A. Acquire parkland/open space	yes	no
B. Preserve natural areas	yes	no
C. Save historic landmarks	yes	no
D. Save agricultural land	yes	no
E. Other _____	yes	no

2. **Roughly what percent of these goals are likely to be achieved given funding levels and/or regulatory authority? (Please circle a percent estimate.)**

	Percentage				
A. Acquire parkland/open space	0	25	50	75	100
B. Preserve natural areas	0	25	50	75	100
C. Save historic landmarks	0	25	50	75	100
D. Save agricultural land	0	25	50	75	100
E. Other _____	0	25	50	75	100

3. **Below are several reasons why communities don't use TDR.**

   A. We have not given TDR much serious consideration.

   B. We rely primarily on zoning and development restrictions to achieve land use goals.

   C. We prefer to use outright purchase to acquire land, easements and development rights.

   D. Our community considers TDR to be legally complex and/or logistically burdensome.

   E. Our community cannot agree on areas suitable to accept the transferred density.

   F. Our property owners want to develop the land they own; they are not interested in transferring development rights even if it would result in the same monetary return.

   G. Our property owners are not convinced that they would achieve as much return on investment with TDR as they would by developing their own land.

   H. Our property owners are not sure there would be much demand for transferred development rights since achieving desired density is fairly easy.

   I. Our property owners are, or may be, concerned about the amount of time needed for TDR projects.

   J. Our property owners are, or may be, reluctant to agree to a process that is unknown or untested.

   For each category in which you indicated a goal in response to Question 1, please circle the letters of the reasons why your community has not used TDR or might be reluctant to use TDR.

	Reason									
A. Acquire parkland/open space	A	B	C	D	E	F	G	H	I	J
B. Preserve natural areas	A	B	C	D	E	F	G	H	I	J
C. Save historic landmarks	A	B	C	D	E	F	G	H	I	J
D. Save agricultural land	A	B	C	D	E	F	G	H	I	J
E. Other _____	A	B	C	D	E	F	G	H	I	J

Appendix B

Selling and Buying Pinelands Development Credits: An Instructional Guide

Source: John T. Ross, Executive Director, Pinelands Development Credit Bank, State of New Jersey.

Selling and Buying
PINELANDS DEVELOPMENT CREDITS

An Instructional Guide

State of New Jersey

Pinelands

Development

Credit Bank

CN 035, Trenton, N.J. 08625

(609) 588-3469

July 1988

THE PINELANDS DEVELOPMENT CREDIT PROGRAM

The Pinelands Development Credit (PDC) Program is designed to encourage a shift of development away from forested and agricultural regions of the Pinelands to more appropriate areas. It provides a way for landowners in areas where land use is restricted to benefit economically from increased land values in areas of the Pinelands zoned to allow significant amounts of new residential development. It also provides a way for developers to increase the number of homes they can build in areas designated for new growth. These two goals are achieved when builders buy development rights (PDCs) and transfer development to specified areas.

The PDC program will encourage residential growth near existing development and employment centers. It will discourage growth near fragile ecological areas, wetlands, and important agricultural acreage.

Under the Pinelands Comprehensive Management Plan, all land and water resources within the million-acre Pinelands Area fall into one of eight basic categories of land use. These categories each have a special designation: i.e., Preservation Area District, Special Agricultural Production Area, Forest Area, Agricultural Production Area, Rural Development Area, Regional Growth Area, Military and Federal Installation Area, and Pinelands Villages and Towns.

The Pinelands Plan sets limits on the type and amount of development that can take place within each of these areas. Within Towns, Villages and Growth Areas, for example, an almost unlimited range of activities is permitted, including relatively concentrated residential development. By contrast, the type and density of development permitted in the Preservation Area District and the two agricultural areas is much more limited.

Through the PDC program, landowners in the growth-restricted Preservation Area District, Agricultural Production Areas and Special Agricultural Production Areas are allocated PDCs. These development credits may be used in Pinelands Regional Growth Areas to allow more homes to be built on property than would otherwise be permissible. Each credit permits four additional homes to be built, within an overall range set by the municipality according to Pinelands Plan criteria.

In simple terms, a person who owns property in the Preservation or Agricultural areas has two options: the property he or she owns can be developed for residential purposes as limited by the Pinelands Plan, or the Pinelands Development Credits can be sold for use in Regional Growth Areas. If the PDCs are sold, the credit seller's property can still be used or developed for various activities.

THE PINELANDS DEVELOPMENT CREDIT BANK

The Pinelands Development Credit Bank is an independent state agency which plays a pivotal role in helping the PDC program run smoothly and efficiently. Among its responsibilities, the Bank

- issues PDC Certificates which then enable PDCs to be bought and sold
- tracks PDC sales to maintain current and accurate records of all transactions
- provides information on people who may wish to buy or sell PDCs
- purchases PDCs itself in certain cases

This booklet is intended to help people who wish to participate in the PDC program successfully complete purchases and sales. We hope that most of your questions will be answered after reading this guide, but don't get discouraged if some things still remain unclear. The PDC program is relatively new and therefore may be difficult to understand at first. Another publication, "Benefits of the Pinelands Development Credit Program," is available from the Bank or from the Pinelands Commission to better acquaint you with the program. Also, the Bank's staff and the Pinelands Commission's Public Programs office are always available to answer your questions.

HOW TO USE THIS GUIDE

IF	PLEASE READ
You don't understand the PDC Program	The publication "Benefits of the Pinelands Development Credit Program" before reviewing this guide.
You own property which is allocated Pinelands Development Credits	Section 1
You wish to find a private buyer of your PDCs	Section 2
You wish to buy PDCs	Section 2
You wish to sell PDCs to the Pinelands Development Credit Bank	Section 3
You are ready to complete a sale of Pinelands Development Credits	Section 4
You wish to get a loan using PDCs as collateral for the loan	Section 5
You are ready to use PDCs in order to build homes in a growth area	Section 6
You wish to review the various forms included in this guide	Section 7
For More Information on The Pinelands Development Credit Program, Please Read:	"Benefits of the Pinelands Development Credit Program"

Or Call or Write to:

Pinelands Development Credit Bank
CN 035
Trenton, NJ 08625-0035
(609) 588-3469

Pinelands Commission
P.O. Box 7   New Lisbon, NJ 08064
(609) 894-9342

SECTION 1

ISSUING PINELANDS DEVELOPMENT CREDIT CERTIFICATES TO CREDIT OWNERS

What is a Pinelands Development Credit Certificate?

A Pinelands Development Credit (PDC) Certificate is a document issued by the Bank which attests to the fact that Pinelands Development Credits are available for sale or use. A Certificate is first issued after the number of PDCs allocated to a particular piece of property is determined by the Pinelands Commission and a deed restriction which controls the future use and development of that property has been recorded. Once the Certificate is issued, the PDCs may then be sold, transferred, or used separate and apart from the sale or use of the property from which they were allocated.

When PDCs are sold or used, the Certificate is returned to the Bank and new Certificates will be reissued as need be. More about reissuing Certificates is included in Section 4. A sample PDC Certificate is included in Section 7.

Do I need a PDC Certificate if I intend to sell my PDCs to the State Pinelands Development Credit Bank or the Burlington County Pinelands Development Credit Exchange?

Currently, the Bank and the Burlington County Pinelands Development Credit Exchange are the only two public agencies which can purchase PDCs.

If you plan to ask the state Bank to buy your PDCs, you don't need to have your PDC Certificate in hand. Section 3 of this booklet explains how to apply for Bank purchase.

The Burlington County PDC Exchange can purchase credits only from Burlington County property owners. The Exchange can *not* buy PDCs from anyone *after* a PDC Certificate has been issued. The Burlington County Exchange will take care of obtaining the Certificate for you. For more information on the Burlington County Pinelands Development Credit Exchange, please call or write to Burlington County Department of Economic Development, 49 Rancocas Road, Mt. Holly, NJ 08080 (609) 265-5787.

How do I obtain a Certificate?

If you own property which is entitled to a PDC allocation, the process entails four steps:

Step 1 Obtain a "Letter of Interpretation" from the Pinelands Commission which states the number of PDCs allocated to the property.

Step 2 Apply to the Pinelands Development Credit Bank for a PDC Certificate.

Step 3   Record a deed restriction (easement) which controls the future use and development of your property.

Step 4   The PDC Certificate is issued by the Bank.

Although the process doesn't need to be complicated, each step must be completed properly to avoid pitfalls and delays. We'll try to explain what needs to be done and how to do it to avoid those problems.

What should I do if I'm not certain whether my property is entitled to a PDC allocation?

The Pinelands Commission can tell you if your property is entitled to a PDC allocation. Write a short note to the Commission asking if your property qualifies. Be sure to include your return address, the municipality in which the property is located, and the tax block and lot numbers for the property. The block and lot numbers are on your property tax bill.

Within two weeks, the Pinelands Commission will tell you if the property is eligible for a PDC allocation. If the property is eligible, you may then decide to apply for a "Letter of Interpretation" which will tell you exactly how many Pinelands Development Credits are allocated to it.

Why must I get a Letter of Interpretation to find out how many PDCs are allocated to my property?

The number of PDCs allocated to each property varies according to the zone it's in (Preservation or Agricultural) and its environmental characteristics (uplands or wetlands). The allocation formula is explained in detail in "Benefits of the Pinelands Development Credit Program."

Although you may be able to estimate the number using this formula, only the Pinelands Commission can establish the precise credit allocation since it must first conduct a detailed analysis of your property.

What is a "Letter of Interpretation" and how do I get it? (STEP 1)

A "Letter of Interpretation" is the document issued by the Pinelands Commission which establishes the exact number of PDCs allocated to a particular piece of property. An example of a Letter of Interpretation is included in Section 7.

To apply for a Letter of Interpretation, a relatively simple application form must be completed and submitted to the Pinelands Commission. Although the Commission attempts to process these applications quickly, it may take up to several months because of the large number of these and other types of applications received by the Commission.

A sample application form along with step by step instructions is included in Section 7.

Once I have the Letter of Interpretation, how do I apply for a PDC Certificate? (STEP 2)

Again, a relatively simple application form must be completed and submitted to the Pinelands Development Credit Bank. A sample application with instructions is included in Section 7.

Two extremely important parts of the application are the title search and the deed restriction.

A 60 year title search is required under state law to ensure that title to the property is marketable. Although the property itself is not being sold, a deed restriction (or easement) must be placed on the property when credits are sold. Only an owner of the property who has the legal right to do so may place such an easement.

The deed restriction is necessary because separation of the PDCs from the property permanently extinguishes the right to use or develop the property for certain things. Although the property may then be sold or transferred like any other property, the new owner's use of the land is limited by those deed restrictions.

Is the title search merely a formality?

We hope so, but there may be instances where it may identify questions as to who owns all or a portion of the property or it may disclose that someone else has an interest in the property. If outstanding title questions exist or the owner can't legally restrict the use of the property because of someone else's interest, the Bank can't issue a PDC Certificate.

For example, a title search may disclose that someone other than the property owner owns the mineral rights to a property. Since the right to mine must be extinguished in order to sell PDCs, the Bank could not issue a Certificate to the property owner unless he controlled the mining rights.

What if the title search discloses potential questions?

Depending on the type and nature of the question, it may be easily resolved or it may not prove to be a hindrance to the placement of the deed restriction. If questions are raised, you may wish to forward the title search to the Bank for review or consult an attorney with expertise in real estate law.

Speaking of attorneys, do I need one to get through the process?

Although there is no requirement that you have an attorney, you may wish to hire one. Some people feel more secure with an attorney to advise them, and others may wish to have an attorney handle the paperwork, make arrangements for the title search, prepare the deed restriction, and so forth.

How do I make arrangements for a title search?

Any reputable title company can conduct the 60-year search. A relatively simple and straightforward search should cost approximately $150.

A word of caution. Be sure that the title company knows in advance that you must receive a certification that it performed a *60-year* search. The certification must state that the title company performed the 60-year search and that a United States District and New Jersey Superior Court search was made against all record owners of the property for the past 20 years.

Since a deed restriction is a legal document, how can I handle it without an attorney?

The Bank's attorneys have prepared three sample deed restrictions which are easy to complete. Although these are samples and variations can be made, they can be used without change. You need only determine which sample applies to your property. Simply match the management area (Preservation Area District, Special Agricultural Production Area, or Agricultural Production Area) to that noted on your Letter of Interpretation.

If I wish to have an attorney prepare the restriction, what must be covered?

The Pinelands Comprehensive Management Plan requires that the deed restriction reflect several things:

1. Future uses of the property are expressly limited in accord with Pinelands Comprehensive Management Plan requirements.

2. The restriction is granted in favor of a public agency or, if you prefer, a non-profit, incorporated conservation organization.

3. The restriction is expressly enforceable by the Pinelands Commission.

Other matters, such as the right for public access, are decided by you as the property owner. More information can be obtained from "Benefits of the Pinelands Development Credit Program."

How do I handle the restriction if I wish to retain the right to build a home in the future?

Under normal circumstances, the right to build a home is extinguished once PDCs are separated from the property. However, the Pinelands Comprehensive Management Plan permits certain property owners (e.g., long-time Pinelands residents) to reserve the right to build one or more homes if the PDC allocation for the property is reduced. For more information, please read "Benefits of the Pinelands Development Credit Program."

These arrangements must be worked out *before* the deed restriction is recorded and the PDC Certificate is issued. The easiest way is for you to inform the Pinelands Commission of your intentions in writing when applying for a Letter of Interpretation. The allocation of PDCs will then be adjusted.

The deed restriction must also specify that this right is being retained. Language reserving the right to build in the future that can be inserted into a deed restriction is included in Section 7. Again, the keys to successfully completing this arrangement are:

1. Make sure that the PDC allocation contained in the Letter of Interpretation reflects the arrangement and that the PDC allocation has been adjusted by the Pinelands Commission

2. Prepare a deed restriction which incorporates the arrangement.

3. Make sure that the arrangements in the deed restriction are identical to those reflected in the Letter of Interpretation.

4. Ask the Pinelands Development Credit Bank to review your application for a PDC Certificate **before** the deed restriction is recorded.

Why should I apply for a PDC Certificate before recording the deed restriction?

Although the Bank can't issue the Certificate until after the deed restriction is recorded, it is advisable to resolve any questions or potential problems beforehand. Once the restriction is recorded, it is extremely difficult to resolve problems. Also, a property owner may not wish to subject his property to a deed restriction if he can't be issued a PDC Certificate because of title questions and the like. Therefore, it's recommended that you submit a draft, but not recorded, deed restriction with your PDC Certificate application. The restriction can be recorded after learning that your application has received a preliminary okay.

Why not just issue the Certificate immediately instead of giving me a "preliminary" okay?

In most cases, the issuance of the Certificate is a formality after you've received the preliminary okay. However, the Bank must double check that the deed restriction submitted for recordation is identical to that given preliminary approval and that the property has not been sold or encumbered since the title search was completed.

How do I go about recording the deed restriction? (STEP 3)

After the deed restriction is signed and notarized, it must be recorded in the same manner as if you were selling the property and transferring fee title to someone else. You should follow the following steps:

1. Mail or deliver the completed deed restriction to the county clerk. (There will be a fee for this.)

2. Send the original of the recorded deed restriction to the State PDC Bank.

3. Send a copy of the recorded restriction to the Pinelands Commission.

4. Send a copy of the recorded restriction to the clerk of the municipality in which the property is located.

5. Send a copy of the recorded restriction to the agency or organization to whom the restriction is in favor.

How long should the entire process take from start to finish? (STEP 4)

Each case is slightly different and it's difficult to predict the exact time. However, you should expect it to take at least three months from the date you apply for a Letter of Interpretation to the date you receive the PDC Certificate. Of course, questions or problems may cause delays.

Can I do anything to avoid some of the more common problems?

Absolutely. We've identified eight items which you may wish to pay particularly close attention to.

1. *Decide if you wish to retain the right to build a home before applying for a Letter of Interpretation.* Since this right affects the number of PDCs allocated, it's best to consider this as early as possible. Although you can decide anytime before the deed restriction is recorded, adjustments at that late date will cause delays.

2. *Make sure your Letter of Interpretation is accurate and current (within one year).* Since PDC allocations are influenced by the use of the property (e.g., amount of land farmed), any change in the property since your Letter of Interpretation was issued will require a re-examination of the PDC allocation. Also, the older the letter, the longer it may take to verify the original PDC allocation.

3. *Make sure your title company conducts a full, 60-year title search and certifies this in the title documents.* In some cases, title companies will research the title for a shorter period if a prior title policy has been issued. Although this is an acceptable practice in many cases, a full 60-year search is a prerequisite for PDC Certificates.

4. *Submit a proposed deed restriction to the Bank with your PDC Certificate application.* Although there is no prohibition against recording a deed restriction prior to applying to the Bank, problems and delays can be avoided this way.

5. *Apply to the Bank for your Certificate immediately after receiving the title search.* The longer you wait, the more difficult it is to double check the title after the restriction is recorded. In some cases, the title company may be unable to update the search without charging an extra fee.

6. *If your property is mortgaged, obtain a release from the mortgage company.* Since a mortgage company holds an interest in your property, a certificate can't be issued unless the mortgage company agrees. A release must acknowledge that the mortgage holder:

   a. Understands that a restriction has or will be placed on the deed to your property limiting the future use and development of the property.

   b. Understands that the landowner will be issued PDCs which the landowner can sell in return for the deed restriction.

   c. Agrees to subordinate his interest in the property to the deed restriction.

7. *Hire an attorney if you feel uncomfortable with or unsure about the Process.* Although an attorney is not essential, you may wish to engage an attorney with expertise in real estate law.

8. *Do not apply to the Bank for a PDC Certificate if you hope to sell your PDCs to Burlington County.* The Burlington County Pinelands Development Credit Exchange can't buy PDCs after the deed restriction is recorded. Also, the County will take care of much of the paperwork for you.

SECTION 2

FINDING BUYERS AND SELLERS

How do I locate a buyer for my PDCs?

There are a number of options which you may pursue including:

1. Selling your PDCs to the State Pinelands Development Credit Bank.

2. Selling your PDCs to the Burlington County Pinelands Development Credit Exchange.

3. Contacting the State Pinelands Development Credit Bank for a listing of people who have expressed an interest in buying PDCs.

4. Contacting builders' and developers' organizations whose members are active in the Pinelands.

5. Contacting secretaries of municipal planning boards in towns where PDCs can be used.

6. Advertising them for sale.

7. Listing them for sale with a Realtor.

8. Selling your property and your PDCs along with it.

Do I need to have a PDC Certificate in hand before exploring these options?

No, but in many cases having the PDC Certificate in advance removes one impediment to a final sale and may help to show that you're serious about selling your PDCs.

In a few cases, getting your PDC Certificate ahead of time is *not* recommended. For example, the Burlington County Pinelands Development Credit Exchange can not buy PDCs unless it obtains the deed restriction (easement) in favor of the county at the same time. Therefore, if you are considering selling your credits to the Burlington County Exchange, do not deed restrict your property in advance.

A PDC Certificate is also not needed if you plan to sell your property together with the PDCs allocated to it. The owner of the property is automatically the owner of the PDCs unless the PDCs have been separated from the property beforehand. Remember that PDCs don't get separated until a PDC Certificate is issued.

A PDC Certificate is not needed for PDCs which were sold prior to the April 4, 1988 establishment of the State Pinelands Development Credit Bank. However, any resale or transfer after April 4, 1988 must be made with a PDC Certificate. The Bank's staff can help you with the arrangements if you're faced with this situation.

If you hope to sell your PDCs to the Pinelands Development Credit Bank, you need not obtain a PDC Certificate in advance. Selling PDCs to the Bank is covered in more detail in Section 3.

In the other cases, you need not have the PDC Certificate in hand until the final sale is to take place. However, as mentioned earlier, it's your choice whether you obtain the PDC certificate before looking for a buyer or waiting until you have a buyer- Remember, however, that it can take several months to get your PDC Certificate and a buyer may be interested in a quicker sale. A potential buyer may also want to know that you do indeed qualify for a specific number of PDCs and the PDC Certificate is the best means of removing any uncertainty.

Are there other advantages in obtaining a PDC Certificate before locating a buyer?

Yes. The Pinelands Development Credit Bank maintains a Registry which identifies people who have been issued PDC Certificates. Anyone interested in buying PDCs may contact the Bank and obtain the names of potential sellers.

The Bank will also periodically send informational bulletins to builders and developers' organizations and to towns where PDCs may be used in development projects. Of course, you may do this on your own as well.

How much money can I expect for my PDCs?

Although the State Pinelands Development Credit Bank will pay at least $10,000 for each PDC it purchases, remember that it may be possible to sell them privately for a larger amount. The State PDC Bank may be able to help you locate an interested buyer with whom you can negotiate a price .

If I'm interested in buying PDCs, can the Bank help?

Here again the Bank can help, but it's not the only choice you have. The Registry of PDC Certificate holders which the Bank maintains can be a ready source of potential sellers. The Bank will also be buying PDCs directly and these will also be available for resale.

What are the other options available for locating people who may wish to sell PDCs?

The Burlington County Pinelands Development Credit Exchange also resells PDCs. The address and phone number are included in Section 1.

As a buyer, you may also contact landowners directly, work through Realtors, and advertise.

How do I find out more about buying or selling PDCs?

We suggest you read the publication "Benefits of the Pinelands Development Credit Program" and contact the Bank. Our staff will be glad to explain the possibilities in detail.

SECTION 3

PINELANDS DEVELOPMENT CREDIT BANK — PURCHASE OF PDCs

Under what circumstances can the State Bank buy PDCs?

The state law which created the PDC Bank authorizes it to purchase Pinelands Development Credits in two instances. The first instance is when the purchase would further the objectives of the Pinelands Protection Act and the Pinelands Comprehensive Management Plan. The second is when the purchase would help to alleviate a hardship.

In either case, however, the State Bank can not buy any PDCs after December 31, 1992.

What does "furthering the objectives of the Pinelands Protection Act and the Pinelands Comprehensive Management Plan" mean?

Basically, both the Pinelands Act and Plan have as their goals the protection of the Pinelands. We have taken this broad goal and identified five specific situations where the purchase of PDCs would be particularly helpful. They are:

1. *When the property to which the PDCs are allocated is of significant ecological or agricultural importance.* Once the PDCs are purchased, the deed restriction will serve to protect the property. If that property has exceptional qualities, it stands to reason that its protection is particularly important. Significant qualities can include, for example, the existence of cedar swamps, habitat for threatened or endangered plants or animals, or a key farm in a relatively large agricultural area.

2. *When the property to which the PDCs are allocated complements or buffers public conservation lands.* The protection afforded to the property once the PDCs are sold may be particularly important if, for example, it is located adjacent to a state park or forest or is located in an area which drains to a state wildlife area.

3. *When the PDCs the Bank is to acquire are likely to be used for an important residential development project.* The Bank can resell or transfer PDCs it buys and there may be developers waiting to use them. If the PDCs are likely to be redeemed in a residential project which, for example, incorporates an environmentally sensitive design or includes housing which is affordable to families with varied incomes, the Bank could purchase the PDCs in anticipation of their use in those projects. Another example is when a developer has expressed an interest in donating property for conservation purposes to the state, a county, or a municipality. In certain cases, the Bank might decide to transfer the PDCs it buys to a developer at little or no cost.

4. *When the timing and nature of the Bank's purchase will result in a significant and positive example of the PDC program at work.* In the early stages of the Bank's operation, the Bank may buy a number of PDCs to demonstrate how the program works. As time progresses, the Bank may become more oriented toward the purchase of PDCs from owners of relatively small properties to show that the

program can work to the benefit of people who don't own large amounts of land. Or the Bank may focus on purchasing PDCs to protect a number of separate properties which are located adjacent to each other.

5. *When the Property owner intends to use the proceeds from the PDC sale to develop or use the property in a manner consistent with the terms of the deed restriction.* The Bank would be interested in buying PDCs if the seller intended to use those proceeds to improve a farm operation (e.g., installation of irrigation, purchase of farm equipment to improve productivity, etc.) or, for example, to establish a wildlife refuge, nature center, or passive recreation area.

A sixth, more general criterion covers other situations of which the Bank might not be aware. The criterion is that:

6. *The transaction otherwise furthers the purposes of the Pinelands Protection Act and the Pinelands Comprehensive Management Plan.* Although this can't be used as a catch-all to cover every instance where someone wishes to sell the Bank his PDCs, we recognize that there may be other situations where our purchase of PDCs might further the Pinelands Act and Plan. The general test we'll use here is whether the purchase has an unusual, rather than universal, characteristic.

What is meant by "to alleviate hardship"?

Again, the Bank has taken this rather broad goal and identified three situations where a hardship can be determined. These criteria relate to the circumstances in which a property owner finds himself. These are:

1. *When the property owner's investment in the land to which the PDCs are allocated is substantial in relation to his **net worth**.* If a property owner has invested lot of money in a piece of property, the sale of the PDCs will help to return to him at Yeast a portion of that investment. The key here is not so much how much money has been invested but whether that investment is substantial in terms of that person's net worth. In simple terms, net worth is the amount of money you would be left with if you sold all of your assets and then paid off all of your debts. Obviously, people with relatively high net worths will be less likely to meet this test even if the investment made in the property is large.

2. *When the Property owner has been denied a "waiver of strict compliance" from the Pinelands comprehensive Management Plan.* The Pinelands Commission may permit property owners to develop their property even though it is not consistent with the standards of the Pinelands Plan. Under state law, however, this can only be done in very limited situations. If a property owner has sought a "waiver" from the Pinelands Commission but has been denied, the Bank can consider buying his PDCs. For more information on "waivers," contact the Pinelands Commission.

3. *When the property owner is experiencing a unique and extraordinary financial hardship which can be helped through a quick sale of PDCs.* Sometimes people find themselves in situations of great personal hardships such as sudden unemployment or the illness of a close relative. In these and similar cases requiring immediate financial resources, the sale of PDCs might help to alleviate the problem.

If I qualify, how much can the State Bank pay for my PDCs?

The State Legislature set an initial price of $10,000 for each PDC that the State Bank purchases. A quarter of a PDC could, therefore, be purchased for $2,500. Although this price can be increased over time, the Bank can not pay more than 80 percent of the price you could expect to receive from a private buyer. To find out if the current purchase price is above $10,000 per credit, please give us a call.

Are there any expenses which I would be responsible for?

Yes, there are, but we expect that they won't be too high. For example, the property owner is responsible for the title search and fees charged by each county to record a deed restriction. There will also be some out-of-pocket expenses for postage, photocopying, etc. Of course, if you decide to hire an attorney or someone else to help you, that's an additional expense.

Although we can't say exactly how much these items will cost, the following estimates should give you a reasonable idea of what to expect, barring some unusual situation.

Title Search	$150
Legal Assistance	$0 to $300
Recording Fees	$19
Miscellaneous Expenses	$10 to $100
Total Costs	$179 to $569

How do I apply if I want the Bank to buy my PDCs?

An application must be submitted to the Bank. A sample application form along with instructions is included in Section 7.

Do I need to have a PDC Certificate in order to apply?

No. In fact, having a PDC Certificate ahead of time means that your property already is protected with a deed restriction. As we discussed earlier, in some cases the Bank can buy PDCs only if the purchase serves to protect property. If the property is already protected, the Bank could not purchase PDCs on that basis.

Many of the other tests don't, however, involve protection of the property, and even if you already have a PDC Certificate, you may qualify under one of those.

Must I submit a formal application in order to find out if I qualify for the Bank to purchase my PDCs

Although our staff is more than willing to informally discuss the matter with you, we can't give you a definite answer unless all of the information needed for the application is available to us.

Once I apply, how long will it take to get an answer?

If your application is complete, we estimate that it will take approximately one month.

Once the Bank approves a purchase what happens next?

Our staff will contact you and schedule a date, time, and place to complete the sale.

At that time, you will be asked to sign the deed restriction (unless you had previously received a PDC Certificate) and to sign the PDC Certificate over to the Bank. You will also receive a check for the sale price, minus the cost for recording the deed restriction, and be asked to sign a receipt.

Please remember that just prior to the actual sale, we will need to contact your title company to make sure that no title changes have occurred since the title search was done. This is necessary to avoid situations where your ability to deed restrict the property has changed.

COMPLETING A PRIVATE PDC SALE OR PURCHASE

Now that I have a willing buyer or seller, how do I complete a sale or purchase?

If the PDCs are to be sold separately from the property, the property owner must first have a PDC Certificate.

The sale itself can be completed in any number of ways, but the buyer must return the Certificate to the Bank within 10 business days of the sale. Keep in mind that PDCs can be sold with the property or sold separately.

Before discussing the PDC Certificate, can you tell me more about the sale itself?

For the protection of the buyer and seller it is best if a contract is written and signed by both parties.

Since the PDCs originate from land, do we need to record any deed information when PDCs are sold?

No. When the PDCs are first separated from the property, a deed restriction is recorded and a PDC Certificate is issued. Once the Certificate is issued, there is no need to record any further information in the county clerk's office.

Why does the PDC Certificate need to be returned to the Bank?

PDC Certificates are issued to the owner of the PDCs. When the ownership changes, a new PDC Certificate must be issued to the new owner.

What information is needed in order to issue a new PDC Certificate?

The back side of each PDC Certificate includes a section identifying the information needed. A set of step by step instructions in included in Section 7.

Can I sell a portion of my PDCs?

Yes, you can. If that occurs, the Bank will reissue Certificates to you and the buyer. For example, you may own 10 PDCs but sell only 4. When the sale is reported to the Bank, a new PDC Certificate will be issued in your name for 6 PDCs. A separate Certificate for 4 PDCs will also be issued in the buyer's name.

Do I need to notify the Bank of anything other than PDC sales?

Yes, anytime the ownership of PDCs changes it must be reported to the Bank. If you were to donate the PDCs to a charity or give them to your children, it must be reported to the Bank. If you were previously the sole owner of the PDCs but formed a partnership with another person, this too must be reported to the Bank.

A good rule to follow is that whenever your ownership interest in the PDCs changes, report it to the Bank.

SECTION 5

USING PINELANDS DEVELOPMENT CREDITS AS COLLATERAL

Can Pinelands Development Credits be used as collateral against a loan?

Yes, they can be used to secure a loan in the same manner as anything else of value. If you have an interest in obtaining a loan, you may wish to discuss the matter with your local bank, credit union, or other lending institution.

Do I need to have a PDC Certificate in order to use PDCs as collateral?

If you own property which is allocated PDCs, you can of course secure a loan using the property itself as collateral. If, however, you wish to use only the PDCs as collateral, a PDC Certificate should first be obtained.

What do I do if my PDCs are going to be used to secure a loan?

The loan arrangements are made between you and the lending institution, but the PDC Certificate must then be returned to the Pinelands Development Credit Bank within 10 business days of the date on which the loan was given.

Why does the PDC Certificate need to be returned to the Pinelands Development Credit Bank?

Because the lender has agreed to give you a loan using PDCs as collateral, the lender now has an interest in your PDCs. If you default on the loan, the lender will then own the PDCs. The actual loan arrangements are likely to be more involved so you should discuss those details with the lender.

In any event, the Pinelands Development Credit Bank will reissue a Certificate with a notation that the PDCs have been encumbered. This means that they can't be sold without obtaining a release from the lender.

What information is needed in order to issue the new PDC Certificate?

The back side of each PDC Certificate includes a section identifying the information needed. A set of step-by-step instructions is included in Section 7.

What happens if I pledge some but not all of my PDCs as collateral?

In that case, the Pinelands Development Credit Bank will reissue two certificates — one which identifies the number of PDCs encumbered and one without that notation. Of course, you are then free to sell any of the PDCs not encumbered.

Who will hold the PDC Certificate while the PDCs are encumbered?

That is between you and your lender. Normally, we will return the newly issued Certificate to you as the owner unless you notify us of a different arrangement.

After the loan is repaid, how do I get the encumbrance notation removed from the PDC Certificate?

We will reissue a PDC Certificate without the notation immediately upon receiving the current Certificate and a release from the lender. A release states that the lending agency is surrendering its claim to the PDCs which have been used as collateral.

SECTION 6

REDEEMING PINELANDS DEVELOPMENT CREDITS

What does the redemption of PDCs mean?

In simple terms, PDCs are redeemed when a developer receives approval to build more homes in a residential project than would normally be allowed. At that point, the PDCs are used and must be retired. For more information on this and other aspects of the PDC program, please read the publication "Benefits of the Pinelands Development Credit Program."

Do I need to have a PDC Certificate in order to redeem PDCs?

Yes. The PDC Certificate must be completed immediately after the project is approved and then returned to the Bank within 10 days.

Since my Project doesn't receive final clearance until the Pinelands Commission has reviewed it, shouldn't I wait until then to send in the Certificate?

No. The Pinelands Commission will not clear the project until it has received evidence that the proper number of PDCs have been used to obtain the final municipal approval. The builder may wish to complete the purchase just prior to this approval. For your protection, the State Bank will not formally retire the PDCs until determining that the Pinelands Commission has cleared the municipal approval. When that happens, you and the municipal official who attested to the redemption will be notified.

How do I complete the PDC Certificate?

The back side of each PDC Certificate includes a section identifying the information needed. A set of step by step instructions is included in Section 7.

Can I redeem a portion of my PDCs and retain the remainder?

Yes. If you redeem less than the full number of PDCs identified on the front of the Certificate, the Bank will issue you a new Certificate for the difference.

SECTION 7

SAMPLE FORMS AND INSTRUCTIONS

1. Application for Letter of Interpretation and Instructions.

2. Sample Letter of Interpretation.

3. Application for Pinelands Development Credit Certificate and Instructions.

4. Sample Deed Restriction for Preservation Area.

5. Sample Deed Restriction for Special Agricultural Production Area.

6. Sample Deed Restriction for Agricultural Area.

7. Language That Should be Inserted into a Deed Restriction When Reserving Future Development Rights.

8. Pinelands Development Credit Certificate.

9. Application for Sale of Pinelands Development Credits to the State Pinelands Development Credit Bank and Instructions.

10. Instructions for Revising PDC Certificate for Sales and Transfers.

11. Instructions for Revising PDC Certificate When PDCs are Used as Collateral.

12. Instructions for Revising PDC Certificate When PDCs are Redeemed.

APPLICATION FOR LETTER OF INTERPRETATION FOR
PINELANDS DEVELOPMENT CREDITS

RETURN TO:
Pinelands Commission
P.O. Box 7
New Lisbon, NJ 08064
(609) 894-9342

For Pinelands Commission Use Only
Date Rec'd _____
App. # _____
LOI # _____
LOI Date _____

(Please see pages 3 and 4 for instructions)

OWNER INFORMATION

[1] Property Owner's Name _____ [2] Phone No. _____

[3] Co-Owner's Name _____ [4] Phone No. _____

[5] Property Owner's Street Address _____

[6] City, State, ZIP Code _____

PROPERTY INFORMATION

[7] Municipality _____ [8] County _____

[9] Block # _____ [10] Lot # _____ [11] Total Acreage _____

[12] Nearest Street or Road _____ [13] Mun. Zoning District _____

[14] Are there any homes located on the property? Yes _____ No _____

[15] If yes, how many, and when were they built? _____

[16] Are there any other buildings on the property? Yes _____ No _____

[17] If yes, how many, what are they used for, and when were they built? _____

[18] Describe any commercial activities taking place on this property (e.g., campground, resource extraction):

_____

_____

[19] Did you own this property prior to February 8, 1979? Yes _____ No _____

[20] Have you ever submitted to the Pinelands Commission an application for development or for a waiver of strict compliance for this property? Yes _____ No _____ [21] If yes, enter the Pinelands Commission application number _____

[22] Do you own any other adjacent property? Yes _____ No _____

[23] Block # _____ [24] Lot # _____

[25] Are there any easements or deed restrictions affecting this property? Yes _____ No _____

Page 1 of 4

APPLICATION INFORMATION: *Is the following information attached?*

[26] Deed to property? Yes _____ No _____

[27] Easements or other restrictions?   Yes _____   No _____   N/A _____

REPRESENTATIVE INFORMATION

[28] Do you authorize a person to act as your representative in all matters pertaining to this application? Yes _____   No _____

[29] Representative's Name _____   [30] Phone # _____

[31] Representative's Street Address _____

[32] City, State, Zip Code _____

[33] Signature of Representative _____

OWNER CERTIFICATION

I hereby certify that the information furnished on this application and the attachments are true. I am aware that false swearing is a crime in this state and subject to prosecution. I hereby authorize the staff of the Pinelands Commission to conduct such site inspections on the property as are necessary to review this application.

| Signature of Owner (Applicant) | Date | Signature of Co-Owner (Co-Applicant) | Date |

SWORN AND SUBSCRIBED TO BEFORE ME

THIS _____ *DAY OF* _____ *19* _____.

_____

NOTARY PUBLIC

Page 2 of 4

INSTRUCTIONS FOR COMPLETING AN APPLICATION FOR
A LETTER OF INTERPRETATION FOR PINELANDS DEVELOPMENT CREDITS

Please print or type

1.   Enter your first, middle, and last name. No nicknames, please.

2.   Include the telephone number, including area code, where you are most likely to be reached during the day.

3.   If you own the property jointly with another person, please enter his or her name. If there are more owners, please attach an additional sheet with their names and telephone numbers.

4.   Enter the telephone number, including area code, where the co-owner may be reached during the day.

5.   Enter the full street address, including apartment number if appropriate, of the home or business where you would like to receive mail.

6.   Enter the city, state, and zip code of your mailing address.

7, 8.   Identify the municipality and county in which the property is located.

9, 10.   Enter the tax block and lot numbers from your most recent property tax bill.

11.   Enter the total acreage of the property.

12.   Enter the name or route number of the road which is closest to your property. If you are uncertain, please identify the road which you believe is the closest.

13.   Enter the zoning district in which the property is located. This information can be obtained from the municipal zoning officer or the Pinelands Commission office.

14.   Note if there is one or more homes located on the property.

15.   Note when (month and year) the home was built. If number 14 was checked "no," please enter "Not Applicable."

16.   Note if there are any other buildings on this property.

17.   Describe the other buildings on this property, what they are used for, and when they were built. If number 16 was checked "No," please enter "Not Applicable."

18.   Note if there are any commercial activities conducted on this property. If there aren't any, enter "None."

19.   Note if you owned the property before February 8, 1979.

20.   Note if you have previously submitted any application to the Pinelands Commission concerning this property or if you have applied for a waiver (exemption) from Pinelands Comprehensive Management Plan regulations.

Page 3 of 4

21. If number 20 was checked "Yes," please enter the number which the Pinelands Commission assigned to your application.

22. Note if you own any additional property adjoining the property listed in 9 and 10.

23, 24. If number 22 was checked "Yes," please identify this property by block and lot number.

25. Note if there are any easements or deed restrictions affecting the property listed in 9 and 10.

26. A copy of the deed to the property must be attached in order for your application to be processed. If it is not available, please check the box marked "No" and attach a sheet explaining why it is not available.

27. If number 25 was checked "Yes," copies of the easement or deed restrictions must be attached in order for your application to be processed. If they are not available, please check the box marked "No" and attach a sheet explaining why they are not available.

28. Please indicate whether or not you have engaged an attorney or someone else to represent you. If you check the box marked "yes," the Commission will correspond and communicate directly with your representative and not you.

29, 30, 31, 32. Please complete only if you checked the box marked "Yes" in number 28.

33. If you have designated a representative (see number 28), he or she must sign here.

Certification

Please read the certification carefully before signing and dating the application. Any and all co-owners identified in number 3 must sign and date the application as well.

Notary The application must be notarized before it is submitted to the Pinelands Commission.

Page 4 of 4

The Pinelands Commission

P.O. Box 7, New Lisbon, N.J. 08064 (609) 894-9342

April 19, 1988

Mr. John Smith
1230 Whitehorse-Mercerville Road
Trenton, New Jersey 08625

> Re: App. No. 88-0000
> Block 21, Lot 10.12.15
> Smith Road
> Pemberton Township

FINDINGS OF FACT

The applicant has owned the above-referenced 19.4 acre parcel in Pemberton Township since 1967. The parcel is located in an Agricultural Production Area. Pursuant to N.J.A.C. 7:50-4.72(a). the applicant is requesting a Letter of Interpretation as to the number of Pinelands Development Credits which are attributed to this lot.

There is a hardwood swamp as defined in N.J.A.C. 7:50-6.5(a)2 located on 9.9 acres of the parcel. The remaining 9.5 acres of the parcel is a blueberry field. There are no easements limiting the use of this parcel to non-residential uses. The parcel is vacant. This parcel is not in common ownership with any contiguous parcel.

CONCLUSION

N J.A.C. 7:50-5 43 grants, with certain exceptions, to every parcel of land in an Agricultural Production Area, a use right known as "Pinelands Development Credits" that can be used to secure a density bonus for lands located in Regional Growth Areas. None of these exceptions apply to this parcel.

N.J.A.C. 7:50-5 43(b)2 establishes the ratio by which Pinelands Development Credits are allocated in an Agricultural Production Area. Two Pinelands Development Credits are allocated for every 39 acres of uplands, except for uplands which are mined as a result of a resource extraction permit approved pursuant to the provisions of the Plan, for areas of berry agricultural bogs and fields and for wetlands in active field agricultural use as on February 7, 1979. There are 0.2 Pinelands Development Credits allocated for every 39 acres of other wetlands.

The hardwood swamp is a fresh water wetlands (N.J.A.C.7:50-6 5(a)2). The applicant is entitled to 0.05 Pinelands Development Credits for these 9.9 wetlands acres. The remaining 9.5 acres is a blueberry field. The applicant is entitled to 0.48 Pinelands Development Credits for this acreage.

There are a total of 0.5 Pinelands Development Credits allocated for this 19.4 acre parcel.

RECONSIDERATION

Any person who is aggrieved by this determination may seek reconsideration for the decision by the Pinelands Commission within 18 days of the date of this letter by giving notice, by Certified Mail, of the request for reconsideration to the Pinelands Commission. Said notice shall include:

1. The name and address of the person requesting the reconsideration;

2. the application number;

3. a brief statement of the basis for the reconsideration request; and

4. a certificate of service, indicating that service of the notice has been made, by Certified Mail, on:

    a. the applicant (unless the applicant is requesting the reconsideration);

    b. Secretary, Pemberton Township Planning Board;

    c. Pemberton Township Environmental Commission.

Sincerely,

William F. Harrison, Esq.
Assistant Director

WFH/mm

c: Secretary, Pemberton Township Planning Board
         Pemberton Township Environmental Commission
         John T. Ross, Pinelands Development Credit Bank

APPLICATION FOR
PINELANDS DEVELOPMENT CREDIT CERTIFICATE

RETURN TO:
State Pinelands Development Credit Bank
CNO35
Trenton, NJ 08065
(609) 588-3469

For Bank Use Only
Date Rec'd _____
App'd _____
Denied _____
Date _____
Cert. # _____

(Please see pages 3 and 4 for instructions)

OWNER INFORMATION

[1] Property Owner's Name _____ [2] Phone # _____

[3] Co-Owner's Name _____ [4] Phone # _____

[5] Property Owner's Street Address _____

[6] City, State, ZIP Code _____

PROPERTY INFORMATION

[7] Municipality _____ [8] County _____

[9] Block # _____ [10] Lot # _____ [11] Total Acreage _____

[12] Nearest Street or Road _____

[13] Letter of Intent # _____ [14] Date Issued _____ [15] Number of PDCs _____

[16] Has the property been altered or developed in any way since the Letter of Interpretation was issued? Yes ____ No ____

[17] If yes, describe the changes: _____

_____

TITLE COMPANY INFORMATION

[18] Name of Title Company _____ [19] Phone # _____

[20] Company's Street Address _____

[21] City, State, Zip Code _____

Page 1 of 4

MORTGAGE COMPANY INFORMATION

[22] Is there a mortgage on the property? Yes _____ No _____

[23] Mortgage Holder's Name _____ [24] Phone # _____

[25] Mortgage Holder's Street Address _____

[26] City, State, Zip Code _____

REPRESENTATIVE INFORMATION

[27] Do you authorize a person to act as your representative in all matters pertaining to this application? Yes _____ No _____

[28] Name of Representative _____ [29] Phone # _____

[30] Representative's Street Address _____

[31] City, State, Zip Code _____

[32] Signature of Representative _____

APPLICATION INFORMATION: *Is the following information attached?*

[33] Deed to property? Yes _____ No _____ [34] Deed Restriction: Draft _____ Recorded _____ None _____

[35] Title Certification: Yes _____ No _____ [36] Letter of Interpretation: Yes _____ No _____

[37] Tax Map: Yes _____ No _____ [38] Mortgage Release: Yes _____ No _____ N/A _____

OWNER CERTIFICATION

I hereby certify that the information furnished on this application and the attachments are true, that I am the legal owner of the property described above, that I have marketable title to the property, and that I have the legal right to restrict the use of the property consistent with the deed restriction attached hereto. I grant permission to the Pinelands Development Credit Bank to seek an update from the Title Company prior to its issuance of a Pinelands Development Credit Certificate.

_____ _____ _____ _____
Signature of Owner (Applicant)   Date   Signature of Co-Owner (Co-Applicant)   Date

Note to Applicants: The State Pinelands Development Credit Bank staff will contact you within two weeks of the receipt of this application.

Page 2 of 4

INSTRUCTIONS FOR PDC CERTIFICATE APPLICATION FORM

Please print or type

1. Enter your first, middle, and last name. No nicknames, please.

2. Include the telephone number, including area code, where you are most likely to be reached during the day.

3. If you own the property jointly with another person, please enter his or her name. If there are more owners, please attach an additional sheet with their names and telephone numbers.

4. Enter the telephone number, including area code, where the co-owner may be reached during the day.

5. Enter the full street address, including apartment number if appropriate, of the home or business where you would like to receive mail.

6. Enter the city, state, and zip code of your mailing address.

7, 8. Identify the municipality and county in which the property is located.

9, 10. Enter the tax block and lot numbers from your most recent property tax bill.

11. Enter the total acreage of the property which will be subject to the deed restriction. If this acreage figure is not the same as that shown on the Letter of Interpretation, please attach an explanation.

12. Enter the name or route number of the road which is closest to your property. If you are uncertain, please identify the road which you believe is the closest.

13. Enter the Pinelands Commission's Letter of Interpretation number. This is noted on your Letter of Interpretation. Please don't confuse this with an application number which is also shown on the letter.

14. Enter the date on which the Letter of Interpretation was issued.

15. Enter the number of Pinelands Development Credits allocated in the Letter of Interpretation. Please make sure that this represents the total number of PDCs to which your property is entitled. If the Pinelands Commission adjusted your allocation because you are reserving the right to build one or more homes, please enter the adjusted number.

16. If you have cleared any land, enlarged or reduced actively farmed lands, or built anything on the property since the Letter of Interpretation was issued, please check the box marked "Yes." If there hasn't been any change, check the box marked "No."

17. If you checked "Yes" in number 16, a brief description of the changes should be included. If you need more space, please continue on another sheet of paper. "N/A" should be entered if number 16 was answered "No."

18. Enter the full name of the title company which performed your title search.

19. Enter the phone number, including area code, of the title company's office.

Page 3 of 4

20.   Enter the full street address of the title company office which conducted the title search. If there is more than one office, please enter the office with which you worked.

21.   Enter the city, state, and zip code of the title company office.

22.   If there is a mortgage, lien, or other financial encumbrance on the property, please check the box marked "Yes." If there is none, please check the box marked "No."

23, 24,   If you checked "Yes" in number 22, please complete these boxes for the mortgage
25, 26.   holder. If number 22 was answered "No," please enter "N/A" in each space.

27.   Please indicate whether or not you have engaged an attorney or someone else to represent you. If you check the box marked "Yes," the Bank will correspond and communicate directly with your representative and not you.

28, 29,   If you checked the box marked "Yes" in number 27, please enter the appropriate
30, 31.   information regarding the representative. If number 27 was answered "No," please enter "N/A" in each space.

32.   If you have designated a representative (see number 27) he or she should sign here. If there is no representative, please enter "N/A."

33, 34,   This information must be attached in order for your application to be processed. If
35, 36,   any item is not available, please check the box marked "No," or "None," and
37.   attach a sheet explaining why it is not available.

34.   Please indicate whether the restriction you are attaching is a draft or whether it has been fully executed and recorded with the county clerk.

37.   A photostat of the municipal tax map which shows the property to be deed restricted can be obtained by contacting the municipal clerk, tax assessor, or tax collector of the town in which the property is located.

38.   If you checked the box marked "Yes" in number 22, you must check either the "Yes" or "No" box here. Remember that your application can't be processed until the mortgage holder has given you a written release. The release must state that the mortgage holder is aware that you intend to place a restriction on the deed to the property, that the restriction will limit future uses of the property, and that the mortgage holder has agreed to subordinate his interest to that of the deed restriction. If number 22 was answered "No," please check the box marked "N/A."

39.   Please read this certification carefully before signing and dating the application. Any and all co-owners identified in number 3 must sign and date the application as well.

Page 4 of 4

PINELANDS DEVELOPMENT CREDIT DEED RESTRICTION
FOR AGRICULTURAL PRODUCTION AREA

THE INDENTURE dated _____, 19___
Made by:

_____

(Name(s) and address(es) of landowner(s)

_____

_____

_____

In favor of the State of New Jersey, Department of Environmental Protection, C/O CN 035, Trenton, New Jersey, 08625, hereinafter referred to as GRANTEE. This transfer is made for no monetary consideration.

WITNESSETH:

WHEREAS, GRANTOR owns in fee simple all that certain Land (location and legal description)

WHEREAS the Land is located in an area designated under the Pinelands Comprehensive Management Plan as eligible for the use right known as Pinelands Development Credits; and

WHEREAS the New Jersey Pinelands Commission has determined that there is/are _____ transferable Pinelands Development Credit(s) allowable to the Land,   number of credits

NOW THEREFORE, for and in consideration of the right to sell, transfer, and assign the Pinelands Development Credit(s) allocable to the Land by means of a Pinelands Development Credit Certificate the GRANTOR hereby conveys, sells, transfers, and assignees to GRANTEE, its successors and assigns, the following conservation restriction:

1. The Land, which is located in an Agricultural Production Area, may only be used in perpetuity for the following uses:

   Agriculture; farm related housing in accord with N.J.A.C. 7:5.24(a)2; forestry; low intensity recreational uses in which the use of motorized vehicles is not permitted except for necessary transportation, access to water bodies is limited to no more than 15 feet of frontage per 1,000 feet of frontage on the water body, clearing of vegetation does not exceed five percent of the parcel, and no more than one percent of the parcel will be covered with impermeable surfaces; agricultural sales establishments, excluding supermarkets and restaurants and convenience stores, where the principal goods or products available for sale were produced in the Pinelands and the sales area does not exceed 5,000 square feet; agricultural products processing facilities; airports and heliports accessory to agricultural uses and which are used exclusively for the storage, fueling, loading, and operation of aircraft as part of an ongoing agricultural operation; fish and wildlife management; and agricultural employee housing as an accessory use.

2. Nothing herein contained shall be construed to convey to the public any right of access to or use of the Land, and GRANTOR, for itself, its successors and assigns shall, subject to Paragraph 3 hereof, retain the exclusive right of access to and use of the Land.

3. This conservation restriction shall be fully enforceable by the GRANTEE as well as by the New Jersey Pinelands Commission, which is a specific beneficiary of the conservation restriction, in an action a law or equity or both. Moreover, GRANTEE and the New Jersey Pinelands Commission and their respective agents shall be permitted access to, and to enter upon, the Land at all reasonable times but solely for the purpose of inspection in order to enforce and assure compliance with the terms and conditions herein contained. GRANTEE and the New Jersey

Page 1 of 2

Pinelands Commission agree to give GRANTOR 24 hours advance notice of their intention to enter the Land, and further, to limit such times of entry to the daylight hours on regular business days of the week.

4. It is understood that this instrument imposes no obligation on the GRANTOR and no restrictions on the development of the Land or the making of construction of improvements thereon in furtherance of the uses of the Land specifically reserved and set forth in Paragraph 1 hereof. Nothing herein contained shall be construed to interfere with the right of the GRANTOR, its successors, assigns, licensees and any party claiming under them to utilize the Land in such manner as they may deem desirable within the scope of the uses herein reserved to GRANTOR in Paragraph 1 hereof.

5. This instrument shall be binding upon the GRANTOR, its successors and assigns.

IN WITNESS WHEREOF, and intending to be legally bound, the GRANTOR has executed this indenture.

WITNESS   GRANTOR

By: _____   By: _____

                                                 GRANTOR

                                                 By: _____

STATE OF NEW JERSEY, COUNTY OF _____ SS: _____

I CERTIFY that on _____, 19 ____,

_____ personally came before me and acknowledged under oath, to my satisfaction that this person (or if more than one, each person):

(a) is named in and personally signed this document; and
(b) signed, sealed, and delivered this document as his or her act and deed; and
(c) this transfer is made for no monetary consideration.

_____
(Print name and title below signature)

STATE OF NEW JERSEY, COUNTY OF _____ SS: _____

I CERTIFY that on _____, 19 ____,

_____ personally came before me and this person acknowledged under oath, to my satisfaction that:

(a) this person is the _____ secretary of _____ _____ the corporation named in this document;
(b) his person is the attesting witness to the signing of this document by the proper corporate officer who is the _____ President of the corporation;
(c) this document was signed and delivered by the corporation as its voluntary act duly authorized by a proper resolution of its Board of Directors;
(d) this person knows the proper seal of the corporation which was affixed to this document;
(e) this person signed this proof to attest to the truth of these facts; and
(f) this transfer is made for no monetary consideration.

_____
(Print name of attesting witness below signature)

Sworn and subscribed to before me on

_____, 19 ____,

_____
NOTARY PUBLIC

Page 2 of 2

PINELANDS DEVELOPMENT CREDIT DEED RESTRICTION
FOR PRESERVATION AREA

THE INDENTURE dated _____ , 19___

Made by:

_____

(Name(s) and address(es) of landowner(s))

_____

_____

_____

In favor of the State of New Jersey, Department of Environmental Protection, C/O CN 035, Trenton, New Jersey, 08625, hereinafter referred to as GRANTEE. This transfer is made for no monetary consideration.

WITNESSETH:

WHEREAS, GRANTOR owns in fee simple all that certain Land (location and legal description)

WHEREAS the Land is located in an area designated under the Pinelands Comprehensive Management Plan as eligible for the use right known as Pinelands Development Credits; and

WHEREAS the New Jersey Pinelands Commission has determined that there is/are _____ transferable Pinelands Development Credit(s) allowable to the Land, <small>number of credits</small>

NOW THEREFORE, for and in consideration of the right to sell, transfer, and assign the Pinelands Development Credit(s) allocable to the Land by means of a Pinelands Development Credit Certificate the GRANTOR hereby conveys, sells, transfers, and assignees to GRANTEE, its successors and assigns, the following conservation restriction:

1. The Land, which is located in an Preservation Area, may only be used in perpetuity for the following uses:

   Berry agriculture; horticulture of native Pinelands plants; forestry; beekeeping; fish and wildlife management; low intensity recreational uses in which the use of motorized vehicles is not permitted except for necessary transportation, access to water bodies is limited to no more than 15 feet of frontage per 1,000 feet of frontage on the water body, clearing of vegetation does not exceed five percent of the parcel, and no more than one percent of the parcel will be covered with impermeable surfaces; and agricultural employee housing as an accessory use.

2. Nothing herein contained shall be construed to convey to the public any right of access to or use of the Land, and GRANTOR, for itself, its successors and assigns shall, subject to Paragraph 3 hereof, retain the exclusive right of access to and use of the Land.

3. This conservation restriction shall be fully enforceable by the GRANTEE as well as by the New Jersey Pinelands Commission, which is a specific beneficiary of the conservation restriction, in an action a law or equity or both. Moreover, GRANTEE and the New Jersey Pinelands Commission and their respective agents shall be permitted access to, and to enter upon, the Land at all reasonable times but solely for the purpose of inspection in order to enforce and assure compliance with the terms and conditions herein contained. GRANTEE and the New Jersey Pinelands Commission agree to give GRANTOR 24 hours advance notice of their intention to enter the Land, and further, to limit such times of entry to the daylight hours on regular business days of the week.

4. It is understood that this instrument imposes no obligation on the GRANTOR and no restrictions on the

Page 1 of 2

to interfere with the right of the GRANTOR, its successors, assigns, licensees and any party claiming under them to utilize the Land in such manner as they may deem desirable within the scope of the uses herein reserved to GRANTOR in Paragraph 1 hereof.

5. This instrument shall be binding upon the GRANTOR, its successors and assigns.

IN WITNESS WHEREOF, and intending to be legally bound, the GRANTOR has executed this indenture.

WITNESS   GRANTOR

By: _____   By: _____

                                                GRANTOR

                                                By: _____

STATE OF NEW JERSEY, COUNTY OF _____ SS: _____

I CERTIFY that on _____, 19 ____,

_____ personally came before me and acknowledged under oath, to my satisfaction that this person (or if more than one, each person):

(a) is named in and personally signed this document; and
(b) signed, sealed, and delivered this document as his or her act and deed; and
(c) this transfer is made for no monetary consideration.

                              _____
                              (Print name and title below signature)

STATE OF NEW JERSEY, COUNTY OF _____ SS: _____

I CERTIFY that on _____, 19 ____,

_____ personally came before me and this person acknowledged under oath, to my satisfaction that:

(a) this person is the _____ secretary of _____
    _____ the corporation named in this document;
(b) his person is the attesting witness to the signing of this document by the proper corporate officer who is the
    _____ President of the corporation;
(c) this document was signed and delivered by the corporation as its voluntary act duly authorized by a proper resolution of its Board of Directors;
(d) this person knows the proper seal of the corporation which was affixed to this document;
(e) this person signed this proof to attest to the truth of these facts; and
(f) this transfer is made for no monetary consideration.

                              _____
                              (Print name of attesting witness below signature)

Sworn and subscribed to before me on

_____, 19 ____,

_____
NOTARY PUBLIC

PINELANDS DEVELOPMENT CREDIT DEED RESTRICTION
FOR SPECIAL AGRICULTURAL PRODUCTION AREA

THE INDENTURE dated _____ , 19___

Made by:

_____

(Name(s) and address(es) of landowner(s))

_____

_____

_____

In favor of the State of New Jersey, Department of Environmental Protection, C/O CN 035, Trenton, New Jersey, 08625, hereinafter referred to as GRANTEE. This transfer is made for no monetary consideration.

WITNESSETH:

WHEREAS, GRANTOR owns in fee simple all that certain Land (location and legal description)

WHEREAS the Land is located in an area designated under the Pinelands Comprehensive Management Plan as eligible for the use right known as Pinelands Development Credits; and

WHEREAS the New Jersey Pinelands Commission has determined that there is/are _____ transferable Pinelands Development Credit(s) allowable to the Land, number of credits

NOW THEREFORE, for and in consideration of the right to sell, transfer, and assign the Pinelands Development Credit(s) allocable to the Land by means of a Pinelands Development Credit Certificate the GRANTOR hereby conveys, sells, transfers, and assignees to GRANTEE, its successors and assigns, the following conservation restriction:

1. The Land, which is located in an Agricultural Production Area, may only be used in perpetuity for the following uses:

    Berry agriculture; horticulture of native Pinelands plants; forestry; beekeeping; fish and wildlife management; and agricultural housing as an accessory use.

2. Nothing herein contained shall be construed to convey to the public any right of access to or use of the Land, and GRANTOR, for itself, its successors and assigns shall, subject to Paragraph 3 hereof, retain the exclusive right of access to and use of the Land.

3. This conservation restriction shall be fully enforceable by the GRANTEE as well as by the New Jersey Pinelands Commission, which is a specific beneficiary of the conservation restriction, in an action a law or equity or both. Moreover, GRANTEE and the New Jersey Pinelands Commission and their respective agents shall be permitted access to, and to enter upon, the Land at all reasonable times but solely for the purpose of inspection in order to enforce and assure compliance with the terms and conditions herein contained. GRANTEE and the New Jersey Pinelands Commission agree to give GRANTOR 24 hours advance notice of their intention to enter the Land, and further, to limit such times of entry to the daylight hours on regular business days of the week.

4. It is understood that this instrument imposes no obligation on the GRANTOR and no restrictions on the development of the Land or the making of construction of improvements thereon in furtherance of the uses of the Land specifically reserved and set forth in Paragraph 1 hereof. Nothing herein contained shall be construed to interfere with the right of the GRANTOR, its successors, assigns, licensees and any party

Page 1 of 2

5. This instrument shall be binding upon the GRANTOR, its successors and assigns.

IN WITNESS WHEREOF, and intending to be legally bound, the GRANTOR has executed this indenture.

WITNESS   GRANTOR

By: _____   By: _____

                                             GRANTOR

                                             By: _____

STATE OF NEW JERSEY, COUNTY OF _____ SS: _____

I CERTIFY that on _____ , 19 ____ ,

_____ personally came before me and acknowledged under oath, to my satisfaction that this person (or if more than one, each person):

    (a) is named in and personally signed this document; and
    (b) signed, sealed, and delivered this document as his or her act and deed; and
    (c) this transfer is made for no monetary consideration.

                                      _____

                                     (Print name and title below signature)

STATE OF NEW JERSEY, COUNTY OF _____ SS: _____

I CERTIFY that on _____ , 19 ____ ,

_____ personally came before me and this person acknowledged under oath, to my satisfaction that:

    (a) this person is the _____ secretary of _____
        _____the corporation named in this document;
    (b) his person is the attesting witness to the signing of this document by the proper corporate officer who is the
        _____ President of the corporation;
    (c) this document was signed and delivered by the corporation as its voluntary act duly authorized by a proper
        resolution of its Board of Directors;
    (d) this person knows the proper seal of the corporation which was affixed to this document;
    (e) this person signed this proof to attest to the truth of these facts; and
    (f) this transfer is made for no monetary consideration.

                                        _____

                                  (Print name of attesting witness below signature)

Sworn and subscribed to before me on

_____ , 19 ____ ,

_____
NOTARY PUBLIC

RESERVING RIGHTS IN ASSOCIATION WITH
PINELANDS DEVELOPMENT CREDITS

Sample Provisions for Deed Restrictions:

1. If a property owner whose land is located in an Agricultural Production Area qualifies for and wishes to reserve a right for residential development after Pinelands Development Credits are separated from the property, the following provision should be inserted at the end of paragraph 1:

   "Not withstanding the above, in addition to homes in existence on the property, not more than _____ residential lots may be subdivided from the property and each such lot shall contain 1 (one) acre of land.

   In consideration of the residential development right(s) retained in this section, the allocation of Pinelands Development Credits has been reduced."

2. If a property owner whose land is located in a Special Agricultural Production Area qualifies for and wishes to reserve a right for farm related residential development after Pinelands Development Credits are separated from the property, the following provision should be inserted at the end of paragraph 1:

   "Not withstanding the above, in addition to homes in existence on the property, not more than _____ residential dwellings accessory to an active agricultural operation may be developed on the property. Each dwelling must be:

   a. For an operator or employee of the farm who is actively engaged in and essential to the agricultural operation; and

   b. Located on a parcel of land of at least 40 (forty) acres in size which is under or qualified for agricultural assessment; and

   c. Located on a property which has an active production history or, if not, where a farm management plan has been prepared which demonstrates that the property will be farmed as a unit unto itself or as part of another farm operation in the area.

   In consideration of the residential development right(s) retained in this section, the allocation of Pnelands Development Credits has been reduced."

3. If a property owner whose land is located in either the preservation Area District, an Agricultural Production Area, or a Special Agricultural Production Area qualifies for and wishes to reserve a right to build one or more homes for himself or members of his immediate family, the following provision should be inserted at the end of paragraph 1:

   "Notwithstanding the above in addition to homes in existence on the property, not more than residential lots may be subdivided from the property to provide a principal place of residence for the property owner or a member of his immediate family. Each such lot must:

   a. Contain at least 3.2 (three and two tenths) acres; and

   b. Be for the property owner or a member of his immediate family:

   i. Who is a member of a two-generation immediate family that has resided in the Pinelands for at least 20 (twenty) years; or

   ii. Whose household income is primarily derived through employment or participation in a Pinelands resource related activity.

   No person may subdivide a lot from the property within 5 (five) years of a prior subdivision for this purpose.

This right shall be extinguished in the event the property owner or a member of his immediate family has not owned the property since February 7, 1979.

In consideration of the residential development right(s) retained in this section, the allocation of Pinelands Development Credits has been reduced.

FOR MORE INFORMATION ON THESE PROVISIONS, PLEASE CONTACT THE NEW JERSEY PINELANDS COMMISSION.

NO: _____
DATE ISSUED: _____
PLI #: _____

State of New Jersey
Pinelands Development Credit Bank
CN 035
Trenton, NJ 08625-0035   (609) 588-34369

Pinelands Development Credit Certificate

Pursuant to the Pinelands Development Credit Bank Act N.J.S.A. 13:18A–30 ET SEQ. and the Pinelands Comprehensive Management Plan N.J.A.C. 7:50–1.1 ET SEQ.

This certifies: _____ hereby owns,

DUPLICATE

_____ Pinelands Development Credits

A restriction on the Deed to Block(s) _____ Lot(s) _____ situated in the Municipality of _____, County of _____ is recorded in Book _____, Page _____ at the County Clerk's Office, _____, New Jersey.

_____
Owner's Signature

This certificate entitles the owner to a density bonus as provided in the Pinelands Comprehensive Management Plan.

_____
Chairman
Pinelands Development Credit Bank

_____
Executive Director,
Pinelands Development Credit Bank

SALE, CONVEYANCE, OR TRANSFER OF PINELANDS DEVELOPMENT CREDITS

Within ten (10) business days the person acquiring a Pinelands Development Credit, or any interest therein, shall deliver to the Pinelands Development Credit Bank this original certificate, properly completed.

Upon receipt, certificate(s) will be re-issued in the name of the person or persons who have secured an interest in the Pinelands Development Credits.

1. Grantee (Buyer)
   Name: _____
   Address: _____
   City/State/ZIP: _____
   Signature: _____

2. Grantor (Seller)
   Name: _____
   Address: _____
   City/State/ZIP: _____
   Signature: _____

3. Number of credits sold, conveyed, or transferred: _____
4. Date of transaction: _____
5. Interest secured: _____
6. Consideration: _____
7. Attach written evidence of the transaction (e.g., Contract of Sale, Bill of Sale).

PINELANDS DEVELOPMENT CREDITS PLEDGED AS SECURITY

When Pineland Development Credits are pledged as security for loans, the lending institution shall return this certificate to the Pinelands Development Credit Bank, properly completed, within ten (10) business days.

Upon receipt, certificate(s) reflecting the encumbrance will be re-issued.

1. Owner (Borrower)
   Name: _____
   Address: _____
   City/State/ZIP: _____
   Signature: _____

2. Lending Institution
   Name: _____
   Address: _____
   City/State/ZIP: _____
   Signature: _____
   Title: _____

3. Amount of Loan: _____
4. Term of Loan: _____
5. Date of Loan: _____
6. Number of Pinelands Development Credits pledged as collateral: _____
7. Attach written evidence of the transaction

NOTE: *When Pinelands Development Credits are released as security, the Pinelands Development Credit Bank will again re-issue a certificate upon notification by the owner and lender.*

REDEMPTION OF PINELANDS DEVELOPMENT CREDITS

When Pinelands Development Credits are redeemed in association with a residential development project approved by a municipal approval agency, the person redeeming the Pinelands Development Credits shall return this certificate to the Pinelands Development Credit Bank properly completed, within ten (10) business days.

1. Owner (Person Redeeming)
   Name: _____
   Address: _____
   City/State/ZIP: _____
   Signature: _____

2. Municipality in which Pinelands Development Credits are redeemed:
   Municipality: _____
   County: _____

3. Municipal Tax Block and Lot Number of property for which Pinelands Development Credits were redeemed.
   Block # _____ Lot # _____
   (Use separate sheet of paper if needed.)

4. Number of Pinelands Development Credits redeemed: _____
5. Municipal development approval was issued:
   Date _____
6. Municipal official issuing development approval:
   Name: _____
   Title: _____
   Signature: _____

THIS DOCUMENT IS FOR INFORMATION AND RECORD-KEEPING PURPOSES ONLY.

APPLICATION FOR SALE OF PINELANDS DEVELOPMENT CREDITS
TO STATE PINELANDS DEVELOPMENT CREDIT BANK

New Jersey Pinelands
Development Credit Bank
CN-O35
Trenton, NJ 08065
(609) 588-3469

For Bank Use Only
App # _____
Date Rec'd _____
Action _____
Date _____

(Please see pages 3 and 4 for instructions)

OWNER INFORMATION

[1] PDC Owner's Name _____ [2] Phone No. _____

[3] Co-Owner's Name _____ [4] Phone No. _____

[5] PDC Owner's Street Address _____

[6] City, State, ZIP Code _____

PINELANDS DEVELOPMENT CREDIT INFORMATION

[7] Has a PDC Certificate been issued for the PDCs which you wish to sell? Yes _____ No _____

[8] If yes, the PDC Certificate number is _____

[9] How many PDCs do you wish to sell to the Bank? _____

Please circle the appropriate answer(s)

[10] The Bank should purchase my PDCs because: ·

a. Yes N/A My property is of significant ecological or agricultural importance.

b. Yes N/A My property buffers or complements publicly owned conservation lands.

c. Yes N/A The Bank is likely to resell or transfer my PDCs for use in a residential development project which satisfies a compelling public need or which will protect conservation or agricultural lands.

d. Yes N/A It will serve as a significant example of the PDC program at work.

e. Yes N/A I intend to use the proceeds from the sale to improve, develop, or use my property in a manner consistent with the terms of the deed restriction.

f. Yes N/A The purchase otherwise furthers the objectives of the Pinelands Protection Act and Comprehensive Management Plan in an unusual way.

Page 1 of 4

Please circle the appropriate answer(s)

[11] The Bank should purchase my PDCs to help relieve a hardship because:

a. Yes   N/A   My investment in the property represents a substantial portion of my total net worth.

b. Yes   N/A   I have been denied a waiver of strict compliance from the standards of the Pinelands Comprehensive Management Plan.

c. Yes   N/A   I am experiencing an extraordinary and unique financial hardship.

REPRESENTATIVE INFORMATION

[12] Do you authorize a person to act as your representative in all matters pertaining to this application? Yes ____ No ____

[13] Name of Representative _____ [14] Phone # _____

[15] Representative's Street Address _____

[16] City, State, Zip Code _____

[17] Signature of Representative _____

APPLICATION INFORMATION: *Is the following information attached?*

[18] PDC Certificate? Yes ____ No ____ N/A____

[19] Application for PDC Certificate: Yes ____ No ____ N/A ____

[20] Statement explaining each of the reason(s) you checked to justify Bank purchase: Yes ____ No ____

[21] A net worth statement and a tabulation of my investment in the property: Yes ____ No ____ N/A ____

[22] A copy of the Pinelands Commission's denial of a waiver of strict compliance: Yes ____ No ____ N/A ____

OWNER CERTIFICATION

[23] I certify that the information included in this application is true, and that I will sell to the Pinelands Development Credit Bank the number of Pinelands Development Credits specified in this application if approved for purchase by the Bank.

_____

Signature of Owner (Applicant)   Date   Signature of Co-Owner (Co-Applicant)   Date

Note to Applicants: The State Pinelands Development Credit Bank staff will contact you within two weeks of the receipt of this application.

Page 2 of 4

INSTRUCTIONS FOR COMPLETING APPLICATION FOR SALE OF PINELANDS DEVELOPMENT CREDITS TO STATE PINELANDS DEVELOPMENT CREDIT BANK

Please print or type

1. Enter your first, middle, and last name. No nicknames, please.

2. Enter the telephone number, including area code, where you are most likely to be reached during the day.

3. If you own the PDC jointly with another person, please enter his or her name. If there are more owners, please attach an additional sheet with their names and telephone numbers.

4. Enter the telephone number, including area code, where the co-owner may be reached during the day.

5. Enter the full street address, including apartment number if appropriate, of the home or business where you would like to receive mail.

6. Enter the city, state, and zip code of your mailing address.

7. Check the box marked "Yes" if the State Pinelands Development credit Bank has already issued a PDC Certificate confirming the number of PDCs. If n Certificate has been issued, check the box marked "No."

8. If the State Pinelands Development Credit Bank has issued a PDC Certificate, enter the Certificate number. If no Certificate has been issued, enter "N/A."

9. Enter the number of PDCs you wish to sell to the Bank.

10. Since the State Pinelands Development Credit Bank can only purchase credits under certain circumstances, please circle which circumstance(s) apply to your situation. If one or more of these items are not applicable, circle "N/A."

11. If you wish to sell your PDCs because of a hardship, please circle those circumstances which apply to you. If one or more of these items are not applicable, circle "N/A."

12. Please indicate whether or not you have engaged an attorney or someone else to represent you. If you check the box marked "Yes," the State Pinelands Development Credit Bank will correspond and communicate directly with your representative and not you.

13, 14, Please complete only if you checked the box marked "Yes," in number 12.
15, 16.

17. If you've designated a representative (see number 12), he or she must sign here.

18. If number 7 was checked "Yes," a copy of your PDC certificate (front and back) must be attached in order for your application to be processed. If it is not available, please check the box marked "No," and attach a sheet explaining why it is not attached. If number 7 was checked "Yes," please check the box marked "N/A."

Page 3 of 4

19. If number 7 was checked "No," you must also submit an *Application for Pinelands Development Credit Certificate* in order for this application to be processed. If you have not completed and attached the *Application for Pinelands Development Credit Certificate*, check the box marked "No," and attach a sheet explaining why it is not attached. If number 7 was checked "Yes," please check the box marked "N/A."

20. A statement explaining each of the items circled "yes" in numbers 10 and 11 must be attached.

21. If you circled "Yes" for number 11a, this information must also be attached for your application to be processed. If it is not available, please check the box marked "No" and attach a sheet explaining why the information is not available. If you circled "N/A" for number 11a, please check the box marked "N/A" here as well.

22. If you circled "Yes" for number 11b, a copy of the Pinelands Commission's decision on your application for a waiver of strict compliance must be attached for your application to be processed. If it is not available please check the box marked "No" and attach a sheet explaining why the information is not available. If you circled "N/A" for number 11b, please check the box marked "N/A" here as well.

23. Please read the certification carefully before signing and dating the application. Any and all co-owners identified in number 3 must sign and date the application as well.

INSTRUCTIONS FOR REVISING PDC CERTIFICATE FOR SALES AND TRANSFERS

Complete the "Sale, Conveyance, or Transfer" section of the PDC certificate	*Following these instructions:*

1. Grantee (Buyer)
  Name:
  Address:
  City/State/Zip:
  Signature:
	Enter the name and address of the person who has bought or who owns the PDCs. The name should be entered as you wish it to appear on the front of the new PDC Certificate. Include the mailing address and signature.

2. Grantor (Seller)
  Name:
  Address:
  City/State/Zip:
  Signature:
  Title:
	Enter the name of the person who sold the PDCs. The name must appear as it does on the front of the Certificate. Include the address and signature.

3. Number of Credits Sold, Conveyed or Transferred:	Enter the number (e.g., 200) of PDCs involved in the transaction. Remember that some but not necessarily all of the PDCs shown on the front of the Certificate can be sold or transferred. In no case can the number be greater than the number shown on the front of the Certificate.
4. Date of Transaction:	Enter the date (e.g., 07/25/89) on which the sale or transfer actually occurred.
5. Interest Secured:	Enter the following as appropriate: • **Fee** is entered if full ownership of the PDCs identified in number 3 has been transferred. • **Partial** is entered if a part interest in the PDCs has been transferred. This would apply where, for example, the prior owner and another person now have joint ownership of the PDC. • **Other** is entered if neither of the above reflects the interest secured by the grantor. If **other** is entered, an explanation signed by both the grantee and grantor must be attached.
6. Consideration:	Enter the total cash price or one of the following as appropriate: • **Other** is entered if the transaction involved consideration other than cash (e.g., financing or other property in lieu of cash). If **other** is entered, the terms must be described in an attached sheet which is signed by both parties. • **Donated** is entered if the PDCs were transferred at no cost.
7. Attach Written Evidence of the Transaction	Written evidence that the sale or transfer was consummated must be attached. This can be, for example, the bill of sale.

• When you have properly noted all of the above and attached required items, forward the PDC Certificate and materials to the Bank to notify it of the transaction.

INSTRUCTIONS FOR REVISING PDC CERTIFICATE
WHEN PDCs ARE USED AS COLLATERAL
(Refer to the back of the PDC Certificate)

Complete the "Pledged as Security" section of the PDC certificate	*Following these instructions:*
1. Owner (Borrower) Name: Address: City/State/Zip: Signature.	Enter the name and address of the person who owns the PDCs. The name must appear as it does on the front of the Certificate. Include the person's mailing address and signature.
2. Lending Institution Name: Address: City/State/Zip: Signature: Title:	Enter the name of the business or person who is providing the loan as well as the mailing address. In the case of a business which is the lender, the signature must be that of an authorized officer of the business and his or her title must be identified. If an individual is making the loan, the title line need not be completed.
3. Amount of Loan:	Enter the total amount of the loan.
4. Term of Loan:	Enter the date (e.g., 07/25/89) on which the loan is to be fully repaid.
5. Date of Loan:	Enter the date (e.g., 07/25/88) on which the loan was granted.
6. Number of Pinelands Development Credits Pledged As Collateral:	Enter the number of PDCs used to secure the loan. Remember that some but not necessarily all of the PDCs shown on the front of the Certificate can be encumbered. In no case can the number be greater than the number of PDCs shown on the front of the Certificate.
7. Attach Written Evidence of the Transaction	A copy of the loan agreement can be attached. If the parties agree, other written evidence that the loan has been made will suffice.

INSTRUCTIONS FOR REVISING PDC CERTIFICATE
WHEN PDCs ARE REDEEMED

Complete the "Redemption" section of the PDC certificate	*Following these instructions:*
1. Owner (Person Redeeming) Name: Address: City/State/Zip: Signature:	Enter the name and address of the person who used the PDCs. The name must appear as it does on the front of the Certificate. The person must also sign in the appropriate space.
2. Municipality in Which Pinelands Development Credits Are Redeemed.	Enter the names of the municipality and county in which the development project is located.
3. Municipal Tax Block and Lot Number of Property for Which Pinelands Development Credits Were Redeemed.	Enter the block and lot number of the property to be developed. If there is more than one block or lot, enter "Attached" and attach a sheet listing them.
4. Number of Pinelands Development Credits Redeemed:	Enter the number (e.g., 2.00) of PDCs redeemed. Remember that some but not necessarily all of the PDCs shown on the front of the Certificate need be redeemed. In no case can the number redeemed be greater than the number shown on the front of the Certificate.
5. Municipal Development Approval Issued: ——————————————— Date	Enter the date on which the subdivision, site plan, or other approval was issued by the municipality.
6. Municipal Official Issuing Development Approval: Name: Title: Signature:	Enter the name and title of the official who issued the approval. If the approval was granted by a planning board or board of adjustment, the secretary to the board or its chairman is acceptable. The official must then sign the Certificate.

**STATE OF NEW JERSEY
PINELANDS DEVELOPMENT CREDIT BANK**

BOARD OF DIRECTORS

Chairman
Jeff Connor
Commissioner of Banking

Francis P. Carr
Chief Examiner, Financial Analysis
Alternate Member

Arthur R. Brown, Jr.
Secretary of Agriculture

Richard Chinery
Public Member

Samuel Garrison
Alternate Member

Robert J. Del Tufo
Attorney General

Ralph A. Sturdivant
Public Member

Gregory C. Schultz, Esq.
Alternate Member

Scott A. Weiner
Commissioner of
Environmental Protection
& Energy

Al Metzger
Public Member

James F. Hall
Alternate Member

Richard J. Sullivan
Chairman, NJ Pinelands
Commission

Ann E. Myles
Public Member

K. Brian McFadden
Alternate Member

John T. Ross
Acting Executive Director

Stephanie A. Wall
Administrative Assistant

John M. Van Dalen, DAG
Legal Counsel

Appendix C

The Land Coverage Program of the California Tahoe Conservancy

Source: Wrtten by John Gussman, Staff Counsel, and other staff members of the California Tahoe Conservancy.

The Land Coverage Program of the California Tahoe Conservancy

The California Tahoe Conservancy—Overview

The Tahoe Conservancy is a California state agency which was activated by the Governor and the Legislature in 1984 and which began operations in 1985. The Conservancy is implementing a number of programs involving land acquisitions and site development activities on the California side of the Lake Tahoe Basin. These programs are designed to:

- Protect the natural environment through acquisition of environmentally sensitive lands, in order to prevent further damage from development in inappropriate areas, and to facilitate the repair of disturbed areas through soil erosion control projects, watershed restoration projects, transfers of development rights, and mitigation projects

- Provide public access and recreational opportunities through the provision of new access and public recreational facilities, the expansion of existing facilities, and the connection of recreational facilities with trail systems

- Preserve wildlife through acquisition and site improvement projects designed to protect habitat for endangered, rare, threatened, sensitive, and special-interest species

- Provide for the management of acquired lands

These programs represent a comprehensive approach to dealing with resource protection and enhancement and public access needs in the Tahoe Basin.

To date, the Conservancy has authorized the expenditure, either directly or through grants, of over $116 million for the acquisition of over 4,700 parcels (involving over 6,000 acres) and the construction of over 150 site improvement projects.

The Land Coverage Bank—Introduction

The Tahoe Conservancy established a Land Coverage Bank program in November 1987, in response to the provisions for mitigation and transfer of ground coverage which were set forth in the 1987 Regional Plan of the Tahoe Regional Planning Agency (TRPA). The Conservancy formalized the program by entering into a Memorandum of Understanding with TRPA, which provided for a Land Coverage Bank and laid down the procedures for transfer of coverage rights through the bank and the assignment of developers' mitigation fees to the bank.

The land coverage program is designed to help landowners comply with regulatory permit requirements, while, at the same time, advancing the resource protection objectives of TRPA and of the State of California.

In recent years, California, like some other states, has enacted land use controls at the state level, for regions which, because of resource-related issues, are of statewide concern. Through these controls, the state is able to manage problems relating to land development and resource preservation which extend beyond the jurisdiction and capabilities of local government. Such controls have primarily been focused on areas with limited carrying capacities for development, such as Lake Tahoe. At Lake Tahoe, special controls have been initiated both under state law and pursuant to an interstate compact between California and Nevada.

In areas like Tahoe, a common method of assuring that carrying capacities are not exceeded is to require that new development be offset by removing or retiring equivalent development (or development potential) from another site in the affected area, embodying the principle of "mitigation." Most often, mitigation requirements can be fulfilled by paying a fee to the regulatory agency; however, there is still the question, for the agency, of how to put the funds to effective use. Some mitigation programs have sidestepped the issue by requiring the permit applicant to carry out the mitigation directly. The results in such cases, however, are often less than optimal, since many landowners find it too costly and time-consuming to carry out the mitigation in the manner desired by the regulatory agency.

In certain transfer of development programs in California, landowners have been able to acquire mitigation or development credits either on the open market or from a central repository. In one Coastal Commission program, landowners were able to purchase density transfer credits on the open market; meanwhile, a cooperating agency, the Coastal Conservancy, acted as a seller of last resort for those permit applicants who either preferred this channel or could not obtain credits elsewhere.

The Tahoe Conservancy's program represents a further evolution of these approaches. The Conservancy's Land Coverage Bank may be the first to bring together, under a single umbrella, (1) the function of acquiring and restoring land, which is then managed by the land banking entity, (2) the function of receiving and utilizing mitigation fees, and (3) the function of selling credits or rights on the open market. The program also is probably the first to carry out open-market sales of development credits or rights which are generated through the direct acquisition *and* restoration of targeted "sending parcels."

Combining all the above functions within a single program not only is efficient, but helps to assure that funds generated from mitigation or transfer requirements are targeted for the highest-priority use. Thus, the resource benefits which can be achieved through a bank are greatly enhanced. At the same time, the combination of functions increases the usability and convenience of the bank for project proponents.

Purposes of the Land Coverage Bank

The main purposes of the Land Coverage Bank are:

▶ To help improve development patterns on the California side of the Lake Tahoe Basin by retiring development potential on, and restoring where necessary, degraded lands and lands whose legally allowable uses do not meet current planning objectives; and by transferring the development rights to new projects which meet the objectives of planning agencies, resource management agencies, and landowners alike

▶ To support regional, state, and local planning objectives, by retiring obsolete or inappropriately located development potential, by restoring degraded lands, and by "banking" an inventory of development rights, for further allocation in a manner consistent with current planning and redevelopment efforts

▶ To facilitate the implementation of public and private projects, involving new construction or rehabilitation of existing structures, by providing a convenient means for project proponents to comply with ground coverage restrictions and other requirements of the TRPA—thus relieving the proponents of the need to acquire and restore lands on their own

Activities of the Land Coverage Bank include: 1) the generation of land coverage and other marketable rights, for use on eligible sites, through acquisition, restoration, and/or retirement of development potential on selected parcels of land; 2) the allocation of such rights for public and private uses and, within these categories, for mitigation of existing development and transfers or mitigation for new projects; and 3) the distribution of such rights within the overall allocations. These activities are discussed in greater detail below.

A. **Generation of Rights through Acquisition and Restoration.** The Conservancy's Land Coverage Bank provides a mechanism for acquiring and restoring lands on which it is a high priority to remove existing or potential ground coverage. By focusing acquisition and restoration activity on priority parcels, the Conservancy is able to maximize the resource benefits from regulation of coverage, while reducing the need for TRPA to "fine-tune" the parcel eligibility criteria by ordinance.

Coverage rights consist of the ability to place (or, if already in place, to maintain) impervious surfaces (e.g., buildings and parking lots) on the ground. The placement of coverage on any given parcel of land is strictly regulated in the Tahoe Basin. This is because the placement of coverage in inappropriate locations has been found to increase the sediment load, and with it the volume of nutrients, coming into Lake Tahoe. It does so by reducing the filtration of sediment and nutrients from runoff, while, at the same time, increasing the velocity of the runoff, thereby causing further soil erosion. This process is of critical concern at Lake Tahoe, because the transparency of lake water has declined by more than 30 feet during the past 20 years, due in large part to the erosion of soil into the lake and its tributaries.

Under the coverage bank program, the Conservancy identifies and acquires parcels with obsolete coverage or development potential, of high priority for retirement or restoration, in each of the six TRPA-defined hydrologic areas which make up the California side of the Tahoe Basin. For example, the Conservancy acquired an old restaurant facility, which had fallen into disuse, in order to remove structures from a wetland area. It has also acquired and restored other areas where there were building foundations, informal parking lots, and other disturbed areas which were likely sources of soil erosion. Often, the process of selecting, acquiring, and restoring land involves the participation of local governments.

Following acquisition, the Conservancy systematically retires the coverage rights on the acquired parcels. First, existing impervious coverage—including structures, asphalt, etc.—is removed. Then, the land is revegetated, and erosion control improvements are installed, where necessary. Areas which have no existing coverage, but which contain potential coverage rights, are permanently restricted against further development. The timetable for restoration is independent of actual sales of coverage rights. This helps to ensure that the benefits to the watershed and the lake are realized as quickly as possible under the program.

Incidental to its acquisitions of land under this program, the Conservancy has also acquired other types of transferable development rights recognized by regulatory agencies at Lake Tahoe, including commercial floor area rights (20,627 square feet), tourist accommodation units (19 units), and commercial or residential sewer units (34). All such rights are considered assets of the Land Coverage Bank.

B. Allocation of Coverage and other Marketable Rights. The next step in the process involves the allocation of the acquired rights between public and private projects. The allocation process recognizes that both public and private projects in the Tahoe Basin must meet various coverage and other requirements, in conditions where coverage and other rights are often scarce, and where project proponents do not necessarily have the ability to satisfy the requirements on their own.

In order to ascertain the various needs within these categories, the Conservancy conducts surveys of local governments, and of other public agencies and private sector entities (e.g., Board of Realtors) to determine the levels and types of near- and long-term needs.

Based on the survey results, the Conservancy allocates its available supply of coverage between the public and private sectors, for various purposes. These include: mitigation of existing excess coverage (to permit the rehabilitation of older structures which exceed current coverage limits); mitigation for public projects on sensitive lands; transfers of coverage for new public projects; reservations of coverage to help meet future local planning objectives; and open-market sales of coverage and other rights.

C. Distribution of Rights. The Conservancy's program utilizes a number of mechanisms to distribute the rights. In all cases, however, the Land Coverage Bank provides a convenient means for project proponents to meet coverage and other requirements because it relieves them of the need to restore, and perhaps to acquire, other land—a costly and time-consuming process for an individual landowner. That is, the program provides "one stop" shopping for parties who need to meet coverage requirements.

Both public and private landowners seeking new permits may be required to mitigate any existing excess coverage on their parcels, either by retiring coverage elsewhere in the same hydrologically-related area, or by paying a mitigation fee based on the amount of excess coverage and the dollar value of the project. In most cases, landowners choose to pay the fee. These fees pass to the Land Coverage Bank by agreement with TRPA and are appropriated to the Conservancy as part of the normal state budgetary process.

Landowners who wish to increase the coverage allowance on their properties may do so through transfers of coverage. This means procuring coverage rights by retiring coverage elsewhere within the same watershed or hydrologically-related area. Such rights can be purchased by private landowners from the Conservancy through auction or other public sale process. In the case of public projects, the agencies concerned may contract directly with the Conservancy for transfer of coverage or purchase of mitigation credits, with payment in cash or in the form of other consideration. The above allocation procedures help to ensure that the coverage is made available to a wide group of participants. Sales of coverage will be held periodically throughout the life of the coverage program.

Summary of Program Accomplishments to Date

To date, under its land coverage program, the Conservancy has authorized the expenditure, either directly or through grants, of $3.2 million for the acquisition of 90 parcels of land, including a total of 970,402 square feet of coverage. The restoration of acquired lands began in 1989. To date, over 80,000 square feet of land has been restored to meet current needs and expected demand under the coverage program.

The Conservancy has allocated a total of 503,120 square feet of coverage and other credits for public service and private projects. Among public projects, coverage has been allocated for excess coverage mitigation purposes (for existing facilities proposed for modification) and for coverage, transfers, and mitigation credits for new public service facilities. Providing this coverage has helped to facilitate public transportation and utility projects, a new jail facility in South Lake Tahoe, and waste recycling improvements for a refuse facility. Among private projects, coverage has been allocated for excess coverage mitigation for commercial and residential rehabilitation projects, as well as coverage transfers through open-market sales.

In the area of other marketable rights, three sewer units have been allocated for a public conference/meeting facility, 21 units have been allocated for open-market sales, and ten units remain unallocated. As a matter of policy, the Conservancy's inventory of commercial floor area (20,627 square feet) and tourist accommodation units (19 units) have been reserved for allocation in a manner consistent with ongoing community planning processes.

Through December 1992, mitigation fees had been collected under this program for over 1,400 projects with existing excess coverage; these fees totaled approximately $910,000. Additional funds (and in-kind consideration) have been received from sales of coverage and from mitigation credits provided to public service projects.

The Conservancy began open-market sales of coverage for private sector projects in March 1990. Sales have been carried out in all of the six hydrologic areas which make up the California side of the Lake Tahoe Basin. A total of 27,458 square feet of coverage rights have been sold. Coverage has been transferred to 93 different projects. Over 1,800 square feet of commercial floor area rights and nine sewer units have also been sold to help implement commercial and residential projects.

In total, over $1.2 million has already been generated for reinvestment in this program. Over the long term the Land Coverage Bank is expected to operate as a revolving fund.

For more information, contact:

Dennis T. Machida, Executive Officer
California Tahoe Conservancy
P.O. Box 7758
South Lake Tahoe, CA 96158
Telephone: (916) 542-5580

August 1993

Appendix D

Cambria/Lodge Hill
Restoration Program

Source: Ray Belknap, Executive Director, and Patricia L. Wirth, Property Manager of the Land Conservancy of San Luis Obispo County.

Cambria/Lodge Hill Restoration Program
Program Review and Status Report

Introduction

In 1986, San Luis Obispo County authorized a Transfer of Development Credit (TDC) program within the community of Cambria that allows the development potential from one lot, measured in square feet of gross structural area, to be transferred to another lot. This is called the Transfer of Development Credit program and is described in the county's Local Coastal Program (LCP).

The purpose of the TDC program is to protect two hillsides in the Lodge Hill portion of Cambria that contain very small lots in areas of sensitive environmental resources. One hillside contains native Monterey pines. The second hillside is located in a scenic area that is visible from Highway 1 as you enter Cambria from the south. The program permits the Land Conservancy of San Luis Obispo County to acquire these lots, obtain a certificate of development credits (measured in square feet of gross structural area), and then sell these credits to other lots within the area that are more desirable, areas without steep slopes or heavy tree coverage. The lots are protected from future development by placing a conservation easement on the property.

Summary

The Land Conservancy has been able to achieve the goals of protecting sensitive resources by retiring lots in the antiquated subdivision located on Lodge Hill. This has been done on a voluntary willing-seller, willing-buyer basis. Funds generated by selling development credits continue to be generated and are used to buy and retire lots on a regular basis.

During a five-year period, the Land Conservancy has purchased more than 75 lots, sold over 21,000 square feet of development credits, and managed a $275,000 revolving fund from the Coastal Conservancy. During this time, we've shown an increase in the value of the fund and demonstrated managing a TDC program according to sound business practices.

The Land Conservancy, the county, and the Coastal Conservancy have developed a business-like working relationship, and we have functioned well as a team. The program has matured and developed during the past five years, sometimes by trial and error, into a program that could never have been achieved by any one party alone.

Background

The initial idea of retiring one lot in Lodge Hill as a prerequisite to building on a second lot began because of Coastal Commission permits being approved between 1984-1986, before the Coastal Commission certified the county's Local Coastal Program. The Coastal Commission would require an applicant for a single-family home to purchase and retire a second lot in the steep and wooded hillside area before approving a coastal development permit for a house on the first lot.

The county later incorporated this practice into its Local Coastal Program. The county's LCP was adopted in several parts by the Board of Supervisors between 1980-1988 and was completely certified by the Coastal Commission in 1988. This certified Local Coastal Program authorized the county to assume the permit authority within the coastal zone of Cambria. The Local Coastal Program is the document that created the Transferable Development Credit program, and spells out the procedures by which credits are bought and sold.

The Local Coastal Plan identified two areas where the county desired to reduce the number of buildable lots. They are called Special Project Areas (SPAs) in the Plan. SPA #1 is a canyon filled with Monterey pines, sometimes called Fern Canyon. SPA #2 is the scenic hillside which is visible from Highway 1. The Local Coastal Program also established the procedures that allow the Land Conservancy to purchase lots in these areas and transfer (sell) the development potential to other lots within Lodge Hill.

Summary of County Ordinances

The San Luis Obispo County Local Coastal Program can be divided into several parts: a land use plan, a package of ordinances, and other supporting information such as maps and technical implementation procedures. The TDC program is described in the land use plan document as well as in the ordinances.

> The land use plan portion of the LCP is also divided into several parts. Part One is the Framework for Planning, which contains information about the county, land use categories, and allowable uses, as well as defining other important ideas used throughout the Local Coastal Program. Part Two, the Land Use Element and Coastal Plan, establishes general policies for the entire coastal zone of the county as well as implementation programs and development standards for each of four smaller planning areas within the county (Cambria is within the North Coast Planning Area).

> Part Three is the Coastal Zone Land Use Ordinance, containing the regulations that implement the policies of the Land Use Element. Lodge Hill falls completely within the Monterey Pine Forest Sensitive Resource Area and is part of the Land Use Element and Coastal Plan policies which set the basic parameters on who can buy TDCs and how TDCs can be used. Additional detail is included within the Planning Area Standards as well as within the Land Use Ordinance.

> The North Coast Land Use Element and Coastal Plan also includes standards on setbacks, square feet of allowable building size, height restrictions, and other similar, very specific subjects. These sections of the Planning Area document do not explicitly reference TDCs, but they do set the minimum standards that may then be exceeded with the purchase of TDCs. If, for example, you wish to build a house of 1,000 square feet in gross structural area, you would consult these standards to determine how large a house you would normally be permitted (900 square feet) and how many TDCs you would be required to purchase (100 square feet) to complete the house.

> It is also within this section of the North Coast Planning Area document that the areas from which development credits may be transferred are defined.

> The Land Use Ordinance section of the Local Coastal Program gives final details on where TDCs can be used, the findings necessary to approve a Minor Use Permit, eligible purchasers, and the requirement for participation by a non-profit corporation, such as the Land Conservancy.

Summary of Coastal Conservancy Grant

In 1986, the California Coastal Conservancy entered into a contract with the Land Conservancy of San Luis Obispo County that funded implementation of the TDC program in SPA #1, Fern Canyon. The Coastal Conservancy approved a revolving fund of $275,000 to be used by the Land Conservancy for a period of ten years. When the ten years have passed, funds remaining will be returned to the Coastal Conservancy.

The funds are provided to the Land Conservancy through escrow as individual lots are acquired. After the lots are acquired and development credits are sold, the money generated from the sale is deposited in a separate checking/savings account managed by the Land Conservancy. The Land Conservancy uses any surplus in this account to purchase additional lots. The Land Conservancy is paid a 5% commission on each sale of TDCs as well as on each lot purchased and retired.

The Land Conservancy operated for many years without drawing heavily on the original grant, due to a large number of TDC sales in the early years of the program. Currently, there is less than $27,000 remaining in the original grant.

Purchased lots are retired from development by recording a conservation easement on the property, in a format developed by the Coastal Conservancy which also contains a continuing offer of dedication to the Coastal Conservancy. Each lot purchased by the Land Conservancy must be approved by the Coastal Conservancy, only after a property appraisal is completed and approved.

One important contractual requirement has been the completion of an annual audit of the revolving fund. This has helped maintain oversight and confidence between the California Coastal Conservancy and the Land Conservancy.

Current Status of the Program

The Land Conservancy has purchased more than seventy-five lots in the past four years, which amounts to a little more than 4.7 acres. Although not a very large area in and of itself, its acquisition has made a significant dent in the priority #1 area. The average size of the lots acquired is 2,800 sq.ft., with a single lot costing about $6,000, which is about $150,000 an acre.

There have been over 120 individual sales of TDCs involving approximately 21,000 sq.ft., for an average sale of about 175 sq.ft. These sales have been for new residences as well as for remodeled older residences.

Policies and Regulations Related to Purchasing Lots

In the future we may work with the Coastal Conservancy to allow us to purchase lots in Special Project Area #2, as well as in other special areas in Cambria which may warrant protection. However, our current policies involve only Special Project Area #1.

A. Price of Lot Acquisition

In Lodge Hill the Conservancy is currently the only buyer of property that is purchased solely for the purpose of transferring development credits. We are, as a result (generally because of the slow real estate market, particularly for lots without water meters), creating our own comparable sales for the purpose of appraising land value. The Land Conservancy has established a policy on land acquisition which is tied to the price of TDCs. This helps to balance the competing interests of offering a good price for lots and a reasonable price for TDCs.

Our policy is to offer a fair price for lots with the final price based on the traditional process of negotiation, offer, and counter-offer. It is therefore important that we offer an equitable purchase price for the lot which will satisfy the seller and still allow the Land Conservancy to sell the resulting TDCs at a low enough price to encourage their use, but not so low so that we do not make a profit to use for the purchase of another lot.

B. Escrow and Tax Procedures

To purchase lots, the Land Conservancy uses the traditional process of escrow, including a title search and title insurance. We rely on the same process any home buyer uses to acquire property (*See* Attachment A).

After a lot is acquired, we apply for tax exemption according to local and state procedures. Although it is much more cumbersome and time-consuming than we had anticipated, this has become a matter of routine. It involves applying for a welfare tax exemption on the supplemental tax bill that accompanies a transfer in property as well as applying for an exemption for each lot every year. We have found that we also need to request exemption from local standby water and sewer fees.

Although the welfare exemptions lower the Land Conservancy's yearly property taxes, the program also has an interesting tax benefit that has helped generate community support. Often, when a property is taken off the tax role, the total income to the county is reduced. Our ability to transfer development from the retired lot to the receiving lot maintains this value. The county receives an increment of property tax from the receiving property because the transfer permitted a larger home to be constructed.

C. Conservation Easements and Long-Term Ownership of Lots

Currently, as each lot is purchased, an easement is recorded on the property and granted to the Coastal Conservancy. This easement prohibits grading, paving, structures, or removal of non-native plants or trees, with a few exceptions such as the need to remove weeds for fire protection.

D. Long-Term Ownership of "Preservation" Lots

Since the very beginning, the program has anticipated that the long-term protection of lots with important or sensitive natural resources should be achieved through public ownership. The role of the Land Conservancy is that of a facilitator in transactions of development credits. It is not an appropriate agency for the long-term ownership of the small lots this program generates.

The issue of long-term ownership has been held in the background for several years pending the creation of a special district for park or forest management. There are a number of reasons unrelated to the TDC program to form a forest management district, which has been discussed within Cambria for several years and is currently being discussed again. If it does come into existence, this district would provide a suitable long-term owner.

Pending the creation of a special district, the Coastal Conservancy has continued to support our ownership of the lots, but this is an important issue that needs resolution.

E. Long-Term Ownership of Low Priority Lots—A Lot "Consolidation" Program

The previous paragraphs describe our policy for the important parcels that fall on the steep hillsides that contain Monterey Pine or occur in the scenic area along Highway 1. The Land Conservancy has acquired other lots (often as the result of a contribution) that are not of such high environmental importance. Even at the edge of priority areas #1 and #2 we have found lots eligible for the transfer of development credits that are level, absent the Monterey pine, and adjacent to existing homes.

We also accept lots outside both priority areas, as a service to the community to reduce the potential build-out of Cambria and as a way of preserving open space, no matter how small. Our policy on accepting lots outside of the priority areas is discussed in greater detail below. However, our policy on the long-term disposition of these lots is different from lots in the high-priority areas. We believe that many of these lots could be resold to the adjoining owner for private open space or, where suitable, could be combined into a larger building site.

In an effort to retire additional lots throughout Lodge Hill, the Land Conservancy has undertaken and funded its own programs outside the TDC program by matching owners of homes with the owners of adjacent open space lots. While this has had only limited success, it demonstrates another vehicle for long-term ownership of existing small open space lots.

F. County Certification of TDCs

After a lot is acquired and a conservation easement is recorded, the Land Conservancy requests a certification on the number of square feet (development credits) that can be transferred off that individual piece of property. This is the first time the county becomes directly involved in the day-to-day administration of the TDC program.

The Land Conservancy fills out the certification form and sends it to the county where the planning department reviews the calculations, and returns a signed copy. The county does this by confirming the characteristics of the site and consulting the building standards of the Local Coastal Program North Coast Planning Area. Only after this form is received by the Land Conservancy can TDCs be sold from the lot.

Application for Use of TDCs

This section of the report describes the procedures and issues related to the purchase of TDCs from the Land Conservancy by a person wishing to build a larger house.

A. Application Form and Procedures

The Land Conservancy publishes a brief brochure for real estate brokers, architects, and residents of Cambria (*See* Attachment B). This brochure is our primary way of describing the program to the public.

The formal process of acquiring TDCs begins when we receive a completed application (*See* Attachment C). The form asks basic information such as name, address, and technical information on the size of house planned as well as the number of TDCs required. The number required is determined by the county as a result of its action on the permit. The number of TDCs requested on the application to the Land Conservancy is the number the county anticipates will be used.

The most important information is the Assessor's Parcel Number for the site, since this is the primary means we use to track the use of development credits.

The Land Conservancy does not monitor or enforce the location where TDCs are used. The county does this through its approval of each individual permit. However, the Land Conservancy does have a special interest in this area. The definition of this area limits the potential market for TDCs and, as a result, the pace by which new lots can be acquired and retired.

B. Reservation of TDCs

At the time it begins to process an application for a Minor Use Permit using TDCs, the county needs to be assured that the number of TDCs necessary for the project are available. County policy on how this is done has changed several times over the years. At one point, the county required all of the TDCs to be purchased in advance. This created problems for both the county and the Land Conservancy that are discussed under "Refund Policy" below. There was also a period when no formal assurance was required due to the close working relationship that existed between the county and the Land Conservancy and the large number of TDCs available. When the program began, it was necessary to make sure TDCs were available for each individual project.

The final policy that has emerged allows an applicant to "reserve" TDCs prior to beginning permit review with the county. This has many benefits. It assures the county that TDCs have been set aside for a particular project from a particular lot, which means that the applicant is not paying for TDCs that may not be used. And, it is easier for the Land Conservancy because accounting and financial headaches associated with refunds are avoided.

This policy is authorized by the county ordinance which specifies that only a "Preliminary Agreement" must be obtained from an authorized non-profit corporation having TDCs for sale. This is required before the application for a Minor Use Permit is considered complete.

If the applicant comes to the office, the time required to reserve TDCs can be less than an hour. Normally, we receive an application in the mail and return the letter of financial agreement the same day. When we receive a signed copy of the financial agreement, we send the original of the "Preliminary Agreement" by return mail (*See* Attachment D). The applicant then presents the Preliminary Agreement letter to the county.

C. Deposit Policy

The current policy is to reserve TDCs for applicants based on the number of applicants and the TDCs available. We also enter into a written financial agreement (*See* Attachment E) with the applicant that allows for the amount of the deposit to be increased at the six-month anniversary and at each yearly anniversary. The Land Conservancy also maintains the right to refund the deposit (less 5%) after one year if there is no activity on the permit.

TDCs have been reserved during recent months on the basis of "no money down" for the first six months, a 50% deposit after the first six months, and the option of increasing this to 100% or offering a refund at each anniversary.

This policy has been well received by applicants because it allows them to begin the permit process at the county level without additional expense. The six-month cut-off for the 50% deposit was chosen because this is often the amount of time necessary to obtain permits. We work with each applicant on an individual basis and can extend the date for the six-month deposit based on the progress they are making with the county.

D. County Processing of TDC Applications

After the applicant has received a letter from the Land Conservancy (the "Preliminary Agreement" discussed above) stating that TDCs have been reserved for the applicant, the county begins a review of the application.

The permit that must be approved is a Minor Use Permit. The Minor Use Permit is used throughout Lodge Hill on hillsides over 25% because of the presence of the Monterey Pine and the difficult site conditions that exist for all the small lots. With the use of TDCs, a Minor Use Permit is particularly important because a public hearing is required before approval. This hearing allows the county the opportunity to notify neighbors that TDCs are going to be used and that the house will be larger than otherwise permitted, which is a useful way of dealing with the community on potential effects of TDCs in the "receiving" area.

The number of TDCs an individual applicant can use is limited, with a ceiling on how large a house can become using transferred development credits. The particular system used by the county in Cambria is based on two factors, the amount of land covered by the house (the "footprint") and the total size of the house ("gross structural area"). An applicant is allowed to increase the footprint to a maximum of 45% of the lot area and the gross structural area to 90% of the lot area. The baseline, or maximum size of house permitted without the use of TDCs, is determined by the Area Plan Development Standards. An applicant cannot, however, assume that his or her individual house can be increased to these maximum amounts. The Local Coastal Program also contains a number of additional standards that must be met. The purchase of TDCs, for example, does not waive height and setback restrictions. The average amount of footprint and gross structural area by which most houses have been allowed to increase through the use of TDCs is far less than the maximum allowed. On houses that have purchased TDCs to increase the gross structural area, our experience has been that the houses average about 55% of the lot size (while the limit is 90%); and that the footprints for houses using TDCs have only been about 31% of the lot area (while the limit is 45%).

Another statistic of interest to the county is that, on the average, houses that purchase TDCs to increase the total gross structural area increase the size of the house by 20%. The footprints of houses using TDCs, on the average, increase by 14% through the use of TDCs.

The size to which a house may grow as a result of a TDC purchase is a substantial long-term concern. The impact on the receiving area should not outweigh the benefits to the sending area.

The Land Conservancy does not participate in the hearings or review of any building permit or Minor Use Permit. We maintain a strict policy of separation. This has been important for gaining acceptance of the Land Conservancy in the implementation of this program. Our role is to help implement a policy established by the county, and we do not act independently to affect the county's action on individual projects.

E. Final Sale and Refund Policy

After obtaining approval for a Minor Use Permit, the applicant writes a check for the full amount of the TDCs (or remaining balance), and we issue a "Final Letter of Sale" (See Attachment F). The applicant presents this to the county as a demonstration of permit compliance, and the county releases the building permit when this and all other permit conditions have been met.

Assuming no refund is needed, this process works well. For several years the Land Conservancy maintained a refund policy which provided a 95% refund if the applicant, for any reason, decided not to proceed with the project. This created problems for both the Land Conservancy and the county.

The problem for the Land Conservancy is that we do not maintain a large cash balance in the checking account. When funds are available, we purchase lots, which is the primary mission of the program.

The problem for the county is the time required to review the files to mark every copy of every document "void" because the TDCs used as the basis for project approval were no longer valid.

We currently do not offer any refund and have made several changes in other parts of our procedures to make this an easier policy to support. We reserve TDCs until the applicant's permit is approved, and we only require the applicant to purchase the exact number of TDCs the permit requires. We also indicate in our correspondence to the applicant that the TDCs should be capitalized into the value of the building just as an architect's plan is capitalized and the costs of permits are capitalized. And, just as building plans can be sold with the associated permits, so TDCs may be transferred as a capital asset to the new owner.

F. Price of TDCs

The funds raised from the sale of TDCs under the Coastal Conservancy grant are used to acquire and retire additional lots. This is also the objective of the county.

The price of TDCs has therefore been set to cover the administrative and property holding costs associated with the program, but it also includes raising funds for the retirement of additional lots. The pricing policy is also designed to keep the price of TDCs within reach of the home builder. As with the marketing of any product, there is a fine line between raising funds and pricing yourself out of the market.

For the sake of simplicity as well as to relate the price of TDCs directly to the cost of land, the Conservancy established a policy of 100% markup based on the average cost of acquiring TDCs during the previous year (depending on the pace of activity). Administrative costs and holding costs reduce the net markup.

The average (wholesale) cost of TDCs to the Land Conservancy has been about $10/sq.ft. In areas where we felt it was very critical to obtain a particular lot, the cost of some TDCs has been more than $20/sq.ft. The high prices paid for selected lots is balanced against other lots that are contributed or cost much less, which results in an average acquisition cost of about $10/sq.ft.

Based on our policy of a 100% markup, the current (retail) price for TDCs results in the current price of $20/sq.ft. We have recently adjusted the price downward by eliminating the sliding scale that raised the price to $25/sq.ft. for smaller purchases (under 100 sq.ft.).

G. Trades for TDCs

Because the Conservancy has been approached by individuals who may own a lot in the priority area and wish to trade this property for TDCs, a new policy has recently been adopted. The Land Conservancy will accept property at its appraised value (as approved by the Coastal Conservancy) toward the full purchase price of TDCs, and a property owner may not trade property for more TDCs than is necessary for a particular project.

H. Demand for TDCs

For the last two years the demand for TDCs has averaged about 6,000 sq.ft. per year. These are TDCs actually sold. Including the amount now committed, the average is about 6,700 sq.ft. per year. This is down from the projection two years ago of 7,500 sq.ft. Because of restrictions on new water meters and the advent of growth control within the county, we expect the demand to decrease. Most of the TDC sales we now see are for remodeling, and we anticipate more of this as small cottages are bought and converted into larger homes simply because they have a water meter.

The demand for TDCs is strictly limited by the area the county authorized for the use of TDCs. The county established the receiving area of Lodge Hill, because this area contains smaller lots (associated with the underlying antiquated subdivision), it is largely committed to urbanization, and the area contains no large areas of sensitive natural resources. And the county had a worthy public purpose in limiting the maximum size of the houses that could be built on these small lots. Elsewhere in Cambria and throughout the county there is generally no upper limit to the size of a house, and therefore no need to acquire TDCs.

There are only two readily apparent means of expanding the market in the near future. The first would be to request the use of TDCs when approving new discretionary projects within Cambria, and the second would be to examine other neighborhoods within Cambria to see if the houses now being constructed without a maximum size limit warrant treatment similar to Lodge Hill. These neighborhoods could include Park Hill and Happy Hill, both areas with a predominance of small lots and sensitive resources. However, no change in the Local Coastal Program should be made without community support and a study of the effect unrestricted development is having on these neighborhoods. For the foreseeable future, the market for TDCs within Lodge Hill will remain constant although slow.

I. Accounting of TDCs

The Land Conservancy maintains the available supply of TDCs, records of purchases, and the specific lots to which they were applied. We currently maintain all financial records for TDC transactions through a computerized accounting program.

Administrative and Long-Term Planning Considerations

A. Transaction Ledgers

Our contract requires notifying the Coastal Conservancy of all financial transactions related to the revolving fund on a monthly basis. Reports submitted during the early years required a separate set of hand-maintained ledgers, which was extremely time-consuming but did not describe the transactions in a simple, clear format. We have recently developed an alternative format listing transactions together with the fund balance less liabilities for refunds and deposits, which has been submitted to the Conservancy and found acceptable. This format is also very helpful to the Land Conservancy Board of Trustees.

B. Impact of TDCs on Receiving Areas

A few residents have expressed concern about the size of houses permitted by the TDC program. Reflected in public comments made during hearings on the LCP revision, the impact of development on a receiving areas is always a concern in any program to transfer development credits.

The size of a new (or remodeled) house that can be constructed is regulated by public policy according to a formula based on the size of the property. The county ordinance contains a table which indicates the house size allowable in accordance with the topography and the size of the lot, with an inherent assumption that a larger lot can absorb a larger house. Through the purchase of TDCs, the house can be larger as long as it remains within overall setback and height constraints. This program has worked well.

The Land Conservancy has recently completed an evaluation of each lot that has used TDCs. We took photographs of each house, evaluated their relative size within the context of the surrounding community, and compared this to the underlying lot size and the square feet of development rights purchased.

As a result of this evaluation, out of more than 110 purchases of TDCs, eight houses looked "large." When we calculated the amount of square feet purchased (as represented by TDCs) and compared this to the size of the house (both in gross structural area and footprint), we could not find a specific reason why the houses appeared to be large. These houses occurred on a variety of lot sizes ranging from 1,750 sq.ft to more than 4,000 sq.ft. The increase in gross structural area averaged only 54% of the total lot size which is lower than the average for all TDC sales. And the increase in footprint for these houses averaged 33% of the total lot size or only slightly larger than the 31% average for all TDC sales.

We can only conclude that the houses looked large for the community due to the specific location of the house on the lot, its orientation to the street (where pictures were taken), and the design of the individual house. The standards established in the ordinance for using TDCs do not appear to be responsible for the "large" houses.

This issue should continue to be monitored, but the original guidelines contained in the Local Coastal Program appear to be working well.

Appendix D *(Attachment A)*

Buying Lots—Selling TDCs—Protecting Open Space

Buying the Lot

The Land Conservancy of San Luis Obispo County has been in the business of buying lots and selling TDCs since 1986. The general information on the background of the TDC program, its authorization in county ordinances, and initial funding of a revolving fund have been described in the body of this book. The following is limited to a detailed description of how lots are acquired and TDCs are sold.

When the original Lodge Hill Restoration Program was implemented, the Land Conservancy was authorized by the State Coastal Conservancy revolving fund to purchase lots in an area designated as Special Projects Area #1 (small, steep lots, with many Monterey pines). Although there is a second area, Special Projects Area #2, visible from Highway 1, we are still only purchasing lots in Special Projects Area #1.

As a result of California's prolonged drought, development has been slow in Cambria until this previous winter and spring, and the Land Conservancy remains one of the few buyers of any lots in Cambria. Most of our property is obtained through a purchase. However, we are periodically approached by landowners who want to donate their property, and we work together to complete a transaction which may provide an income tax benefit for them.

When approached by a seller, we ask for the assessor's parcel number, the street location, and, when possible, whether the seller has a predetermined price. With this information we can consult our map to determine if the lot is in Area #1. If the parcel is located outside our designated area, we convey our regrets to the property owner and explain our procedures for buying the lot, placing a conservation easement on the property, and selling its transferable development credits.

However, if the lot is one located in Area #1 that we feel should be protected, we contact the seller (or the realtor, as is often the case) and let it be known that we are interested. If the seller agrees to work with us, we immediately order an appraisal of the property, a requirement which is part of our contract with the California State Coastal Conservancy. We also explain that our contract prohibits us from paying more than its appraised value.

Once we have an appraisal, actual negotiations begin. Our property manager, executive director, and a member of the board of trustees who lives in Cambria usually meet to discuss the merits of the lot and what our initial offer will be. With a figure in mind, we send an offer to the seller (or realtor) stating that we would like to purchase the lot, the amount of our initial offer, and that all transactions will need to be approved by our Board of Trustees and the Coastal Conservancy.

It has been a very important part of our TDC program that lots are purchased on the open market through voluntary negotiations. If our original offer is rejected, we then begin negotiations toward an agreed-upon price. Occasionally, we simply cannot reach an agreement with the owner. Once we have agreed on a price, however, we then send a formal sales contract which states the terms of the purchase (splitting the fees, with the seller responsible for paying special escrow costs and paying off any existing bonds or liens). Once we have the signed sales contract, we open escrow. Escrow documents are prepared and sent for signature by the seller and the Executive Director of the Land Conservancy. As with any home or property purchase, we require a title search and title insurance. Most of our escrows require very little time to complete.

While the lot is in escrow, we prepare a resolution for signature by the president of the Board of Trustees. The resolution, referring to our efforts to preserve open space in Lodge Hill and to retire development credits in that area, simply states that the Land Conservancy wishes to purchase the lot. During escrow procedures, we also prepare a Conservation Easement stating that the property will not be used for any development and will remain as perpetual open space. The Land Conservancy retains ownership of the property, but assigns the Conservation Easement to the California State Coastal Conservancy. The easement is signed by the Executive Director and one of our trustees, who also serves as our real estate advisor.

When all the paperwork is completed and escrow is ready to close, we provide the signed and notarized Conservation Easement, to be recorded at closing, as well as a cashier's check for the purchase price. Title to the lot is held in the name of the Land Conservancy of San Luis Obispo County. We usually receive the recorded Conservation Easement and Deed within about two weeks.

Once notified that a lot has changed hands, the county Appraiser's office immediately prepares a reappraisal of the property under Proposition 13 guidelines. Before the reappraisal occurs, we receive a Notice of Supplemental Assessment, which is not *yet* a tax bill but a notice that one will be forthcoming. Upon receipt of this notice, we immediately file for a welfare exemption. This involves several forms and documents provided by the county, as well as a copy of our Internal Revenue Exemption Letter, copies of any amendments to our Articles of Incorporation, and a current year income statement. Usually granted by both the county and the State of California, the welfare exemptions considerably lower our annual property taxes.

As part of our ongoing tax liability, each year between March 1st and 15th we refile for welfare exemptions for *all* our property. It is a major undertaking, but we are required to refile on a yearly basis.

Requesting TDCs

Once the signed deed is received, we prepare a form which requests certification of the number of Transfer Development Credits available on the newly purchased property. Each lot has a certain amount of TDCs available based on the size of the lot (single, double, or triple) and whether or not the lot is considered very steep. Very steep lots are usually assigned a fewer number of TDCs. If the lot dimensions are very irregular, the number of TDCs may vary. Using county guidelines, we complete a form requesting certification of the TDCs and send it on to the planning department.

The planning department will check our computations and return the signed form, specifying the number of TDCs we now have available to sell. These new TDCs are entered into our Lodge Hill bookkeeping system for future sale.

Selling TDCs

The Land Conservancy is the only organization currently authorized to "make a market" in TDCs, so, if a builder is planning a home which will be larger than the size currently authorized by county building standards, he or she will be sent to the Land Conservancy to buy the extra square footage needed. When initiating the Minor Use Permit process, a builder is usually advised if additional footage is needed for the project, either for gross structural area (the part of the building that is off the foundation) or for the footprint (the actual part that sits on the ground). TDCs may be required for a new building project or for a modification or enlargement of an existing house.

To begin the process of buying TDCs, a builder will be required to fill out an application form listing the appropriate assessor parcel number, street address, size of parcel in square feet, and a brief legal description. We also require information on the size of the home being planned, the maximum size allowed by the planning department, and the amount of gross structural area or footprint required. The builder only buys the amount needed. We then prepare a preliminary letter, indicating that the builder has the required number of TDCs reserved. The letter states where the TDCs will be used, as well as from which Land Conservancy lot the TDCs have been taken. The builder will also sign a contract of sale, again stating where the TDCs are going, where they are from, and the total number of TDCs reserved and their cost. To help ease the cost of obtaining all the required permits, we currently do not require any payment until six months have elapsed. These letters are then presented to the planning department for reference during the permit process.

The final building permit will not be issued until the sale is completed, so shortly before that stage the builder usually pays us for the TDCs. We then issue a letter stating that the TDCs have been paid for in full, and that the presentation of this letter to the planning department will allow the builder to pick up the building permit and begin the project.

The Land Conservancy deposits the check in the appropriate account to begin the process of using the proceeds to buy yet another lot. One of the nicer aspects of our Lodge Hill Restoration Program is that we color code our lots on a large map of the Cambria Lodge Hill area, so that, when a TDC purchaser comes to the office, we can actually point out the lot which is being protected.

Appendix D *(Attachment B)*

CAMBRIA/LODGE HILL TDC PROGRAM

HOW TO PURCHASE AND USE TRANSFERABLE DEVELOPMENT CREDITS FROM THE LAND CONSERVANCY OF SAN LUIS OBISPO COUNTY

This brochure was prepared by the Land Conservancy of San Luis Obispo County to help the general public, especially landowners, builders, architects, and others, who are interested in our Transferable Development Credits (TDC) program in the Lodge Hill neighborhood in Cambria.

The Transfer Development Credit (TDC) program, unique to Cambria and managed by the Land Conservancy of San Luis Obispo County, began in November, 1986, as an outgrowth of the San Luis Obispo Local Coastal Program (LCP) which was adopted in 1984.

The purpose of the program is to protect environmentally sensitive open areas in Cambria, specifically, the Lodge Hill area. Existing lots in this area are very narrow, usually 25' wide, many are quite steep, and all contain Cambria Pines; one of only five natural stands or Monterey Pines found in California.

Under the county's Local Coastal Program, the owner (of one of those lots) is authorized to build a certain size structure on the property, based on the total gross structural area allowed by county building codes. The Land Conservancy buys lots in environmentally sensitive areas in the Lodge Hill area of Cambria and then sells (transfers) the development potential, measured in square feet, from these lots to landowners, builders, and architects who purchase the area square footage to complete their building plans at other locations within Lodge Hill. This development potential is called a "transferable development credit" or TDC. The environmentally sensitive lots are then maintained in perpetual open space through legally recorded conservation and scenic easements.

WHAT ARE TDCS AND HOW CAN I MAKE USE OF THEM?

Transferable Development Credits are measured in square feet of either "Gross Structural Area" or "Footprint Area", as defined in the county's Local Coastal Plan. Gross structural area refers to the total overall square footage area of a proposed new or enlarged home, including a garage or carport. This does not include open exterior decks or certain interior lofts.

Footprint area refers to the actual area of the lot covered by the structure, excluding decks, balconies, or eaves. If your proposed home would exceed either of the limits as set forth in the LCP for your type of lot, you will need to buy additional TDCs.

NOTE: If you exceed both limits, you need only to buy the type of TDCs which you exceed the most. For example, if your new home exceeds the GSA by 100 square feet and also exceeds the footprint limit by 200 square feet, you would need to purchase 200 square feet of TDCs from us.

TDCs are sold on a first-come, first-serve basis. The Land Conservancy can not however, guarantee the county will approve the use of TDCs on any particular lot. The county determines where and how many TDCs can be used on an individual project through their approval of a Minor Use Permit. Once you have this permit, we call complete the transaction within two-three days.

HOW TO PURCHASE TDCS

1. Step One. Complete an Application Form to Purchase TDCs, available from the Land Conservancy office. The application requires the following information:

- Name, address, and daytime telephone number.

- Assessor Parcel Number, street address, size of parcel, and legal description of the parcel where TDCs will be used.

- Size of home being planned, including both gross structural area or building footprint.

- Maximum size permitted by the LCP standards, for both gross structural area or building footprint.

- Amount of GSA or footprint, in square feet, in excess of that permitted by county ordinance without the use of TDCs; the difference between the previous two calculations.

2. Step Two. Once we receive your completed form, we will prepare a "Preliminary Agreement — Financial Terms and Conditions." This document lists the number of

LAND CONSERVANCY OF SAN LUIS OBISPO COUNTY

CAMBRIA/LODGE HILL "TDC" PROGRAM

PO Box 12206
San Luis Obispo, CA 93406
(805) 544-9096

If you need any additional information concerning the Cambria/Lodge Hill TDC program, please contact our office at (805) 544-9096.

Since the inception of our TDC program, we have been able to increase the open space area in Lodge Hill by over 70 parcels containing some 110 individual 25' lots. The TDC program has made a substantial contribution to the quality of Cambria. Your purchase of TDCs will provide even greater protection.

The Land Conservancy of San Luis Obispo County is a private, non-profit organization dedicated to preserving sensitive open space areas throughout the county. Some of our other projects include the San Luis Creek Restoration project and preserving the Black Lake Canyon area in Nipomo.

We depend upon membership and private tax-deductible donations for funding along with the TDC program. If you are interested in learning more about the Land Conservancy, please contact the office.

TDCs being purchased, the sending lot (the one we are transferring the TDCs from), the receiving lot (your lot for building purposes), and the total purchase price.

A deposit may be required. We establish our policy for deposits on a case-by-case basis, depending on the number of TDCs available. Often, we can reserve TDCs without a deposit for up to six months. Depending upon the status of your Minor Use Permit, we may either extend your permit time or refund your deposit, less five percent (5%) retained by the Land Conservancy for expenses.

As of May 1, 1991, our current price is $20 per sq.ft. We require a minimum purchase of 50 sq.ft. and will sell uneven amounts above that, i.e., 53 sq.ft.

3. Step Three. Once the financial agreement has been signed by both Parties, we will provide you a letter of "Preliminary Agreement" which documents the number of credits you require, the sending lot, and the receiving lot. This letter is required by the county and should be presented to the appropriate office for completing your Minor Use Permit (MUP) application.

4. Step Four. Once you have obtained your MUP and upon payment of the remaining balance due for the TDCs, we will issue a "Final Letter of TDC Sale" which again lists the total number of TDCs required, total payment price, sending lot, and receiving lot. This can be done very as quickly and is presented by you to the county a demonstration of permit compliance. All TDC sales are final.

Appendix D *(Attachment C)*

Application Form to Purchase TDCs from the
San Luis Obispo County Land Conservancy

This form will provide information to the Land Conservancy for purchasing TDCs from us under our Lodge Hill Restoration Program.

Note: Many people will need to purchase additional Gross Structural Area and do not need additional Footprint. If that applies to your situation, you don't need to include any information on Footprint area. If, however, you need to purchase additional Footprint Area, you may ignore the items dealing with Gross Structural Area and include only Footprint items.

Date: _____

Property Owner: _____	Agent, if any: _____
Address: _____	Agent Address: _____
City: _____	City: _____
State: _____ Zip: _____	State: _____ Zip: _____
Daytime Telephone: _____	Daytime Telephone: _____
Evening Telephone: _____	Evening Telephone: _____

RECEIVING LOT INFORMATION

Assessor Parcel Number of lot to be built upon: _____

Street Address: _____ Size of Parcel: _____ Square Feet

Legal Description: Cambria Pines Manor Unit #: _____ Blk: _____ Lot(s): _____

ESTIMATED TDC REQUIREMENT

Size of the home being planned:

Gross Structural Area (GSA): _____ sq.ft. (LINE A)
OR
Building Footprint (*OPTIONAL*): _____ sq.ft. (LINE A-A)

Maximum size permitted by the LCP standards:

Gross Structural Area (GSA): _____ sq.ft. (LINE B)
OR
Building Footprint (*OPTIONAL*): _____ sq.ft. (LINE B-B)

Amount of GSA – or Footprint – that I need:

Gross Structural Area: _____ sq.ft. (LINE A minus LINE B)
OR
Footprint Area (*OPTIONAL*): _____ sq.ft. (LINE A-A minus LINE B-B)

_____
(Signature of property owner/agent)

Submit this form with a check for the amount required according to the price schedule, made out to the San Luis Obispo County Land Conservancy, and mail to us at P.O. Box 12206, San Luis Obispo, CA 93406. Keep a copy , if you wish. We will then provide the Letter of TDC Sale for your use, as explained in the "procedures" brochure.

Appendix D *(Attachment D)*

"Preliminary Agreement"

May 23, 1991

P.O. Box
Cambria, CA 93428

RE: _____ Property

Dear Mr. (or Ms.) _____ ,

This letter will acknowledge that we have reached a preliminary agreement for the purchase of Transferable Development Credits in the amount of 549 square feet of Gross Structural Area from the following lot(s).

SENDING LOT:

   Assessor Parcel #23-241-008 (34 GSA)/Assessor Parcel #23-233-028 (515 GSA)

It is our understanding that you will use these Credits as follows:

RECEIVING LOT:

   Assessor Parcel #23-332-
   Street Address: _____ Burton Drive, Cambria, CA 93428
   Cambria Pines Manor Unit #5, Block 114, Lots _____

This letter is provided to you, in accordance with County Ordinance 23.04.440 (d.), to facilitate completion of your application for a Minor Use Permit. This purchase is reflected in the attached inventory that has been updated to reflect this sale. The county will want to see a copy of this inventory as part of your application. Copies of the Deed and Deed Restrictions applicable to the sending lot(s) are maintained in our files and can be provided on request.

We will be pleased to complete a final sale of the TDCs upon final approval of your Minor Use Permit. The county may place a hold on your building permit until we provide a "Final Letter of TDC Sale."

The TDCs reserved for your project have been allocated under the terms of our separate financial agreement. If the final sale is not completed, or the TDCs you have reserved are abandoned, we are required to notice the county of that transaction.

Sincerely yours,

Raymond K Belknap
Executive Director

Appendix D *(Attachment E)*

"Preliminary Agreement"
Financial Terms and Agreement

May 23, 1991

P.O. Box
Cambria, CA 93428

RE:_____ Property

Dear Mr. (or Ms.)_____,

This letter will acknowledge that we have reserved 549 square feet of Gross Structural Area Transferable Development Credits from the following lot.

SENDING LOT:

Assessor Parcel #23-241-008 (34 GSA)/Assessor Parcel #23-233-028 (515 GSA)

RECEIVING LOT:

Assessor Parcel #23-332-
Street Address:_____ Burton Drive, Cambria, CA 93428
Cambria Pines Manor Unit #5, Block 114, Lots _____

Our reservation policy is based on a case-by-case analysis of TDCs available for sale, and our desire to make it convenient for the applicant of a Minor Use Permit to begin the processing of this permit with as little financial commitment as necessary. The terms of this reservation are as follows:

1. No deposit is required to reserve the TDCs for six months.

2. Fifty percent (50%) of the total purchase price of the TDCs reserved is due and payable six months from the date of this reservation. The total purchase price of the TDCs reserved for this project is $10,980.00.

3. One year from the date of this reservation, and at each subsequent anniversary date, the Land Conservancy may at its own discretion request payment in full, or, after corresponding with the applicant on the status of the Minor Use Permit, refund the amount of the reservation less five percent (5%) of the amount paid to date.

4. If the final sale is not completed, or the TDCs you have reserved are abandoned by failure to pay the reservation fee according to the terms herein, or the payments for reservation are refunded, we are required to notice the county.

_____   _____
Raymond K. Belknap
Executive Director

Appendix D *(Attachment F)*

"Final Letter of TDC Sale"

February 13, 1991

Morro Bay, CA 93442

Dear Mr. (or Ms.) _____ ,

This letter will acknowledge **FINAL RECEIPT AND SALE** in the amount of $13,000.00 for the purchase of Transferable Development Credits in the amount of 650 square feet of Gross Structural Area from the following lot(s).

SENDING LOT(s): Assessor Parcel #23-242-31 for 446 sq.ft.
Assessor Parcel #23-234-08 for 204 sq.ft.

It is our understanding that you will use these Credits as follows:

RECEIVING LOT: Assessor Parcel #23-222-
Street Address: _____ Trenton Ave.
Minor Use Permit # _____

This letter is provided to you in compliance with the conditions imposed by your Minor Use Permit. A copy of this letter should be sufficient to obtain final approval from the county and the release of your building permit. Copies of the Deed and Deed Restrictions applicable to the sending lot are maintained in our files and can be provided on request.

The terms of this sale are final. The cost of the TDCs should be included in the capital costs of the house in the same way that architecture and permit fees are included.

Sincerely yours,

Raymond K Belknap
Executive Director

Glossary

Compensation

Throughout most of this book, the term "compensation" is used simply to mean payment. However, the "Legal Issues" section of Chapter I explores the more specific term "just compensation" which is required if a court determines that a taking has occurred.

General Plan

A municipality's or county's general plan establishes the community's goals for future land use patterns, intensities, and other characteristics. By state law, a general plan must contain seven elements: Land Use, Circulation, Housing, Open Space, Conservation, Noise, and Safety. Public improvements as well as private developments must be consistent with the general plan. The zoning code implements the general plan through specific code requirements which also must be consistent with the general plan.

Receiving Site

The site identified by a community as appropriate to receive transferred development rights.

Sending Site

The site containing a resource which a community wants to protect by transferring its development rights to another site.

Specific Plan

A specific plan allows a community to adopt in one document a clarification of general plan goals for a particular area and the measures needed to implement those goals. California law establishes the components needed for a specific plan.

Taking

A court can determine that a governmental regulation is so restrictive that it has "taken" private property and that the owner of that property should receive "just compensation." The courts have not clearly established a formula for determining when a taking has occurred but some of the parameters created by past cases can provide some direction, as discussed in the "Legal Issues" section of Chapter I.

TDR Banks

TDR banks are agencies which purchase development rights from the owners of sending sites, "bank" those rights, and then sell them to the owners and/or developers of receiving sites.

Transfer of Development Credit (TDC)

Some communities use the term "credit" rather than "right" to indicate that the ability to develop land is a privilege. Aside from this philosophical distinction, TDC is the same as TDR.

Transfer of Development Right (TDR)

A procedure in which the right to develop one property, a sending site, is transferred to another property, a receiving site. As a result of the transfer, the owner of the sending site receives compensation, even though no additional development occurs at that site. Conversely, the owner of the receiving site can develop that site in a manner that would not otherwise be allowed.

Transfer Ratio

Many communities encourage the transfer of development rights by allowing more development on a receiving site than can be transferred from a sending site. The multiplication factor used by these communities is the transfer ratio.

Zoning

Zoning is the part of a city or county's municipal code which implements the goals and policies of the general plan by establishing zones where various land uses can be located and development restrictions such as building height, bulk, setbacks, and parking requirements apply . Zoning codes also establish the procedures for processing development applications and requests to deviate from the established code.

Acronyms

CDO	Cluster Development Ordinance
CMP	Comprehensive Management Plan
CUP	Conditional Use Permit
EDR	Existing Development Right
FAR	Floor Area Ratio
HRO	Hillside Residential and Open Space
IBC	Irvine Business Complex
NJPDCB	New Jersey Pinelands Development Credit Bank
OPR	California Governor's Office of Planning and Research
PAD	Planned Agricultural District
PDC	Pinelands Development Credit
PUD	Planned Unit Development
RDCS	Residential Development Control System
ST	Special Treatment
TDC	Transferable Development Credit
TDR	Transferable Development Right
TEDR	Transfer of Existing Development Rights
TIPS	Traffic Intensity Performance Standard
TRPA	Tahoe Regional Planning Agency

Index